# IPOs and Equity Offerings

**Butterworth-Heinemann – The Securities Institute**

A publishing partnership

**About The Securities Institute**

Formed in 1992 with the support of the Bank of England, the London Stock Exchange, the Financial Services Authority, LIFFE and other leading financial organizations, the Securities Institute is the professional body for practitioners working in securities, investment management, corporate finance, derivatives and related businesses. Their purpose is to set and maintain professional standards through membership, qualifications, training and continuing learning and publications. The Institute promotes excellence in matters of integrity, ethics and competence.

**About the series**

Butterworth-Heinemann is pleased to be the official **Publishing Partner** of the Securities Institute with the development of professional level books for: Brokers/Traders; Actuaries; Consultants; Asset Managers; Regulators; Central Bankers; Treasury Officials; Compliance Officers; Legal Departments; Corporate Treasurers; Operations Managers; Portfolio Managers; Investment Bankers; Hedge Fund Managers; Investment Managers; Analysts and Internal Auditors, in the areas of: Portfolio Management; Advanced Investment Management; Investment Management Models; Financial Analysis; Risk Analysis and Management; Capital Markets; Bonds; Gilts; Swaps; Repos; Futures; Options; Foreign Exchange; Treasury Operations.

**Series titles**

- **Professional Reference Series**
  The Bond and Money Markets: *Strategy, Trading, Analysis*
- **Global Capital Markets Series**
  The REPO Handbook
  Foreign Exchange and Money Markets: *Theory, Practice and Risk Management*
  IPOs and Equity Offerings
  European Securities Markets Infrastructure
  Best Execution in the Integrated Securities Market
- **Operations Management Series**
  Clearing, Settlement and Custody
  Controls, Procedures and Risk
  Relationship and Resource Management in Operations
  Managing Technology in the Operations Function
  Regulation and Compliance in Operations
  Understanding the Markets

**For more information**

For more information on **The Securities Institute** please visit their web site:

www.securities-institute.org.uk

and for details of all **Butterworth-Heinemann Finance** titles please visit Butterworth-Heinemann:

www.bh.com/finance

# IPOs and Equity Offerings

*Ross Geddes*

ELSEVIER
BUTTERWORTH
HEINEMANN

AMSTERDAM • BOSTON • HEIDELBERG • LONDON • NEW YORK • OXFORD
PARIS • SAN DIEGO • SAN FRANCISCO • SINGAPORE • SYDNEY • TOKYO

Butterworth-Heinemann is an imprint of Elsevier
Linacre House, Jordan Hill, Oxford OX2 8DP, UK
30 Corporate Drive, Suite 400, Burlington, MA 01803, USA

First edition 2003



**British Library Cataloguing in Publication Data**
A catalogue record for this book is available from the British Library

**Library of Congress Cataloging-in-Publication Data**
A catalog record for this book is available from the Library of Congress

ISBN: 978-0-7506-5538-5

For information on all Butterworth-Heinemann publications visit our website at books.elsevier.com



*Transferred to Digital Printing 2010*

# Contents

*For HBG and HDAG*

# Preface

This book is written for those with an interest in the process of raising new equity funds. Professionals (either banking, legal, accounting or other) who are involved in IPOs, Finance Directors and CFOs of companies about to go public, graduate students in finance and MBA programmes, and academics who wish a fuller understanding of the process will all find the book useful.

The goal of the book is to help the reader understand the complete IPO process. In a financial world of increasing sophistication, few participants in an IPO see all aspects of the deal. There are a number of good guides written by lawyers and accountants that cover the legal and procedural aspects, but these do not say much about marketing or syndication. Other books tell the story of specific deals, but do not cover the topic in a comprehensive manner. I have tried to capture the whole process, using as many examples as possible. As it is written by a former banker, readers should understand the biases and perspective taken in this volume.

The book is global in outlook, but necessarily spends much time on the American and British markets – two of the largest markets for IPOs and international equity offerings. In particular, the majority of the academic papers that I cite are based on research into US IPOs. However, the implication of much of the research is global and the examples that I use are more heavily weighted to European offerings. I am sure that I have missed some important work, but that is what second editions are for.

This book is the culmination of a number of years' work, both in practice of managing IPOs and in researching them as an academic. The first two chapters are based on a teaching note that I wrote while at the University of Greenwich. I thank my former colleagues for their support and comments on the initial paper, in particular Pat Baynes, Nick Hand and Z. Sevic. Chapter 5 on determining value is derived from an earlier book, *Valuation and Investment Appraisal* (R. Geddes, 2002), published by Financial World/Association of Corporate Treasurers, who kindly gave permission to include the material.

I received help and direction from a number of former colleagues and current industry participants. Thank you to Christopher Ridge and Paul van Isseum of Dresdner Kleinwort Wasserstein; Debra Wilson of the Securities Institute; and Mike Cash and his team at Butterworth-Heinemann. All writers need to thank those around them who put up with writer's block, deadlines (often missed in this case) and the need for quiet. For their forbearance and support in this venture, I thank first and foremost Christina Butler, but also Alexander, Bruce, Clare, Ellery, Gillian, Ian, Mom, Neil, Rachelle and Sheila (note to you all, the list is alphabetical).

# About the author

Ross Geddes writes and speaks on financial topics, particularly corporate finance and equity new issues. Mr Geddes worked in investment banking for 10 years, primarily in corporate finance and equity capital markets. He has taught MBAs and MSc finance courses at City University Business School, the University of Greenwich and the University of Reading. Mr Geddes is now a director of a number of companies. *IPOs and Equity Offerings* is his fourth book.

# 1 The decision to go public

It is an oft-repeated cliché in business that for a company to survive it must grow. It must grow its market share. It must grow its customer base. It must increase its R&D spending in order to find new products or new uses for existing products. It must increase its manufacturing capacity in order to make the products. And then it must market and distribute these products.

All of this takes money. And lots of it. One of the most tried and tested methods of raising cash is through an initial public offering. An initial public offering (IPO) is, as it sounds, the first sale of a company's shares to the public and the listing of the shares on a stock exchange. In the UK, IPOs are often referred to as flotations.

Many companies need more cash than provided by an IPO. They return to the stock market in secondary offerings or rights issues. While not as monumental as the first decision to go public, any decision to raise equity is not taken lightly.

Issuing companies are not the only parties that raise money on the stock market. Existing shareholders may decide to offload their holding either in the IPO or secondary offering. The existing shareholder may be an individual, venture capital firm, parent company or even a government, in the case of privatizations.

Whoever is raising the funds, the process of flotation is arduous, involves significant time commitments from the company's management and advisors (investment bankers, stockbrokers and solicitors amongst others), and is not cheap. This effort is expended in order to raise the cash required at a price that keeps both the vendor and the purchaser of the shares happy.

The three main interested parties in an IPO (the vendor, the company and the investor) have complementary objectives.

The *Company* will want to:

- Maximize proceeds
- Build broad and stable ownership base
- Raise its profile
- Facilitate future fund raising and possibly future acquisitions
- Ensure that there is good liquidity in secondary market trading
- Be seen as launching a successful IPO.

The *Vendor*, or selling shareholder, wants to:

- Maximize proceeds
- Maximize value of retained interest/share price performance
- Be seen as part of a successful transaction

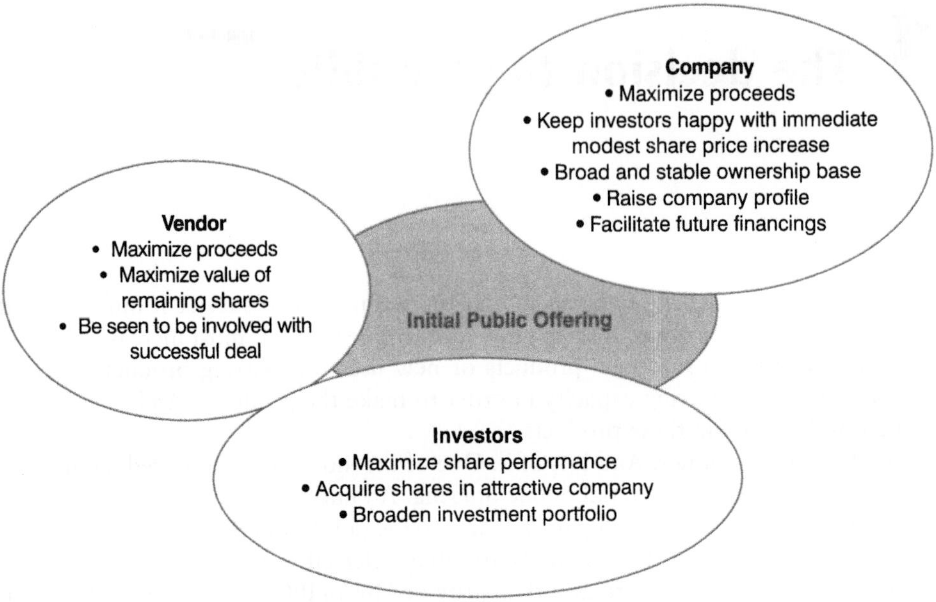


**Figure 1.1** Various IPO objectives

*Investors* will want to:

- Maximize share price return (short-term and long-term)
- Broaden and diversify portfolio
- Accumulate a position not easily found in the secondary market.

In an IPO, the objectives of the vendor, company and investor are complementary, but not identical. The role of the investment bank that is managing or sponsoring the offering is to ensure that a balance of interests is maintained amongst the three parties. One of the difficulties of managing an investment bank is managing the inherent conflicts between issuing clients and investing clients. This became particularly notable in the aftermath of the IPO bubble in the late 1990s and 2000, particularly in the USA.

## The company

Corporate objectives in a flotation are numerous and both financial and non-financial. The company will wish to attain a high valuation that is maintained in the secondary market. Companies are in business to create value for their shareholders. The last thing a firm wants is for its first public shareholders to lose money. So, while a high price is desirable, one that will go even higher in the aftermarket is more so. High prices minimize the dilution experienced by existing shareholders, so two groups are happy.

Sustainable valuations are supported by core long-term shareholders. Core shareholders do not want to sell their investment, but they want to see regular trading in the company's shares (called liquidity), so that they know they can sell if necessary.

Other objectives include increasing the company's profile and facilitating future fund raising and acquisitions. These objectives will be discussed in greater detail below.

## The vendors

The company may not be the vendor of the shares in the following situations:

- Founders are selling out
- Other investors are selling shares
- Venture capital 'exits'
- Reverse leveraged buy-outs (LBOs)
- Parent companies selling subsidiaries
- Privatizations.

When the vendor and the company are not the same party, the vendor's number one objective is to maximize the value of its shareholding. This may mean accepting a 'low' price on the IPO or not selling any/all shares when the company first comes to market. In fact, many selling shareholders do not divest all their shares at the time of the IPO. Therefore, a strong share price performance in the aftermarket is important. Shareholders such as venture capitalists (VCs) recognize that they will need to return to the stock market at least one more time to fully realize the value of their investment in the company undertaking an IPO.

For example, Citicorp Venture Capital realized the value of patience by not selling any of its shares in Fairchild Semiconductors' 1999 IPO at a price of $18.50 per share. Five months later when the company returned to the equity market Citicorp sold shares at $33.44, increasing its proceeds by 80 per cent compared to the IPO price.

## The investors

Finally, investors wish to maximize share price performance after the flotation. This will be the product of both the traditional opening day premium and continued strong stock market performance on the part of the company's shares.

IPOs are ideal opportunities for investors to obtain a sizeable stake in companies that would not easily be found in the secondary market. The fact that the issuing company pays all commissions also helps the performance of an investor. To see how much an investor can potentially save, let's look at the following hypothetical example.

**Commission savings by buying shares in new issues**

An investor has the choice of investing in two nearly identical companies: one through buying shares in new issue (either an IPO or secondary), the other through accumulating shares in the stock market.

In the first instance, the investor buys 500 000 shares in the new issue at $12.00 for an aggregate cost of $6 million. The investor incurs no additional costs – there are no trading commissions on the purchase (the issuer pays them), there is no bid–ask spread, and stamp tax (where applicable) is also paid by the issuer.

The alternative investment is already listed on the stock exchange. For simplicity, assume that the other company's shares are currently trading at $12.00. The investor may be paying $0.05 per share, or an aggregate commission of $25 000, plus a bid–ask spread of say $0.02, or $10 000. Therefore, the investor's initial cost base for the shares would be $6 035 000, or 0.563 per cent higher than in the IPO. Remember that institutional fund managers measure their performance after trading costs and commissions for performance measurement purposes, and 0.5 of 1 per cent can be a significant factor in the fund's overall performance.

This example assumes that the investor would be able to accumulate 500 000 shares without moving the price higher than $12.00 in the secondary market. If the average daily trading volume of the second company was only 50 000 shares, the purchase of 500 000 might be expected to move the share price up – for simplicity, say it increases the average cost per share to $12.10, another 0.833 per cent. Depending on the free float and average trading volume of the company's stock, the investor may find that its purchases forces the price 2 to 3 per cent higher, or even more for companies with illiquid shares.

During the technology IPO bubble in the late 1990s, it was alleged that some US investors were so desperate to get allocations in hot IPOs that they willingly paid 'excess' commissions to the IPOs' lead managers. The commissions would be paid on trades in other stocks around the time of the IPO. By agreeing to pay a commission of, say, $0.12 per share rather than the normal four or five cents per share in a secondary trade, the investor hoped to gain a favourable IPO allocation.

## What is the commonality?

The area of overlap that we find is in maximizing the aftermarket performance of the company's share price – which is a factor of good performance, appropriate IPO pricing and good liquidity in the aftermarket. Aftermarket liquidity is itself a function of the number of shares in issue, the number of markets on which the shares are traded, the amount of research coverage and number of market makers (where applicable) for the shares.

We find that IPOs in every country give investors in the offering an immediate positive return. On average, IPOs finish the first day of trading 16.6 per cent above

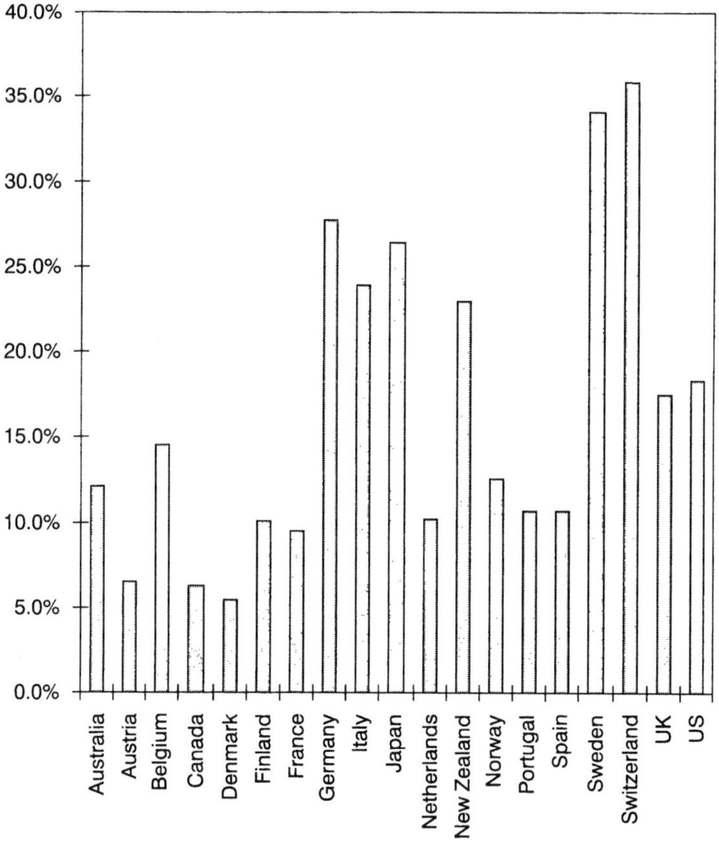


*Source*: Loughran et al. (1994); updated by Ritter (2001a).

**Figure 1.2** IPO one-day premia in selected major markets

the offering price (see Figure 1.2).[1] The 'pop' ranges from a low of 5 or 6 per cent in Austria, Canada and Denmark to around 35 per cent in Sweden and Switzerland. The first-day premium is even higher in a number of emerging markets – 257 per cent in China, 104 per cent in Malaysia and 47 per cent in Thailand (Loughran et al., 1994; updated by Ritter, 2001a). The existence of the first-day premium has exercised the minds of many leading academics and is known as the underpricing phenomenon. Although IPOs may appear to be underpriced, the issuer and its investment bank(s) price IPOs to open at a premium of between 10 and 15 per cent. That is they deliberately underprice issues by 10 to 15 per cent.

This 'underpricing' keeps everyone happy – investors have achieved an immediate return, while vendors/companies have not 'left too much money on the table'. In bull markets like the late 1990s, much more money is left on the table as young, very risky companies are brought to market at a much earlier stage of their development than would normally be the case. The average first-day premia during the bubble years (1998–2000) far exceeded long-term averages.

[1] This figure is the simple average of studies in 18 countries, as summarized by Ritter (2001a).

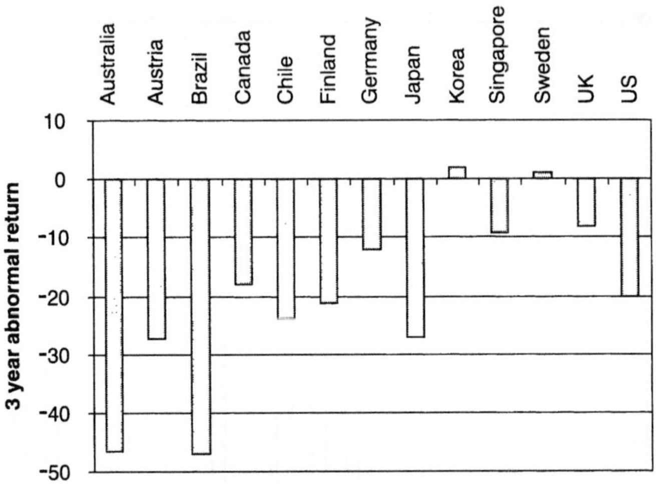


**Figure 1.3** Long-run overpricing of IPOs

The short-run underpricing phenomenon of IPOs is interesting, because the one thing that we can say about the long-run performance of equity offerings is that they underperform the market and peer groups – exactly the opposite of the shared goal of an IPO. Long-term underperformance has been identified in markets as diverse as Australia and Brazil, Japan and Korea, and is summarized in Ritter (1998a). Figure 1.3 indicates that in only two of 13 markets examined do IPO firms outperform non-issuing firms in the three years following the offering. In the two countries that exhibit positive returns (Korea and Sweden), the positive returns are 2.0 per cent and 1.2 per cent, respectively.

The common bond that keeps the three parties (vendors, issuers and investors) happy is the team of investment bankers assigned to manage the process. For their part, the investment banker must keep multiple constituencies within the bank satisfied: equity research analysts; salesmen and traders; and, of course, their own bonus pool.

In May 1999, Antoine Schwarz, Goldman Sachs' head of European Equity Capital Markets, was quoted in RISK magazine: 'The buyer wants to think you're favouring them; the seller wants to think you're favouring them. But you have to be the person in the middle trying to optimise it.'

At the end of this chapter we'll discuss some of the factors that make an IPO successful. First, why do companies go public?

## Why do companies go public?

Companies undertake an IPO for one of two reasons:

1 To raise capital for the company's use (a 'primary' offering).
2 To raise funds for the existing shareholders (including venture capitalists and governments, as in privatizations, etc.) (a 'secondary' offering).

The terms primary offering or primary issue and secondary offering or secondary issue are often used to classify the recipient of the proceeds. Proceeds from a primary offering go to the company – it creates and issues new shares for sale to the public. Secondary offerings sell existing shares to the public. Many IPOs combine primary and secondary offerings.

These differences are notable in the naming of public offers in the UK and Italy, where Offers for Subscription and *Offerta Publicca di Sottoscrizione*, respectively, refer to the sale of new shares and Offers for Sale and *Offerta Publicca di Vendita*, respectively, refer to the sale of shares by an existing shareholder.

The reader should be aware, however, that in some markets subsequent (or follow-on or seasoned equity offerings (SEOs)) are also called 'secondary offerings', regardless of whether primary or secondary shares are being sold. So one might have a 'secondary–secondary' offer, where existing shareholders sell further shares, or a 'secondary–primary' offer, where new shares are sold by a company already listed on an exchange. In this book, I regularly use the term secondary offering for follow-on offering.

During the 1990s, the global volume of IPOs rose from around \$11 billion in 1990 to \$155 billion in 1999. The following year, 2000, saw another record, with \$176 billion raised for companies coming to the market for the first time. The pace of flotations slackened dramatically in 2001, as the global technology bubble burst, leaving bankers, lawyers, accountants and other advisors to fight over the fees from a 'mere' \$75 billion of offerings. When one considers that the fees and commissions payable on most IPOs range from 2 to 7 per cent of the proceeds, one shouldn't feel too sorry. IPO fees are generally the highest in the USA. The New York Stock Exchange reported in early 2001: 'Wall Street investment banks earned an average fee of 6.67 percent of deal proceeds for underwriting IPOs in 2000, down from 6.83 percent in 1999' (The New York Stock Exchange, 'The year 2000 in review', pp. 6–7).

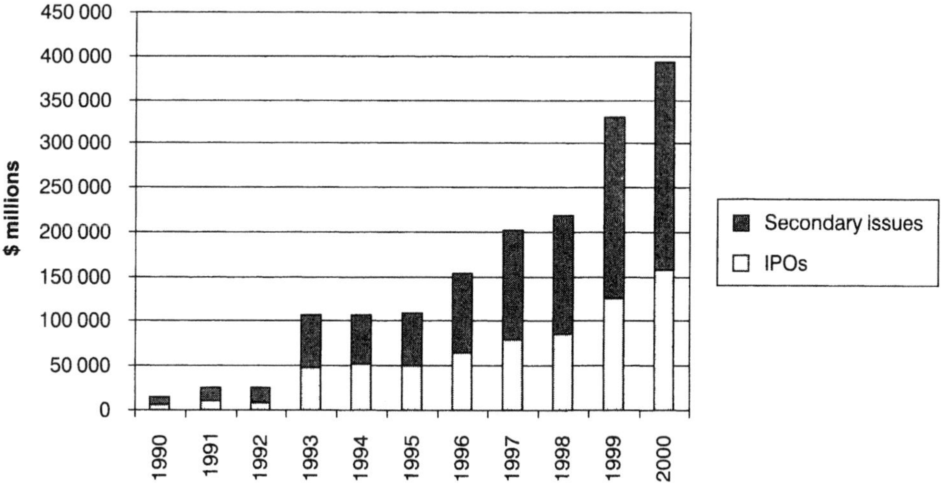


*Data sources*: Various.

**Figure 1.4** Funds raised in equity offerings (1990–2000)

The growth in follow-on (secondary) offerings was equally dramatic, increasing at an annual clip of 32 per cent from 1990, reaching $250 billion in 2000.

## Capital raising

Companies that are raising capital by creating and selling new shares do so to improve the financial health of the business. Equity has two great advantages over bank loans and other forms of debt: it does not have to be repaid, nor are there regular payments to be made – dividends are paid at the option of the directors. In general, capital raising IPOs are undertaken in order to:

- raise cash in order to expand the business of the company, or
- reduce the debt levels (leverage or gearing) of the company.

The decision to go public for many companies is a strategic decision, not just a fund raising decision. The IPO process can be a catalyst for developing the company's strategy more fully. It can also be seen as the final step in the financial development of a company.

There is a mythology of company development, particularly strong in the USA, that culminates in the IPO. The IPO company of lore is founded in a garage and sees its financing needs met with ever more sophisticated instruments, as illustrated in Figure 1.5. On establishment, the founders' savings typically finance companies. As the business grows, the founders may borrow or seek investment from friends and family. At a certain level of development, bank financing is sought. If a company is growing rapidly, it may require additional equity capital, provided by a venture capitalist or institutional investors. Finally, the company goes to the public markets by flotation to finance the next stages of its growth.

When considering an IPO, the company must critically assess itself to determine whether it is truly ready to sell shares to the public. Upon reflection, it may decide to raise funds from an alternative source – either late stage venture capital or private equity returning to them a second or even third time if necessary. We will look at a company's readiness for flotation in Chapter 3.

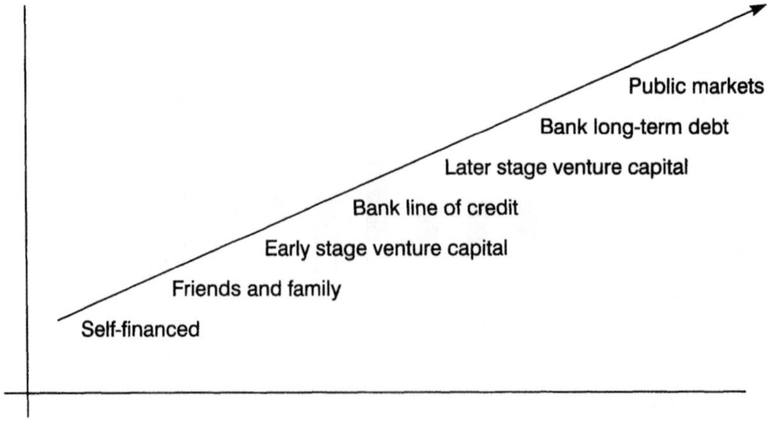


**Figure 1.5** Typical sources of new venture financing

### *Use of proceeds*

When a company is raising funds for its own use, smart investors look closely at the 'Use of Proceeds' section of the offering prospectus and evaluate how the firm will create value for its new shareholders. A firm's IPO will be more successful the more clearly it can explain the use of proceeds and how the funds will assist in the company's future growth.

During hot new issues markets or bull markets, companies can raise funds from investors in IPOs with much less detailed discussion of how they intend to use the funds, as illustrated by the following example from Docent's IPO prospectus dated 29 September 2000:

> 'We do not have specific uses committed for the net proceeds of this offering. The size of the offering has been determined primarily based on our desire to raise a sufficient amount of capital to afford us significant business flexibility in the future.
>
> The principal purposes of this offering are:
>
> - to obtain additional working capital;
> - to create a public market for our common stock;
> - to facilitate future access by Docent to public equity markets; and
> - to enhance our ability to use our stock to make future acquisitions due to the fact that our shares will be publicly traded. We may use a portion of the net proceeds to acquire or invest in complementary businesses . . .'

This was typical of the use of proceeds section from the tech boom of 1998–2000. The company gives reasons for the shares to be listed, but only vague spending plans and nothing for why an investor should buy the shares.

A little better was the use of proceeds section from the IPO prospectus for Brokat Infosystems AG, a German software company that developed products for the e-commerce industry and went public in September 1998. The offering released funds for the management shareholders as well as raised capital for the company. The use of proceeds was outlined as follows:

> '. . . serve to intensify the marketing of the Company's goods and services, especially abroad, and to finance the Company's rapid growth, including potential corporate acquisitions.'

In April 1998, Ottakar's, a UK chain of book stores, made a £15 million offering, of which £6 million went to the company. In the section of the prospectus titled 'Reasons for the Placing and Use of Proceeds', the company stated:

> 'The Directors believe that the listing will provide greater flexibility for financing the future development of Ottakar's and will facilitate the Group's pursuit of its strategic plans and initiatives. It will also enable the Company to provide a partial

> exit for Foreign & Colonial who, prior to the placing, hold approximately 70 per cent of the equity shares.
>
> In addition, the listing will help attract and retain high calibre staff by providing share incentive schemes to executive directors and employees.
>
> The placing will raise approximately £6.037 million (net of expenses) for the Company. This will enable the Company to redeem £1.737 million of its preference share capital and initially to reduce bank borrowings, with the balance placed on deposit, thereby allowing the Group flexibility to fund further store expansion.'

None of the three examples are particularly useful to a potential investor who really wants to know what his money is going to be spent on. These examples are not particularly bad compared with other IPO disclosures, just typical of the times.

Finally, Mobile TeleSystems OJSC, a Russian mobile telephone operator, made a public offering to US investors in June 2000. This was a company in a risky industry in a risky market. Therefore, its investment bankers ensured that there was a very detailed use of proceeds in its prospectus:

> 'We have budgeted the following amounts that we intend to fund using the net proceeds from the offering for the period through 2002:
>
> - $135 million to fund investments in network infrastructure in the Moscow license area;
> - $75 million to expand our business in our regional license areas;
> - $45 million to acquire existing GSM operators and license holders, although we have no present understanding or agreement relating to any material acquisition or investment; and
> - $50 million to fund investments in new mobile data services such as Internet access, higher speed data transmission, and other advanced technology mobile telecommunication technologies.'

Investors in risky industries and in risky markets will typically demand greater disclosure of the use of proceeds. In MTS's case, the disclosure does not tie management's hands entirely, as it is worded loosely enough that if an opportunity arose, the company would likely be able to take it.

## Sale by existing shareholders

There are numerous reasons why existing shareholders may wish to sell part or all of their shareholding through flotation. As noted above, in some markets a sale by existing shareholders is referred to as a secondary offering. In secondary offerings, no new shares are sold and the company receives no cash. With the exception of privatizations, very few IPOs are purely secondary offerings. Existing shareholders usually 'piggyback' on a primary offering. Reasons for secondary sales include:

- Sale by entrepreneur
  - Succession
  - Tax and other personal reasons
  - 'Cashing in'
- Sale by professional investors
  - Venture capitalists and private investors seeking an 'exit'
  - Reverse LBOs
- Funds required by parent company/major shareholder
  - Equity carve-outs
  - Demergers (spin-offs)
- Demutualizations
- Privatizations of state-owned enterprises.

### *Sale by entrepreneur*

Investors look very closely at the reasons behind the sale of shares by the founding entrepreneur or founding management group. They know that these insiders have better knowledge of the business and its prospects than anyone, and are rightly suspicious of the timing of any sale.

#### Succession

Succession is the cause for the flotations of many small- and medium-sized companies. Flotations resulting from succession factors increased during the late 1990s, particularly in continental Europe. If younger members of the owner's family have no interest in, or aptitude for the business, the owner may sell the company. Many entrepreneurs prefer to introduce professional (i.e. non-family) managers and float the company, rather than sell the company to a competitor.

#### Tax reasons

In order to encourage the development of their capital markets, a number of countries have introduced lower, preferential tax treatment for companies that list on the stock market. Italy provides an example.

In 1994, the Italian Government introduced tax incentives for Italian companies going public. The corporate income tax rate for newly listed small- and medium-sized enterprises (SMEs) issuing new shares was reduced to 21 per cent (from as much as 50 per cent). Then in 1997, the rate of income tax for these companies was reduced to 19 per cent. Again in a further attempt to induce firms, particularly SMEs, to go public, the 19 per cent tax rate was reduced to 7 per cent for three years (Arosio et al., 2000).

Whether it was the reduction in tax rate, the opening of the Nuovo mercato (market for smaller companies) or just buoyant markets, IPOs in Italy did increase from 1998 onwards, as illustrated in Figure 1.6.

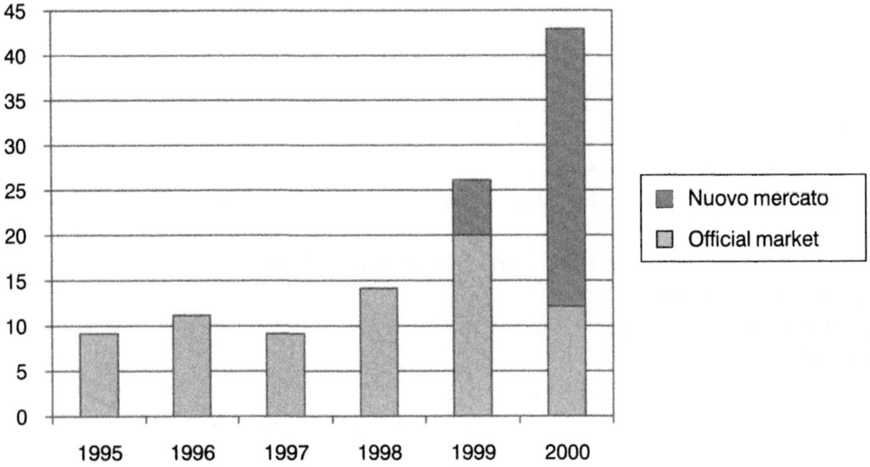


*Source*: CONSOB, Annual Report 2000, Table III.1.

**Figure 1.6** Number of Italian IPOs (1995–2000)

In January 2002, the German Government abolished a longstanding 50 per cent capital gains tax applied to profits earned by corporations that sold stakes in other companies. These cross-shareholdings are a major feature of the German economy. Abolition of the tax was anticipated to result in a flurry of secondary offerings, as companies unwound intricate cross-holdings and focused on their core business.

The change to the law was announced approximately 18 months in advance, leading to a dramatic increase in the issuance of exchangeable bonds in Germany. Exchangeable bonds are an example of an 'equity-linked' security, whereby a company issues a bond that is exchangeable for the shares of another company at the option of the bondholder. The exchange feature on these issues was set so that bondholders were unable to swap their bonds for shares prior to 1 January 2002. Thus the bonds' issuers avoided the swingeing capital gains tax, but were able to monetize their investment in advance of the change.

### 'Cashing in'

It is the rare IPO that consists entirely of shares being sold by the founding shareholder(s). Investors are extraordinarily suspicious, and rightly so. Who knows better the future prospects of a company than its founder and senior executives? If they are cashing in, potential investors will wonder what is over the horizon. When entrepreneurs want to sell their shares, the lead investment bank will usually force them to bundle the sale with the sale of new shares to raise capital for the company, and will usually not allow them to sell all their shares at once. This helps to ensure that the entrepreneur's interests remain aligned with those of the company's new shareholders.

Entrepreneurs and managers can benefit from an IPO, even when they don't sell shares in the offering. The collateral value of shares in a public company is much greater than that of a private company. So an entrepreneur could borrow a larger amount using his shares as security. There are other ways that entrepreneurs can monetize the value of their assets, as described in Chapter 11.

## *Raising capital for shareholders/parent company*

Majority shareholders, whether they are corporations, venture capitalists or charitable foundations, may have different reasons for selling some or all the shares in a company's IPO or secondary offering. Starting in the 1980s, investors have increasingly rewarded focused companies. Shareholders downgrade the share of diversified groups, or companies with subsidiaries that don't fit. This leads to asset sales, equity carve-outs and demergers.

Venture capitalists and private equity providers are never long-term shareholders. Most have a target time horizon of three to seven years from the date of investment to 'exit'. If stock markets are favourable, flotation may maximize their returns. Finally, shareholders, such as charitable foundations, may seek diversification to reduce risk or increase income.

### Charitable foundations: diversifying investments

Like an entrepreneur selling a company for succession reasons or estate planning, corporate or foundation owners may decide that they no longer wish to have their entire wealth bound up in the company. By selling a portion, the owner is able to diversify its investments.

In one of the major IPOs of the 1950s, the Ford Foundation sold a majority stake in Ford Motor Company to investors on the New York Stock Exchange. The Foundation continued to hold a significant minority (approximately 40 per cent) of the voting securities of Ford. With the proceeds, the Foundation was able to invest in a broad range of securities and to finance its donations.

The Wellcome Trust paid millions in investment banking fees as it reduced its stake in Wellcome plc from 100 per cent in 1986 to under 2 per cent (of the successor company) in 2001.The Wellcome Trust is a British charitable foundation that funds medical research. The Trust used the income from the company's dividends to make donations to medical research.

It began selling its shares because it found that the income from Wellcome plc's dividends was insufficient to meet the demands of the various research projects to which the Trust contributed. The Trust invested the proceeds of the offerings in a widely diversified portfolio of securities that reduced its investment risk and raised its income from investments. This allowed the Trust to increase its donations to medical research, as a result of the increased investment income.

Over 15 years, the Trust used each method of offering described in this book. The process began with the company's IPO in 1986, when 26 per cent of the shares were sold to the public. This was followed six years later by the £2 billion plus marketed secondary offering of Wellcome plc shares, lead managed by Robert Fleming & Co.

The Trust's ownership stake was diluted through a series of mergers during the late 1990s and 2000, when Glaxo and Wellcome merged to form GlaxoWellcome, and then the next merger which saw the disappearance of the Wellcome name. In December 2000, GlaxoWellcome merged with SmithKlineBeecham to form Glaxo-SmithKline, or GSK.

In late 2001, the Trust decided to reduce its stake in GlaxoSmithKline, where its ownership stake had dwindled to 2.5 per cent. However, prior to the sale, GSK accounted for 20 per cent of the Trust's £13 billion of assets.

For the sale of 100 million GSK shares (worth £1.8 billion), which took the Trust's holding in the company to just under 1 per cent, Schroder Salomon Smith Barney managed an accelerated bookbuilding. The shares were placed at a 1.9 per cent discount to the previous day's closing price, a narrow discount given the size of the offer. Just 10 years earlier, the Trust went through an eight-week marketing period to raise a similar amount.

## Equity carve-outs, spin-offs and demergers

Spin-offs, equity carve-outs (ECOs) and demergers gained in popularity throughout the 1990s in many markets. As noted above, investors were crying out for focused companies. Those companies with more than one core business, or with related businesses that were growing faster than the core business, gave serious consideration to becoming more focused.

Some large, well-known companies, particularly in the Internet sector, began public life as carve-outs: Compuserve (from H&R Block); Expedia (from Microsoft); Freeserve (from Dixons); and McAfee (from Network Associates). During the boom, several carve-outs were valued at more than their parent company.

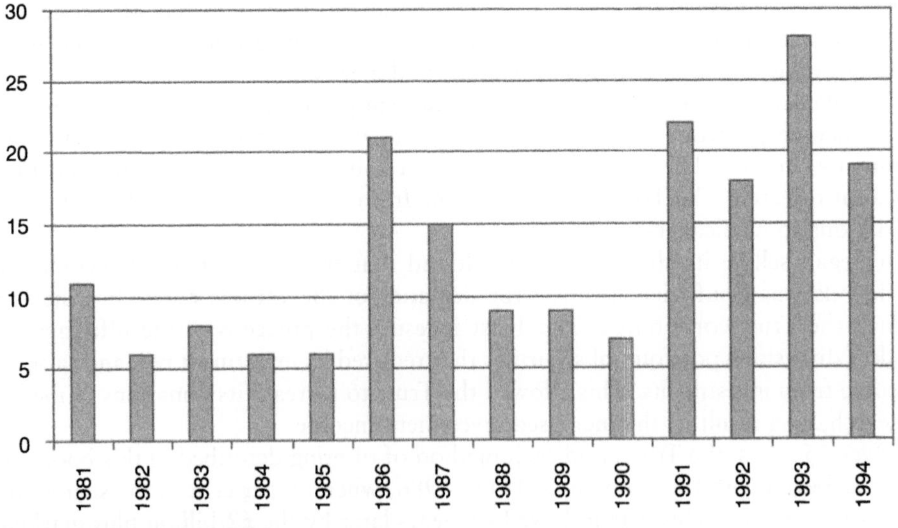


*Source*: Hulbert et al. (2002).

**Figure 1.7** Equity carve-outs in the USA (1981–1994)

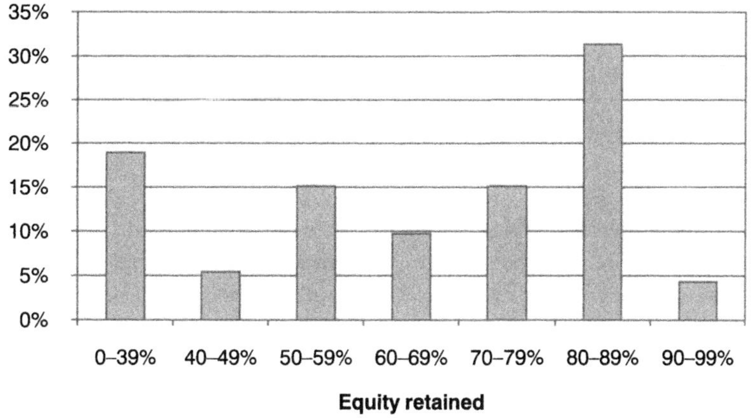


*Source*: Hulbert et al. (2002).

**Figure 1.8** Proportion of equity retained in US equity carve-outs (1981–1994)

In the first instance, a company can undertake an equity carve-out where it sells a portion of the shares in a subsidiary to the public. The funds raised can stay with the selling shareholder or fund the newly independent business's operations.

It is not unusual for a company to spin off a portion of a subsidiary, say 25 per cent of the shares, prior to a full demerger. The initial spin-off raises money for the parent and sets a price on the subsidiary. Figure 1.8 illustrates the proportion of equity retained by the parent company in US equity carve-outs. Fully 50 per cent of carve-outs sell less than 30 per cent of the subsidiary's equity.

Research by McKinsey & Co., the consultants, found that after five years less than 10 per cent of carve-outs were still controlled by their parent (i.e. over 50 per cent ownership). Approximately 31 per cent of parents held minority stakes of less than 25 per cent.

| | |
|---|---|
| Acquired or merged | 39% |
| Repurchased by parent | 11% |
| Delisted | 3% |
| Independent | 31% |
| Parent controlled | |
| 50–75% owned | 8% |
| 25–50% owned | 8% |

**Table 1.1** What happens to carve-out companies?

Carve-outs, spin-offs and demergers occur for a number of reasons, four of which follow:

1 The division/subsidiary doesn't fit with the parent company's strategy or a division is in a different sector than the parent and may be more highly valued as a separate investment than as part of a group.

2 The parent company is heavily indebted and needs to raise fresh capital to repay debt.
3 The parent company follows a regular policy of carve-outs in order to maximize shareholder value.
4 The parent company sells a portion of a foreign division in a foreign stock market to local investors.

Aside from raising money for the parent company, the benefits of an equity carve-out include an increase in information to shareholders regarding the division, and an increase in management accountability, focus and incentives. Investors usually believe that the subsidiary will perform better and therefore the value of the parent's investment will increase.

In 1997, McKinsey & Co. published the results of a study of equity carve-outs that took place in the USA between 1985 and 1996. They examined the performance of companies where the parent retained at least 50 per cent ownership. During the three years following the carve-out, the subsidiaries' shares achieved an average compound annual return of 20.3 per cent, nearly double the return of the Russell 2000 Index.

In addition, research indicates that the announcement of an equity carve-out increases the parent company's stock price (Schipper and Smith, 1986; Klein et al., 1991; Mulherin and Boone, 2000). Hulbert et al. (2002) found that in the two days surrounding the announcement of US equity carve-outs, the parent company's share price increases by a market-adjusted 1.92 per cent.

### The division/subsidiary doesn't fit

In the early 1990s, ICI decided that its mixture of chemicals and pharmaceuticals businesses didn't make sense. The company felt that shareholder value could be maximized by demerging its pharmaceuticals business, which was named Zeneca.

Often times the carve-out firms are viewed as having higher growth prospects than their parent companies. For example, Dixons, a UK retailer of electronic equipment, successfully 'carved out' 20 per cent of its holding in Freeserve, an Internet service provider, in a July 1999 flotation. On flotation, Freeserve's market capitalization was £1.5 billion, almost the same as its parent company.

Many European telecoms companies, including Telefonica of Spain, carved out portions of their high growth mobile telephone businesses during the late 1990s, when investors were willing to pay high premiums for the growth mobile telecoms promised.

### The parent company is heavily indebted and needs to raise fresh capital to repay debt

In 2000, British Telecommunications plc (BT) found itself with nearly £30 billion of debt, after paying very high prices to win 3G (third-generation wireless) licences in the UK and Germany. The company announced a strategy that was centred on a number of carve-outs. BT announced that over the following 18 months it would: (a) prepare BT Wireless, the mobile telephone operating subsidiary, for an IPO; (b) float 25 per cent of Yell, the Yellow Pages directory business, for a hoped for £1 billion; (c) float a similar portion of Netco, its network division; and (d) later in 2002, launch an IPO for BT Ignite, its broadband and Internet business.

As of early 2001, the turn in stock market sentiment had precluded the ability of BT to raise funds through the planned equity carve-outs. To reduce debt, the company launched the UK's largest ever rights issue, and demerged its mobile telephone business.

#### Regular policy of carve-outs in order to maximize shareholder value

An American company, ThermoElectron, is an expert on equity carve-outs. The parent company has partially spun off six subsidiary companies, while those six have in turn partially spun off a further 16 companies. Other serial 'carve-outers' include Safeguard Scientifics, Genzyme Corporation in the USA and MDS in Canada.

The McKinsey study found that the average shareholder return over three years for the serial 'carve-outers' was 31.1 per cent, compared with 36.6 per cent for their carved-out subsidiaries, and 10.2 per cent for the Russell 2000 Index.

### *Demergers*

A more dramatic move is the complete separation of subsidiary from parent. This is called a demerger in the UK and a spin-off in the USA. A demerger is a 100 per cent separation – it raises no new capital for either parent or subsidiary. In a demerger, a business is split into two new, separately listed companies. Investors retain the same proportionate interest in the two successor companies as they had in the original business. For example, in BT's demerger of $mmO_2$ (discussed below), a shareholder who had 10 000 BT shares prior to the demerger received 10 000 new shares in $mmO_2$ and 10 000 new BT Group shares.

Demergers can result in temporary downward pressure on the demerged company's shares, as investors who are not interested in the newly independent company sell their shares in the market.

When German pharmaceutical giant Hoechst merged with France's Rhône Poulenc, management of the new entity prepared to demerge Hoechst's subsidiary in the chemical business, Celanese. Hoechst's shareholders were offered one Celanese share for every 10 Hoechst shares owned. For investors who were not interested in holding Celanese shares, Hoechst organized a bookbuilding process managed by CSFB and Dresdner Kleinwort Benson. Shareholders had 10 days in October 1999 to decide whether to hold the new shares or to sell them. In offering an orderly sale, by seeking new investors through the bookbuilding, Hoechst helped to prevent weakness in the initial trading price of Celanese shares.

Demergers don't always work. In the six months following the demerger of Conoco by DuPont, both stocks underperformed the market by around 20 per cent. If spin-off (demerged) companies are too small, in a market that values size, shareholder value may be destroyed. This happened when Hillsdown Holdings, with a pre-demerger market capitalization of £800 million, split into three. Six months later, the three companies were worth around £725 million, and had underperformed the market by 40 per cent.

### Tracking stock

In the USA, a number of companies issued tracking stock during the 1990s. Tracking stock simply follows the performance of a division or business unit, even if the division is closely integrated with the parent's operations. Tracking stock does not give shareholders ownership of the business's assets, nor do shareholders have voting influence over the business in which they are investing. Some companies that have issued tracking stock include General Motors (EDS and Hughes), AT&T (AT&T Wireless) and Ziff Davis (ZD Net).

### Sale by professional investors

Many companies are backed by development or venture capital firms at an early stage, or have undergone a management buy-out backed by private equity capital. These financial investors typically want to cash in their investment ('exit') within three to seven years. Flotation is often the optimal method of maximizing proceeds, although sale to a strategic buyer is also very common.

I define venture capitalists as those investors that look at start-up, early stage and follow-on financings. Private equity capital is defined as institutional investors who only invest in well-established companies, usually in some sort of leveraged acquisition as described below. You should be aware that many private equity firms in the UK and Europe describe themselves as venture capitalists, but never invest in early stage companies.

Venture capitalists and private equity investors typically monitor their investments much more closely than a portfolio investor in publicly quoted companies. Good venture capitalists provide more than just funds – they provide advice, contacts in industry, knowledge of when and how to do an IPO. Most funds are organized as limited partnerships, with the general partners acting as the managers of the funds as well as the monitors of the investments – generally by sitting on the board of directors of investee companies.

### Sale by venture capitalists

During the IPO boom of the late 1990s, a significant proportion of US flotations were for companies that had venture capital financing at an earlier stage of development. The National Venture Capital Association (NVCA) and Venture Economics reported

| Year | Total IPOs | Number with VC backing | Proportion (%) |
|---|---|---|---|
| 1997 | 629 | 138 | 21.9 |
| 1998 | 373 | 78 | 20.9 |
| 1999 | 544 | 271 | 49.8 |

**Table 1.2** Venture capital exits via IPOs

that 50 per cent of 544 IPOs in the USA in 1999 were backed by VCs, compared with 20 per cent in each of 1997 and 1998.

Work by Barry et al. (1990), Megginson and Weiss (1991) and Brav and Gompers (1997) indicates that companies with VC backing tend to have lower underpricing (i.e. lower first-day premia) than non-VC backed companies. However, Rittter (1999), who examined a later period of IPOs (1989–1995), found that venture capital backed issues were associated with larger initial returns.

Megginson and Weiss (1991) found that the presence of venture capitalists as shareholders in the offering firm 'certifies the quality of the IPO through their investment in financial and reputational capital'. Their study compared 640 IPOs, 50 per cent of which had VC financing and a control group of firms which did not, during the period 1983–1987. Among their findings were:

- VC backed firms are younger, have higher asset values and larger percentages of equity in their capital structures.
- VC backed firms are able to attract higher quality underwriters and auditors as well as a larger institutional following than non-VC backed IPOs.
- They are able to reduce the costs of going public: significantly lower underpricing and underwriter compensation.
- VCs do not cash out on the IPO. In only 43.3 per cent of IPOs did VCs sell shares and in less than 1 per cent of offerings did the VCs cash out entirely. On average 8 per cent of VC holdings were sold at the IPO.

A study of VC investments in the biotechnology industry between 1978 and 1992 showed that VCs are able to successfully time IPOs, when the companies' valuations are at their absolute and short-run peaks (Lerner, 1994). This would seem to be borne out by the increase in proportion of VC backed deals in 1999. The same study indicated that experienced VCs were better at timing IPOs than less experienced VCs.

> 'Successful timing of the IPO market provides significant benefits to VCs, even though they rarely sell shares at the time of the offering. Taking companies public when equity values are high minimizes that dilution of the VC's ownership stake . . .'
>
> (Lerner, 1994: 294)

The deliberate underpricing of IPOs builds support in the market for future offers.

### Reverse LBOs

Leveraged buy-outs (LBOs) are the purchase of companies or divisions utilizing a high proportion of debt to finance the acquisition. LBO is the generic term, which encompasses: MBOs – management buy-outs; MBIs – management buy-ins; and BIMBOs – buy-in management buy-outs. The equity portion of the funding is usually provided by a 'private equity' fund, although in Europe this is often called venture capital as well. Like risk venture capitalists, private equity buyers look for an exit within three to seven years from the date of their investment.

The exit may take the form of the sale of the business to a strategic buyer, the sale of the business to another buy-out firm or an IPO. A reverse LBO is the transaction that brings the company to the public markets in an IPO. The IPO is often the first of several equity offerings required before the equity backers can sell 100 per cent of their investment in the company. The backers realize this and will often accept a lower price in the IPO than they might otherwise have received in order to maximize the long-term stock price.

We'll look at two examples of reverse LBOs – one American and one British.

In August 1999, Fairchild Semiconductor completed its IPO and listing on the New York Stock Exchange. Two and a half years previously, management had bought the company with the equity backing of Citicorp Venture Capital. National Semiconductor, Fairchild's parent company, retained a 10 per cent interest following the buy-out.

Between 1997 and the summer of 1999, Fairchild made two large acquisitions with an aggregate purchase value of $575 million and raised a total of $1.5 billion in bank loans and high-yield bonds. At the financial year end 31 May 1999, Fairchild had $1.06 billion in debt outstanding. Its total stockholder equity was in deficit to the tune of $240 million. By any measure, its balance sheet was stretched.

Credit Suisse First Boston (CSFB) and Salomon Smith Barney (SSB) were appointed the lead managers for the IPO, continuing their strong relationship with the company. CSFB had co-led the syndicated loans and was lead manager on Fairchild's two high-yield bond offerings, while SSB is the investment banking arm of Citigroup.

In the IPO, Fairchild sold 20 million new shares and National Semiconductor sold three million shares all at $18.50 to raise a total of $425 million. Citicorp Venture Capital sold no shares in the IPO. Fairchild used the fresh capital of $370 million to repay debt.

Less than six months later, Fairchild returned to the equity market with a $903 million offering. The shares were priced at $33.44, an 80 per cent premium to the IPO price. In the second offering, Fairchild raised $200 million in new equity, while National Semiconductor and Citicorp sold $700 million of existing shares.

An example of a particularly fast 'exit' via flotation was the case of Collins Stewart, a UK stockbroker, bought by management from Singer and Friedlander in April 2000. Collins Stewart management, backed by CVC Capital, Bank of Scotland and Parallel Ventures, paid £122 million for the company. In October 2000, six months after the purchase closed, the business was floated with a value of £326 million (or 316p per share). By the end of the first day's trading the company's share price was 365p, a further increase of 15 per cent.

### *Demutualizations and introductions*

Introduction is the term used in the UK when a company's shares are listed on the stock exchange, but in which no money is raised for the company or selling shareholders. They are not strictly IPOs, but many of the documentation, marketing and timetable issues are similar. Introductions may occur when a mutual organization decides to list and distribute shares to its members or policyholders, or when a company already listed on a stock market seeks a listing on a foreign exchange. The other main sources of introductions are corporate demergers, as discussed earlier.

| Country | Companies |
| --- | --- |
| Australia | AMP, Colonial Mutual |
| Canada | Canada Life, Clarica, Laurentian Life, Manulife, Sun Life |
| UK | Abbey National, Clerical Medical, Halifax Building Society, NPI, Norwich Union |
| USA | Prudential Financial, Metropolitan Life, John Hancock |

**Table 1.3** Selected demutualizations of financial institutions

Numerous customer-owned (mutual) savings institutions and insurance companies joined stock markets in the 1990s, in a process known as demutualization. Demutualization takes a company from ownership by its customers (e.g. policy-holders, account holders) to ownership by shareholders. On conversion, which requires 'membership' approval, shares are distributed to the firm's policy or account holders. The shares are then listed on a stock exchange through an introduction.

Once a firm has demutualized it is able to raise external equity capital or use its shares to acquire assets or other companies. The process has occurred in the UK, USA, Canada, Australia and France.

## *Privatizations*

Privatizations (the sale of state-owned enterprises) are a special form of sale by existing share owners. In addition to the objectives of selling shareholders introduced at the beginning of the chapter are political objectives. The political objectives may or may not conflict with the objectives of the company or the investors, but will always make the investment banker's job more difficult. Privatizations by way of share offerings have contributed to the development of equity markets in countries as diverse as the UK, Chile, Germany and Malaysia.

Following the initial success of large privatization offerings in the UK (British Telecom, British Gas, British Airways, BAA, etc.), governments around the world launched ever larger IPOs and secondary offerings. Privatizations by way of public share offerings were a significant driver in the growth and development of international equity offerings. The sale of £3.9 billion of BT shares in late 1984 provided the precedent for multi-tranche international offerings.

### Goals of privatizations

The sale of state-owned enterprises to investors has to meet multiple objectives for the privatizing government:

- Raising funds for the treasury.
- Imposing private market disciplines on management and workers – thereby increasing efficiency and service to customers.
- Fostering a shareholders' democracy.
- Winning votes (although this is not explicitly stated).

Privatizations in countries like the UK and Chile were driven in large part by ideological reasons. The British Government of Margaret Thatcher had an inherent distaste of government ownership. It also found that the inefficiencies in the operations of organizations like British Telecom, British Gas and others would be impossible to eliminate under state ownership. This meant that many UK privatizations were able to show operating improvements for years after they went public.

In many other countries privatizations occurred simply because the government needed funds. In Europe, reduction of government debt to levels below those imposed by the Maastricht Treaty for entry into monetary union led to massive volumes of issuance in the mid to late 1990s.

Finally, many governments wished to create a 'share-owning democracy'. Some believe that the success of the first Deutsche Telekom offering in 1996 increased German interest in the equity market and indirectly spurred the growth of the Neuer Markt (market for smaller companies) after it was established in 1997.

## The results

Privatizations have been incredibly successful in raising funds. In aggregate, privatizations raised over $835 billion globally during the 1990s. Of the total amount, approximately $500 billion was raised through stock market flotations or follow-on offerings, as illustrated in Figure 1.9.

One estimate suggests that 11 per cent of IPOs between 1992 and 1999 were privatizations (Ljunqvist et al., 2002), but because most privatizations are sizeable, the proportion of privatization funds raised as a total amount of IPO funds raised is higher.

In fact, the 19 largest and 27 of the 30 largest common stock offerings in history have been privatizations. First in the UK and then around the world, privatizations accounted for some of the largest flotations recorded, including €18 billion raised by the Italian Treasury in the sale of 35 per cent of its interest in Enel, the electricity

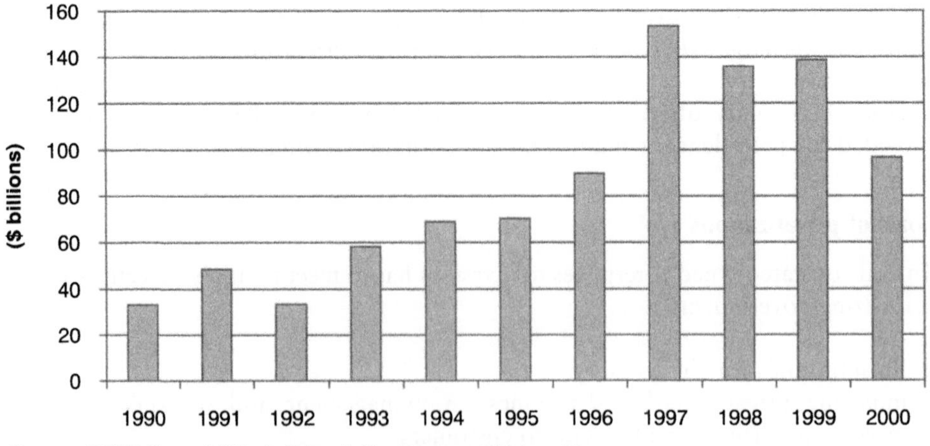


*Source*: *OECD Financial Market Trends* No. 79, June 2001, p. 44.

**Figure 1.9** Global privatization volumes

| Rank | Date | Company | Country | Amount ($m) |
|---|---|---|---|---|
| 1 | Nov-99 | ENEL | Italy | 18 900 |
| 2 | Oct-98 | NTT DoCoMo | Japan | 18 000 |
| 3 | Feb-87 | NTT | Japan | 15 097 |
| 4 | Nov-96 | Deutsche Telekom | Germany | 13 330 |
| 5 | Nov-97 | Telstra | Australia | 10 530 |
| 6 | Dec-90 | Regional Electricity Companies | UK | 9 995 |
| 7 | Dec-89 | UK Water Authorities | UK | 8 679 |
| 8 | Dec-86 | British Gas | UK | 8 012 |
| 9 | Oct-93 | Japan Railroad East | Japan | 7 312 |
| 10 | Oct-97 | France Telecom | France | 7 080 |

*Source:* Megginson, Nash, Netter and Schwartz (2000)

**Table 1.4** Largest privatizations (IPOs) to 2000

generator and supplier, in October 1999. At the time the Enel offering was the largest ever privatization or equity offering in the world.

### Special issues surrounding privatizations

In undertaking a privatization offering, a government faces several interrelated decisions: how to transfer control, how to price the offer, and how to allocate the shares. These are not dissimilar issues to a corporate IPO, but governments face the added political factor. In pricing, many governments are thought to have deliberately underpriced privatizations in order to encourage a 'share-owning' class.

Allocation decisions relate not only to rewarding investors who have indicated the strongest interest at the highest price, but also whether or not to favour one group of investors over another (e.g. retail vs. institutional, domestic vs. international, etc.). The choice of lead manager in the privatization is often fraught – should a government use an international investment bank with global distribution, or should it choose a local bank, in an attempt to build a local champion?

Privatizations involve a greater degree of paperwork, as the selling government may have to prove that it is receiving value for money in the process. For example, Britain's National Audit Office (NAO) reviews each privatization and sale of government-owned shares to ensure that the government has received the best price possible for the lowest fees.

BT's one-day opening premium of 80 per cent led the way for a series of greatly underpriced offerings. Privatizations became viewed as one-way bets. Perotti and Guney (1993), Vickers and Yarrow (1988), Jenkinson and Mayer (1988) and Menyah et al. (1990) all document that privatization issues had higher levels of underpricing than corporate IPOs. However, not all privatizations leap in value and investors must take the same caution that they apply to the purchase of a corporate IPO. One investment banker said:

> 'When a government is the seller, it has to balance the need to make people who invest happy, with a fiduciary duty to the rest of

> the country to sell assets at their real value. At this level of volume (referring to ENEL's privatization in October 1999) even a one percent difference in price is very meaningful. It is worth a lot of hospitals and highways.'
>
> (Caplen et al., 2000)

## Advantages and disadvantages of going public

The above section presented the main reasons that firms go public. This section highlights the additional advantages as well as some of the disadvantages.

### *Advantages*

The advantages of going public include:

1 Liquidity and increased share price
2 Management and employee motivation
3 Enhanced image/prestige
4 Access to alternative sources of capital
5 Ancillary benefits.

#### Valuation and liquidity impact

Companies listed on a stock exchange are typically worth more than similar companies that are privately held. The information contained in an IPO prospectus and subsequent annual reports reduces the uncertainty around performance and hence increases the value of a business.

In addition, investors are willing to pay a premium for liquidity: the ability to easily buy or sell shares. Private companies have limited or no liquidity. The liquidity premium varies over time and economic conditions, but a reasonable estimate would be in the 30 per cent range. This means that if two identical companies exist, one listed and the other not, the listed company will be worth approximately 30 per cent more than the private company.

Daily liquidity means that insiders know the value of their holdings more accurately, as well as facilitating further sales of shares. As noted above, one of the reasons given for the Docent and Ottakar's IPOs was the ability for the shares to trade on a public market.

#### Motivate management and employees

The use of incentives such as stock options and stock bonuses to attract and retain both employees and management became widespread particularly in the USA and UK during the 1990s. Equity-based awards and ownership tend to be spread more broadly among management and employees in public companies compared to private companies. In addition, management and employees of public companies can see the results of their efforts in the share price more immediately.

## Prestige/enhanced image

A significant, but intangible, benefit of a flotation is the increased visibility of the company through its ongoing disclosures to the stock exchange or securities commission. Many believe there is considerable prestige attached to managing and working for a publicly listed company. This can lead to the recruitment and retention of higher quality employees.

A quotation may bring marketing benefits, by making the company seem stronger and more substantial. Press coverage of public companies is typically greater than that of privately owned firms.

> 'While both good and bad news must be disseminated to enable investors to make well-informed decisions, a public company that is well run and compiles a record of success can gain a first class reputation that can prove an immeasurable benefit in many ways. As a company's name and products or services become better known, not only do investors take notice, but so do customers and suppliers, who often prefer to do business with well-known companies.'
>
> (Garner et al., 1994: 17)

## Access to alternative sources of capital

Another benefit ascribed to flotation is the ability to gain access to alternative sources of capital in the future. Quoted companies are often able to raise money for expansion more easily and at better rates than private companies of similar size. The public debt markets are more accessible to stock exchange quoted companies than to companies without a listing.

Moreover, going public generally improves a company's debt–equity ratio and may enable it to borrow on better terms in the future. One study by Pagano et al. (1998) found that Italian companies that went public were able to borrow more cheaply after their IPO. They also found that the number of banks willing to lend to a company increases after its flotation. However, they report that a similar study conducted in Spain (Planell) uncovered no significant decrease in interest rates paid after the IPO.

## Ancillary benefits of flotation

The flotation process often forces a company's management to formulate and articulate a clear business strategy for the first time. This clearly should be beneficial to the future success of the business.

Along similar lines, the anticipation of public ownership leads many companies into improving their management and financial structure. Fast growing medium-sized companies often neglect the formal structures which will help them in their attempts to become large companies.

## *Disadvantages*

Flotation does bring about some disadvantages, although each company will perceive these differently. There are the costs involved: both the direct costs (in time and money) of the flotation process as well as the costs of underpricing of the offering and the costs of increased disclosure to public shareholders (again, this is comprised of both time and money).

Some of the disadvantages of going public are:

1 Increased disclosure
2 Costs of IPOs
3 Potential loss of control
4 Separation of ownership and control
5 Perceptions of short-termism
6 Meeting investor expectations.

### Increased disclosure

When a company moves from private ownership to public, it vastly increases the number of people who have access to its financial records. This can be a huge shock to the existing owners, not just the reporting of the company's results, but the disclosure of management salaries and perks that often piques the interest of newspaper editors on a slow day.

Companies are required by stock exchanges, securities commissions and regulators to disclose information on a regular basis so that investors and potential investors can make buy, sell or hold decisions. A much greater amount of information is required at the time of the IPO and is included in the offering prospectus.

Disclosure requirements vary by country. Those countries with the largest stock markets, relative to the economy, typically have the highest disclosure requirements (e.g. Australia, Canada, UK, USA). The development of efficient capital markets in Central and Eastern Europe has been hindered partially by the reticence of corporate executives to disclose information about their firm's operations and performance.

It's not all bad though. Botosan (1997) has found that increased disclosure on the part of the company can reduce its cost of equity. By reducing its cost of equity, a company is able to invest in more projects, raise capital more cheaply, and enhance its valuation.

### Costs of IPOs

Initial public offerings aren't cheap. Investment bankers take commissions of between 2 and 7 per cent of the total amount raised; lawyers and accountants bill by the hour, and many hours are required. The ancillary costs, such as public relations, printing, corporate advertising and others can add several hundred thousand more dollars, euros or pounds.

In addition to the initial costs of the IPO, there are the costs of maintaining a quote (stock exchange fees, management time, more extensive audits and reporting, reconciliation of accounts to US GAAP if listed on a US exchange, etc.).

However, the direct costs of an IPO can pale beside the indirect cost of underpricing. Because no cash is coming directly out of the issuer's pocket, underpricing can sometimes be ignored as a cost. It should not be. IPOs around the world are underpriced compared with their short-term performance. On average, an IPO will close at a price that is 15 to 20 per cent above its issue price, although this varies by market and industry and over time (see Figure 1.2). This means that selling shareholders and the company are leaving significant sums of money on the table when they go public.

Jay Ritter, a Professor at the University of Florida and leading IPO researcher, keeps track of the money left on the table in US offerings as illustrated in Figure 1.10. Note that the aggregate amount and amount per deal surged in 1999 and 2000, and that while the aggregate amount left on the table dropped back in 2001, as a result of a 75 per cent reduction in IPOs, the amount per deal ($40 million) continues to be significantly above historical norms.

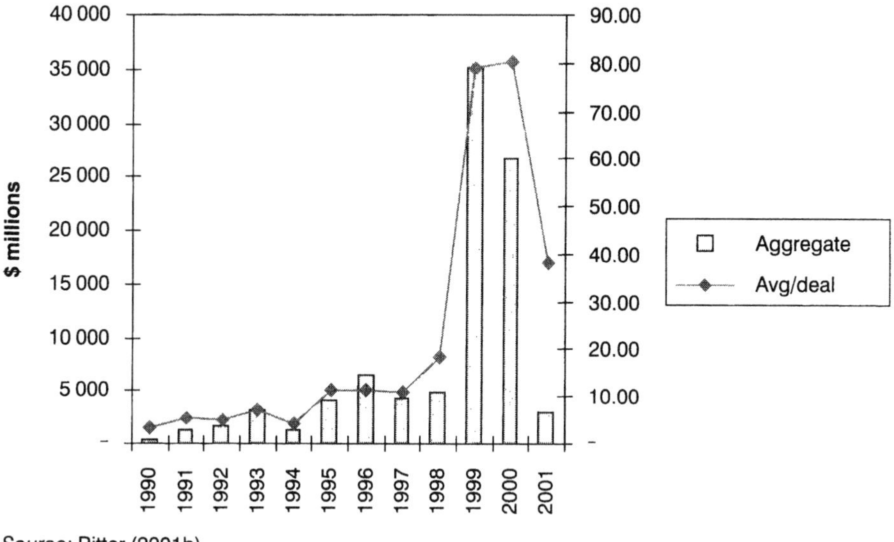


*Source*: Ritter (2001b).

**Figure 1.10** Money left on the table in US IPOs (1990–2001)

The amount of money left on the table is calculated by subtracting the offer price from the first day closing price and multiplying by the number of shares offered (excluding the overallotment option). By excluding the overallotment option (see Chapter 11), this calculation is probably understating the amount of money left on the table.

## Potential restrictions on management action

In many private companies, the managers are the owners. Therefore there are few restrictions on management action other than statutory and legal regulations and common sense. However, this is not a problem as the linkage of ownership and control should lead to little divergence of opinion about the appropriate course of action for the company.

In public companies, the managers are the agents of the shareholders – they should be acting on behalf of, and in the best interests of, the shareholders. In order to ensure that they do, public companies have boards of directors who are meant to oversee management's actions on behalf of shareholders. In some circumstances a strong board of directors may limit the actions of management.

## Potential loss of control

Not all IPOs are for more than 50 per cent of the issuer's voting shares, in fact, the average is around 30 per cent. So although control is not lost at the IPO, if the company requires further equity to fuel its growth, existing shareholders will suffer dilution. For most companies, at some point in time control will pass to public shareholders.

> 'This risk [passing of control] can be minimized by limiting the number of shares sold to the public, seeking to ensure a broad distribution of shares to the public, creating tiered classes of stock with differential voting rights, entering into voting agreements among pre-IPO shareholders, adopting supermajority provisions or staggering the terms of the directors. Creating a dual class voting structure can depress the price of the shares with less voting power. While some structures may prove more effective than others, there is no guarantee that a public company will not be threatened by a hostile acquiror.'
>
> (Greenstein et al., 2000: 7)

## Perceptions of short-termism

One of the most common complaints of corporate management is that Wall Street or the City are too 'short-termist'. That is, investors and analysts focus exclusively on the current quarter/reporting period, without giving due consideration to the long-term impact of decisions. Shareholders generally judge management's performance in terms of profits and stock price. Significant pressure exists to increase profits each period and to meet analysts' expectations. This pressure may cause management to emphasize near-term strategies instead of longer-term goals (Garner, Owen and Conway, 1994).

In order to meet investors' quarterly or semi-annual earnings expectations a company may be forced off the long-term strategy that was in place prior to the IPO. Managers may feel compelled to follow strategies that support the share price in the short term, rather than over a long time horizon. Other potential constraints on management's activities include:

- Restrictions on future sales of shares.
- Possible tax implications in different countries.

### Dealing with institutional investors

Along with the above complaint about short-termism, many chief executives (usually heading a company with poorly performing stock prices) complain that the stock market doesn't understand entrepreneurs, and that entrepreneurial decision making and creativity are stifled by the men in blue pinstripe suits.

Finally, dealing with shareholders, financial analysts and the press is time consuming. The CEO and CFO/Finance Director should expect to expend, on average, at least one day per month meeting with and discussing the company's strategy, performance and operations. Those companies that do not establish good relationships with the financial community can find themselves without friends in times of need, such as when faced with a hostile take-over.

> 'The performance expectations of Wall Street can only be described as brutal. Miss your earnings forecasts, especially in the first year after your IPO, and you could see a catastrophic decline in the price of your stock of 50 percent or better. Once a young management team has discredited itself with Wall Street, there may be no recovery.'
>
> (American Lawyer Media, 'The Survival Guide to IPOs', p. 15)

While the advantages of going public outweigh the disadvantages, every year dozens of companies voluntarily leave the stock market in what is called a 'public to private transaction'. These transactions are typically management buy-outs of the public shareholders and come after periods of a depressed share price.

## What makes a deal successful?

In the USA, Dunbar (1998) examined unsuccessful US IPOs. Of the companies in his study that filed a registration statement with the Securities and Exchange Commission (SEC), 30 per cent didn't make it to market. There may have been a variety of reasons, both company-specific and relating to market conditions. However, less than 10 per cent returned and completed a successful IPO. This research suggests that a company only has one chance to get it right.

In determining what makes a deal successful, we first need to decide how we define success. A successful offering is one that meets the objectives of the three main parties to the deal: company, vendors and investors. There are numerous indicators of success, some of which are listed here:

- Reasonable first day premium
- Broad distribution
- Stable core holdings
- Minimal flowback
- Strong aftermarket share price performance
- Trading volume, market/investor confidence.

In pricing terms, an opening premium of approximately 10 to 15 per cent above the offering price keeps both vendors and investors happy. Vendors don't like to think that they've left too much money on the table, while investors are happy to show a modest initial return on their investment.

If both vendor and investor are happy with the price achieved, so will be the investment bankers (who are always conscious of serving two masters in IPOs and subsequent equity offerings).

On completion of an IPO, particularly large ones, the distribution of shares among investors is important. Companies will want to see a balance between institutional supporters and retail investors. A typical distribution might be 30 per cent retail, 70 per cent institutional. International investors will also account for a proportion of the demand and allocations. If the company opts for a second stock exchange listing, it will hope to see sufficient shares placed in the foreign market so that decent liquidity will develop on its stock exchange.

The company wants to see most shares allocated to long-term supportive investors, shareholders who will continue to hold and increase their investment as long as the company delivers what it has promised. Issuers understand, of course, that it is necessary to place some shares with short-term investors (commonly called flippers or stags), who will sell in the immediate aftermarket, thereby creating liquidity.

In international offerings, the issuer wants to make sure that the foreign shareholders are 'sticky', and that the shares allocated do not 'flow back' to the domestic market.

Offerings in which shares are widely placed are more likely to succeed. If investors don't know each other and don't share information, they will not know whether early demand for an issue is strong. In this case, they must make up their own mind as to the company's merits rather than jumping on the bandwagon for a short ride.

In general, firms with the following characteristics will have more successful offerings:

- Larger rather than smaller
- Profitable rather than loss-making
- Primary offering rather than existing shareholders selling
- Lower number of risk factors disclosed in the prospectus
- High insider (i.e. management and directors) ownership.

This chapter has concentrated on issuers (and to a lesser extent, selling shareholders); their motivations and the benefits that accrue to public companies. The next two chapters will address details regarding the people involved in an IPO and the IPO process itself.

# 2 The players

Preparing a company for flotation requires the involvement of a large number of players, each with a specific role to play. The leading participant, and generally the first advisor appointed, is a merchant bank or an investment bank. Occasionally other professional advisors, such as stockbrokers or chartered accountants, can take this important role. In the UK, this financial advisor is formally known as the sponsor, as it sponsors the company in its application to join the stock exchange. If the issuer is launching its IPO on Britain's Alternative Investment Market (AIM), the sponsor is called the nominated advisor.

In international offerings, the lead bank will be known variously as the lead manager, bookrunner or global coordinator. In the USA, the principal bank is known as the lead manager, but members of the offering syndicate (including the lead) are called underwriters. Chapter 10 contains more information on syndicate terminology.

In general, I will use the terms lead manager and lead banker when referring to the most senior bank's role. Occasionally I will use the term sponsor when referring to exclusively UK deals.

As the markets have developed and become more sophisticated, the personnel involved in a new issue have become specialists. Now, only a few people at the lead investment bank involved in the transaction will have a full understanding of the status of both the legal and marketing aspects of the offering.

The sponsor, or lead manager: develops the structure of the offering; helps to appoint other participants (solicitors, public and investor relations advisors, ADR (American Depository Receipt) depository bank and registrars); coordinates all aspects of the issue; leads the drafting of documentation; organizes the due diligence and verification process; and, in traditional UK offerings, is the primary underwriter. The sponsor also formally backs the company's application for listing on the stock exchange.

The initial public offering of any company is one of the most important moments in its corporate life – it only happens once, and while companies can become skilled at acquisitions and divestitures, they do not have a similar opportunity to become skilful at executing IPOs. Thus, the role of the lead manager in guiding companies and their management to market is crucial.

A member of the Corporate Finance or Equity Capital Markets (ECM) group usually takes the coordinating role within an investment bank. ECM professionals specialize in the flotation of companies and their subsequent equity offerings. They work closely with relationship managers, corporate financiers, the syndicate desk and equity sales and research – blending the knowledge gained from each of the specialist groups. ECM groups are usually physically located close to the equity sales and trading floor, often in a restricted access area just off the main trading area. The ECM is 'behind the Chinese Wall' (see below).

**The Chinese Wall**

Corporate financiers and ECM professionals are said to work behind Chinese Walls – separating them from other members of the firm, in particular those who have daily contact with investors. The name is presumably taken from the Great Wall of China.

Chinese Walls are simply established arrangements in the form of procedures, systems, management and physical location which act as barriers within a firm to ensure that information generated within one part of the firm, or obtained from a client in one part of the firm (i.e. Corporate Finance), does not penetrate another part of the firm (i.e. Research, Sales and Trading). They exist (or should do) in integrated securities firms, investment banks, accounting firms, or any other organization where some members of the firm have access to and deal with information that could affect the share price of clients.

Corporate Finance departments in large investment banks are almost always located on a separate floor to other departments. At the very least, access is restricted to those who work in the area or escorted visitors who are signed in and out.

Chinese Walls provide a mechanism for firms to function as multidisciplinary operations. Without Chinese Walls, a firm could not offer both corporate finance advice *and* research, sales and trading with clients. They work like porous membranes that allow information to flow only in one direction toward Corporate Finance and ECM, as illustrated below:

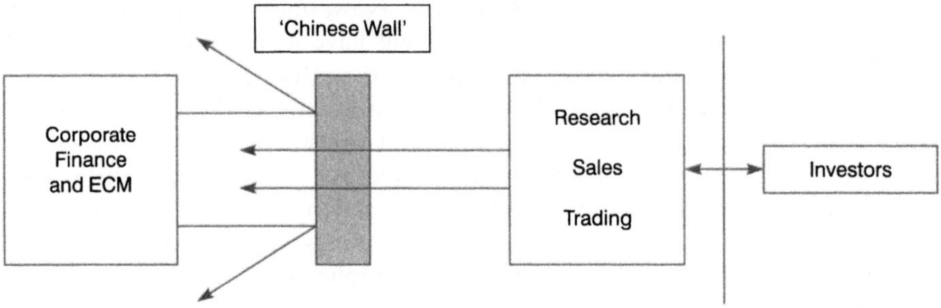


In order to advise clients, corporate financiers must receive information regarding the market, investors' attitudes, etc. from research analysts and salesmen who are in contact with investing institutions. However, the confidential corporate information received by corporate financiers must not flow in the other direction, as it could have an impact on the price of the shares.

Throughout the book, when referring to 'corporate financiers' and 'bankers', the reader should understand that this includes equity capital markets personnel.

Once the mandate to lead an offering has been awarded, in most banks the ECM takes over the 'project management' of the IPO, coordinating the input of the bank's specialist departments as well as external advisors. Figure 2.1 provides a schematic of the interested parties in a flotation. The corporate financier keeps everything together: he or she is the main interface with the company, although solicitors, accountants and investor relations people also have direct, but less wide-ranging, contact with the issuer.

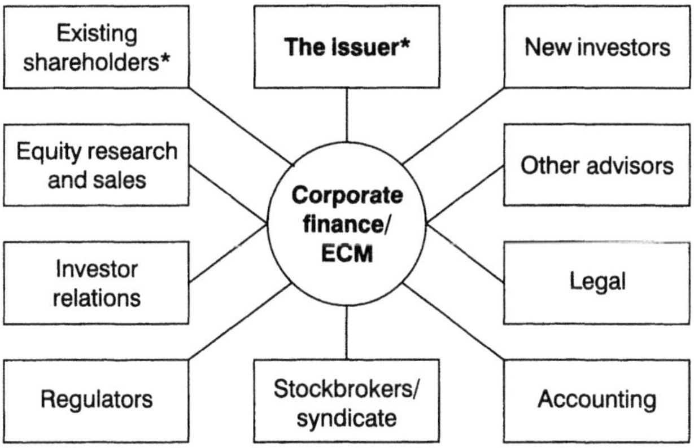


*Either one or both of the issuer and existing shareholders may be the banker's client, depending on the type of shares being sold (primary or secondary).

**Figure 2.1** Parties involved in IPOs and equity offerings

Within the investment bank, corporate financiers and ECM people deal primarily with the company and develop an ongoing relationship with the issuer. Salesmen and research analysts maintain their primary relationship with investors. Sitting between the two groups – literally in many banks – is the syndicate desk.

Syndicate managers do not develop relationships – in the corporate world, anyway. Their role can be likened to a series of short intense affairs, where the object of their affection is the deal itself. The syndicate desk is where the interests of the issuer, as represented by the corporate financiers, must be balanced with those of investors, represented by the sales force.

The lead manager is usually the first appointed external advisor, after the issuer's traditional accountants and lawyers. It then aids the company in selecting the other advisors to work on the transaction. The lead bank provides advice on: the capital structure; developing the investment story; appointing external directors; determining the timing of an issue; and other matters that require a market perspective. They then coordinate the new issue timetable. From start to finish, the flotation process takes from three to six months, sometimes longer if there are particularly difficult corporate structuring issues to be resolved. Corporate financiers deal with documentation (listing particulars, prospectus, underwriting agreement) and the regulators. They are also responsible for the coordination of the different departments in their investment bank and members of the syndicate (i.e. making sure that research analysts know the publication deadlines, the sales departments know the timetable and devote sufficient time to the new issue, the back office is prepared etc.).

Finally, junior members of the corporate finance team are responsible for the organization of the closing dinner; a gala affair for all the participants in the transaction that usually takes place a month or so after the shares have been trading on the stock exchange. In late 2001, the financial press had some fun with an internal memo leaked by someone at CSFB. The memo stated that because of poor market conditions, staff were limited to spending $10 000 on celebratory meals at the conclusion of transactions.

## Selecting the lead investment bank

When selecting the lead investment bank, the issuer or selling shareholders look to a number of criteria (adapted from Greenstein et al., 2000):

- **Industry experience.** The bank should have substantial experience in IPOs of companies in the issuer's industry and a good familiarity with the company and its business. It should be able to tell the issuer how the market would receive an issue at the time it is considering going public.
- **Experienced analyst.** The bank should have a well-known analyst in the industry. Having an analyst with a high profile in the relevant sector is a factor typically accorded great weight by companies considering an IPO. The analyst must describe how the IPO should be positioned in order to appeal to the broadest base of investors.
- **Individual bankers.** Issuers should be aware, if they are not already, that the senior bankers who roll in and pitch for the business frequently are not involved with the deal on a day-to-day basis. The company should feel comfortable with the individual bankers assigned to the transaction.
- **Reputation and attention.** While reputation is important, the most well known investment banks may not give smaller companies as much attention as less well known investment banks. On the other hand, less well known investment banks may not be able to provide the resources that a better known underwriter can.
- **Distribution strength.** The potential lead manager and the company should discuss the offer structure. Will shares be distributed outside the domestic market? Should the issue be sold primarily to retail or institutional investors? The investment bank(s) selected should have the appropriate international, institutional or retail distribution capabilities, as required.
- **Aftermarket support.** The underwriter should have a strong record of aftermarket price performance for the stock of the companies it has recently taken public. A strong record would indicate how well the investment bank priced recent transactions.
- **Conflicts of interest.** Will the bank be involved with any other offerings in the same sector at the time the company's IPO is being marketed?

The academics also have something to say about the selection of lead managers. Booth and Smith (1986) predicted that choosing a highly rated lead manager leads to lower underpricing of IPOs. This hypothesis has been verified in the American market by Carter and Manaster (1990) and Michaely and Shaw (1994).

To generalize, highly reputable investment banks only underwrite less risky IPOs, while less reputable banks are left with the riskier IPOs. Carter and Manaster predict that the initial return on an IPO is negatively correlated with the banker's reputation. This seems to have been true prior to the late 1990s bull market, but during the bull market, deals managed by some of the most 'reputable' banks had the highest degree of underpricing (i.e. the highest opening premium).

Other research (Beatty and Vetsuypens, 1995; Nanda et al., 1995; Carter et al., 1998) investigated the relation between long-run IPO performance and investment banks' market share. The studies suggest that market share is adversely affected by the poor long-run performance of the companies whose IPOs they manage. Beatty and Ritter (1986) also found that lead managers that regularly misprice (i.e. overprice) IPOs tend to lose market share.

Nanda and Yun (1997) investigated the impact of mispriced IPOs on lead underwriter market value (capitalization). When a bank launched an IPO that dropped in price on the first day of trading, they found that the lead underwriters' market value dropped. They suggest that this reflects damage to the lead underwriters' reputation as a result of overpricing the IPO. On the other hand, underpriced offerings are associated with increases in lead manager value.

### Pitching for business

A large part of the life of an ECM professional lies in pitching for mandates to take companies public. Banks typically prepare pitch books the contents of which include:

- Initial thoughts on valuation
- Initial thoughts on the selling story
- Initial thoughts on structure of offering and distribution
- Bank's credentials
  - deal team and profiles
  - research analyst and ranking
  - similar transactions
  - league table positions
  - league table position in specified industry
  - number of sales and trading personnel.

The appendix to this chapter contains the contents of a letter sent to potential syndicate members asking them to submit their credentials by the advisors to a European government. The letter is an invitation to 'pitch' the recipients' credentials to participate in the deal. Such letters and their contents were typical in 1990s privatizations.

### Reputation

Carter and Manaster (1990) devised a ranking system for banks involved in US IPOs to support their hypothesis that underpricing will be less for deals lead managed by underwriters with greater prestige.

| Bookrunner | Amount $US million | Number of Issues |
|---|---|---|
| Goldman Sachs | 76 112 | 241 |
| Morgan Stanley | 71 983 | 255 |
| Merrill Lynch | 52 350 | 222 |
| Credit Suisse First Boston | 35 474 | 113 |
| UBS Warburg | 20 992 | 56 |
| Citigroup–Salomon Smith Barney | 20 276 | 55 |
| Mediobanca | 15 376 | 11 |
| Dresdner Kleinwort Wasserstein | 13 648 | 36 |
| Nikko | 10 573 | 2 |
| ABN–Rothschild | 10 459 | 55 |

*Sources:* Various

**Table 2.1** IPO Bookrunners (1995–2002)

By examining 501 deals from 1979 to 1983, a scale from 0 (least prestigious) to 9 (most prestigious) was developed. Firms with the rank of 9 'were not dominated in the tombstone announcements; no firms were ever found to rank above them'. The ranking reflects 'the company an underwriter keeps'. A bank that leads a large number of deals may not rank highly if it is included in a low(ish) position in the syndicates of other lead managers.

Of the 117 underwriters that were ranked in that period in the US, only five received the top assigned rank of 9:

First Boston Corporation
Goldman Sachs & Co.
Merrill Lynch White Weld
Morgan Stanley & Co.
Salomon Brothers Inc.

These firms are the traditional 'bulge bracket' firms.

In a 1998 update, Carter, Dark and Singh (CDS) again ranked the underwriters, in the context of examining the long-run returns of IPOs and the reputation of the lead manager. This time, only four made the top rank of 9, although there were more firms ranked between 8 and 9. The top four in 1998 were First Boston, Goldman Sachs, Hambrecht & Quist and Salomon Brothers.

Remembering from Chapter 1 that IPOs typically underperform the market over the long term, CDS found that 'On average, the long-run market adjusted returns are less negative for the IPOs brought to market by the more prestigious underwriters.'

In 2001, Ritter and Loughran updated the rankings again (see Table 2.2). Ritter used slightly different criteria to come up with a list of 'prestigious' investment banks. This group of 18 banks would have a rank of 8 or 9 on the Carter–Manaster or CDS scales.

| |
|---|
| ABN Amro |
| Banc of America Securities |
| BancBoston Roberston Stephens |
| Bear Stearns |
| CIBC World Markets |
| Credit Suisse First Boston |
| Chase H&Q (since merged with JP Morgan) |
| Deutsche Banc Alex Brown |
| Donaldson Lufkin Jenrette (since purchased by CSFB) |
| Goldman Sachs |
| JP Morgan (since merged with Chase Hambrecht & Quist) |
| Lehman Brothers |
| Merrill Lynch |
| Morgan Stanley |
| Paine Webber (since purchased by UBS) |
| Salomon Smith Barney (successor to Salomon Brothers, now part of Citigroup) |
| Thomas Weisel Partners LLC |
| UBS Warburg |

**Table 2.2** 'Prestigious' US investment banks

During the late 1990s, concentration in the award of lead manager mandates for equity offerings increased in the US market that is, the big got bigger. As measured by the Herfindal Index, the index increased from 573 to 1188 for IPOs (higher figures mean greater concentration) and from 746 to 1096 for secondary offerings (SEOs).

| | IPOs (2069) | SEOs (2214) |
|---|---|---|
| 1995 | 573 | 746 |
| 1996 | 460 | 665 |
| 1997 | 514 | 661 |
| 1998 | 590 | 907 |
| 1999 | 1188 | 1096 |

*Source:* Roten and Mullineaux (2001).

**Table 2.3** Concentration in equity underwriting

Perceptions of increasing concentration in international offerings were first noted in a *Euromoney* article, 'The start of a global bulge bracket', in April 1993.

## *Commercial banks vs. investment banks*

During the 1990s, many commercial banks made significant investments in building up their investment banking capabilities. Banks were attracted to the higher margin business of investment banking and the regulatory relaxation in major markets such as the USA. Their growth occurred by internal investment or acquisition, depending on the predilections of management. The banks wanted to capture high margin business like equity financings and corporate advisory work to supplement the traditional low margin lending business.

By the turn of the century, commercial banks were linking their willingness to provide debt finance with getting a piece of the high margin business. No longer were they satisfied with vague promises made by CFOs and chief executives. This is illustrated in the late 2001 €8 billion financing for KPN, the Dutch telecommunications operator. When the company ran into difficulties, eight banks supplied the company with a €2.75 billion loan. The same eight (ABN Amro, Deutsche Bank, Bank of America, CSFB, ING, JP Morgan, Rabobank and Schroder Salomon Smith Barney (Citigroup)) underwrote the company's €5 billion secondary equity offering.

## The syndicate

### *International/American practice*

The lead bank, called the lead manager or global coordinator, will assemble a *syndicate* of banks and brokers to assist in the selling of the offering. A new and different syndicate is formed for every deal, although some banks feel more comfortable with certain other banks and include them in most transactions.

Syndicate members are usually selected on the basis of their ability to distribute shares to investors and to provide company research following the offering. The number of syndicate members will depend on the size and structure of the offering and existing banking relationships the issuer may have.

> 'Historically, syndicates existed partly for regulatory capital requirement and risk-sharing purposes, and partly to facilitate the distribution of an issue. Today, there is little reason to form a syndicate to perform the traditional roles of risk sharing, distribution, and meeting capital requirements.'
>
> (Chen and Ritter, 2000)

In addition to the reasons noted by Chen and Ritter, syndicates are formed:

- To broaden the distribution (some brokers/banks have specific geographic niches).
- To encourage research support following the offering.
- To encourage market making (where applicable) following the offering.
- Reciprocity ('You invited me into your last deal, I'll invite you into mine').

While the lead manager and, for large offerings, senior syndicate roles are appointed by the issuer or selling shareholders, other members of the syndicate tend to be appointed (with issuer approval) by the lead manager. The syndicate structure and number of members depend on the size and nature of the transaction and the country of origin.

Research support following the offering is a major reason to syndicate the offering. Michaely and Womack note that analysts at syndicate firms tend to issue buy recommendations when the company's shares have dropped (by an average of 2 per cent) in the previous month. Unfortunately, the buy recommendations don't seem to have much effect, as their study indicated that the shares continue to perform poorly in the year after the 'buy' recommendation was made.

The researchers looked at the recommendations made by underwriters (syndicate members) and non-syndicate members of 391 companies for two years after they went public in 1990 or 1991. They found that analysts' recommendations were biased in favour of companies that had been IPO clients. In addition, they found that stocks of companies that were recommended *only* by analysts from the underwriting syndicate were 'terrible performers'.

### *The traditional UK system*

In traditional UK flotations, the company hires one merchant bank to act as 'sponsor' of the offering and two stockbrokers if it is a listing on the London Stock Exchange. The merchant bank deals with the UK Listing Authority (UKLA), the main regulator on behalf of the company. The appointed stockbroker handles communications with investors prior to the issue, assists in marketing the shares, arranges the sub-underwriting (see below) and is largely responsible for setting the issue price.

If the company is seeking a quote on the AIM, it must appoint a 'Nominated Advisor' and ensure that there are two brokers willing to make a market in its shares.

## Other advisors and involved parties

### *Solicitors/lawyers*

Two law firms work on new issues: the company's counsel and the lawyers who act for the banking syndicate (known as Solicitors to the Issue in traditional UK offerings). The solicitors ensure that the documentation is accurate and draft the various legal agreements (e.g. underwriting agreement) that are required. The syndicate's solicitors typically take primary responsibility for the legal due diligence during the flotation. This will include a verification process on the statements made in the prospectus in UK offerings.

One of the law firms usually takes responsibility for the 'master' of the prospectus. They will control the drafting of the document until it is in sufficiently good shape to go to the financial printers.

In US offerings, the law firms involved in the transaction take primary responsibility for dealing with the regulator, while in UK offerings, the sponsor is the primary point of contact with the regulator.

### *Accountants*

The issuer's accountants, known as the Reporting Accountant in the UK, also have a major role. They must ensure that the most recently audited financial statements are properly presented in the prospectus, they conduct financial due diligence, and conduct an investigation of the company and in UK offers produce a 'long-form report'. In addition the firm may be asked to produce a short-form report and will also be required to report on any profit forecast included in the listing particulars/ prospectus and examine the company's working capital requirements. If a US public offering is being considered, the accountants must prepare the company's accounts according to US GAAP (generally accepted accounting principles).

Companies that are about to take the step of going public often decide to switch from their existing auditors, who may be a smaller regional firm, to one of the Big Four accounting firms (PricewaterhouseCoopers, Deloitte & Touche, KPMG and Ernst & Young). Institutional investors take comfort from a Big Four audit opinion, although in the post-Enron world, many would argue that the Big Four are no better than a good second-tier firm.

If they have not been the company's auditors in prior years, the national firm should audit the financial statements for at least the most recent financial year and preferably the two most recent financial years. If changing auditors, the company should remember that auditing a company for the first time is a time-consuming process and should plan accordingly.

When looking for a new auditing firm, an issuer will want to ensure that the accountants have strong industry knowledge. Accounting issues can vary widely from industry to industry – the issuer's auditors should be well versed in them. The company will also want a firm, and the professionals assigned to the deal, to have experience of IPOs. The process can be fraught and the last thing you want to be doing is providing on-the-job training for a team of auditors (American Lawyer Media, 'The Survival Guide to IPOs', p. 10).

### *Public and investor relations*

It is common to hire public relations and investor relations consultants. These advisors coordinate any advertising to be undertaken, media relations and press conferences. The larger the deal, the more important it is to ensure that the issuer is well known in the investment community. If the offering is planning to include a high proportion of individual investors, the PR programme is that much more important.

Following the flotation, the investor relations advisor assists the company in the preparation of its interim and annual report and accounts and press releases related to the company's results and any other significant events. The investor relations advisor will also organize regular presentations to investors and research analysts who follow the company.

### *Transfer agent and receiving bank*

In UK public offerings it is customary to appoint a receiving bank, to which investors send their applications and payment for shares. After allocations have been made, the receiving bank arranges for share certificates to be sent to the investors, as well as returning any funds not used if the offering was scaled back.

Once a company is trading, it requires a transfer agent, someone to ensure that its shareholder register is kept up-to-date and facilitate payment of dividends, distribution of annual reports, etc.

## *Financial printers*

Financial printers do more that just print the legal documentation: they provide meeting rooms for drafting sessions; have contacts with all the best carry-out food places in town, to feed the hungry team at midnight and beyond; and are generous with corporate trinkets such as golf balls and umbrellas. In many jurisdictions, electronic filing of documents is now possible, and in some cases mandatory (e.g. EDGAR in the USA for domestic issuers). The main financial printers all have facilities capable of making both electronic and paper filings.

## Appendix: Selection criteria

*The following is the text of an appendix of a letter sent by a European government and its advisors to investment banks interested in participating in the privatization of a utility company. This letter is representative of the way that the syndicates for privatizations are assembled. Those invited typically have 10 days to formulate their response and deliver it to the global coordinator/government advisor.*

*You will note that questions E and F ask for considerable detail regarding the bank's research and sales personnel as well as their client base. When questionnaires of this sort were first sent by global coordinators, there was considerable resistance from the second tier of investment banks who feared that their best salesmen and analysts would be poached.*

### A. *Form of response*

If you wish to participate in the International Offering you should respond to the following topics in no more than 10 pages, normal type size inclusive of Appendices.

The written presentation should cover the issues set out below:

### B. *Primary equity experience*

Provide details of your organisation's relevant experience (i) in distributing shares of [country] companies, (ii) in privatisation offerings, (iii) in the electricity sector and (iv) in sector(s) that you consider relevant to the Offering since [199x]. Please restrict these details to transactions in which you have been involved as Lead or Co-lead Manager, noting the date and overall size of such other share offerings, your role, your underwriting, the demand generated and allocation received by your organisation.

### C. *Cross-border equity distribution capabilities*

Provide a breakdown of your international equity distribution staff by location, and within location by those devoted to European stocks or any relevant industry specialisation. For the UK, Switzerland, Continental Europe, Middle East, Asia ex-Japan, Japan and North America, note whether accounts are covered locally or cross-border and, if so, how.

### D. *Secondary market activity*

Please give details of your firm's secondary market activity in relevant peer group shares and in the [country] and other Southern European equity markets as a whole.

### E. *Analyst coverage*

Provide the name(s) of the research analyst(s) you propose to use in connection with the Offering and the countries, sector(s) and any relevant other companies which they cover. Please indicate your analysts' current and previous investment recommendations on relevant other shares and on the [country] market as a whole stating whether you are currently recommending an overweight, underweight or neutral stance towards the market. Please also include a list of relevant publications over the last 2 years as well as the current and previous rankings of your analysts over the last 3 years by the various relevant rating agencies. Please state whether you publish economic or equity market research on [country].

You should confirm your willingness to publish a research report on [company] prior to the Offering subject to regulatory restrictions.

State which analyst(s) would cover [company] following the Offering and how often you would intend to publish follow-up research.

### *F. Sales team and other relevant personnel*

State the sales team you would propose to devote to the exercise, including the names, specific and relevant experience, geographic location and responsibilities of key sales staff you would propose to use.

Please indicate other staff which you would intend to use during the Offering, including staff from capital markets/syndication and corporate finance departments.

### *G. Positioning and valuation*

Please indicate how you would position [company] vis à vis other European comparables and outline the valuation methodologies you would consider most appropriate to value [company] shares.

### *H. Demand*

Outline your preliminary views on the likely composition of demand for [company] shares. Please differentiate between the following regions: UK, Continental Europe, Rest of World and United States. State the basis on which you have arrived at your views, and indicate which investors you expect to provide leadership in the offering.

### *I. Conflicts of interest*

State any conflicts of interest which you may have and any privatisations or major share offerings on which your firm is currently working and specify which (if any) of the individuals named under E. and F. above are involved or may become involved in them.

# 3 The offering process, part 1

Whether an IPO or a marketed secondary offering, corporate issue or privatization, fund raising exercise or exit for existing shareholders, domestic or international, the same basic process applies to managing a successful offering. Bankers and advisors must be hired; the investment case must be developed or refined; decisions taken on listing location and markets and investors to be targeted; pricing and allocating shares to investors; and ultimately the menu for the closing dinner.

The new issue process has five stages. The main issues, as set out here, need to be dealt with in order, with the exception of documentation and marketing, which run in parallel. The three items in the marketing segment (marketing, pricing and allocation) run sequentially:

- Corporate issues
- Offer structure
- Regulation and documentation
- Marketing, pricing and allocation
- Aftermarket.

The offering process for an IPO will be necessarily more complex than that of a secondary offering. In the first place, many of the strategic issues that need to be addressed only apply to companies issuing shares to the public for the first time. Secondly, preparing the documentation is easier the second or third time, because the drafters can rely on the precedent set by the IPO prospectus and the company's annual reports. Finally, marketing and pricing are made easier by the fact that the company's shares are trading. Investors are at least somewhat familiar with the firm's investment case, and the market price of the shares gives a target price for a new issue.

This chapter provides a high-level view of the issues involved in: documentation and regulation; marketing; pricing, allocation and closing; and the aftermarket. Each of these receives fuller treatment later in the book. We will take a more detailed look at the strategic and offering structure issues that may face the company and its advisors. But first, the most important question that an investment banker (or any advisor) can ask: Is the company ready to go public?

## Is the company ready to go public?

One of the main strategic issues that needs to be addressed is whether the company is ready for an IPO. Despite the dot.com mania, most IPOs, particularly on the main markets, are for companies that have been established for years, if not decades.

In the USA the median age of an issuing firm was seven years during the 1980s and eight years between 1990 and 1998, before dropping to five years in 1999 and 2000 (Loughran and Ritter, 2001). In other markets, companies are more established before they go public. For example, the average age of a company listing in Japan during the period 1997–2001 was 23.2 years (Kaneko and Pettway, 2001).

In general, younger firms have a greater degree of underpricing (i.e. first-day increase) than do older firms. During the period 1990–1998, US firms that were less than 10 years old shot up by 17 per cent on their first day of trading, while older firms rose by a more sedate 11 per cent. This could mean that investors view younger firms as riskier and demand higher initial returns to compensate for the risk.

Age obviously is not the only indicator of whether a company is ready to go public, but does give some indication of its stability and ability to generate earnings year after year. This book was written shortly after the end of one of the hottest new issues markets the world has ever seen. On the Nasdaq Stock Market and other markets around the world, companies with practically no history and certainly no earnings and sometimes with no revenues were floated and achieved billion dollar market capitalizations before crashing back down to earth, and delisting.

In hot new issues markets, far more companies are deemed ready for the public markets than in calmer times. Clearly for many entrepreneurs and their backers, the period 1998–early 2000 was the time to do an IPO. Whether the market is hot or cold, a company is ready to go public if it can present a compelling investment case. An investment case is made up of many components, chief among them being:

- capability of management;
- financial track record;
- industry prospects and growth potential;
- position within industry/competition;
- valuation/comparative value.

The first issue to consider is management. Credit officers at banks talk about the six C's, with character of management being foremost. Venture capitalists often say that they back the person, not the plan. Similarly, investors in IPOs and subsequent equity offerings place heavy reliance on the management team's competence. By the time a company goes public, it must have a management team in place. If it does not, it should consider delaying the offering and seeking private equity or venture capital. Venture capitalists may back an entrepreneur and allow him to build a management team – public equity investors need to see the team in place.

The IPO prospectus for LinuxOne in early 2000 contained the following warning: 'Our management team may not be able to successfully implement our business strategies because it has only recently begun to work together.' One must laud the company for its disclosure, but it didn't help. LinuxOne's offering failed.

Bankers will also look to the firm's historical financial performance, but as importantly, its prospects for earnings and cash flow growth. In the USA, IPOs for companies with positive earnings per share during the 12 months prior to the issue are priced more fully than those companies reporting losses. During the period 1980–2001, the average first-day premium for firms with losses was 31.4 per cent, compared with a 12.5 per cent one-day premium for companies reporting positive earnings per share (Ritter, 2001d). Again this suggests that investors require a higher initial return to compensate for perceived risk.

The company must also evaluate its position in its industry. Investors like firms that hold one of the top three spots with respect to market share.

The price or relative value of the shares being offered is the final aspect of the investment case. It is more difficult to sell shares that are deemed 'expensive' by the market than those viewed as cheap. Chapter 5 goes into the valuation aspects of the investment case.

## *Junior exchanges*

The requirements of junior stock exchanges like the UK's AIM or Canada's CDNX are lower than the main market. The exchanges have been established expressly to provide a source of equity capital for junior growth companies. Even so, in addition to evaluating the management team, investment bankers will check that the company has a viable product or service, reasonable market size, solid business plan including a sound financial plan and use of proceeds, before bringing it to market.

Smaller companies coming to market must demonstrate their ability to grow quickly to a minimum market capitalization of $100 million and preferably much more. If the size of the company's market is unlikely to permit a decent company size, the investment bankers looking at the deal may be well advised to send the company to different sources of financing. Later stage venture capital or private equity funds are two major sources.

Institutional interest in small cap stocks has declined, reflecting the desire for increased liquidity and greater earnings reliability. In the UK, small cap is usually defined as market capitalization between £50 million and £250 million, while 'micro-cap stocks' are those valued at less than £50 million.

Three factors discourage institutional support of IPOs of small companies: the difficulty in getting a stake that is significant in terms of the overall portfolio; lack of liquidity in the aftermarket; and the effort to monitor relatively under-researched companies. Of course, specialist 'small cap' funds exist and invest in smaller companies, but many mainstream portfolio managers ignore companies that don't achieve a minimum size.

## *Suitability for listing*

Not only does a company have to determine whether it is ready to go public, the regulators and stock exchanges must come to the same conclusion. Typically, the regulator will examine the nature of the business – for example, if the company is involved in illegal or unsavoury activities, say an agribusiness whose main crop is heroin poppies or an escort service. The definition of unsavoury can be broad. Playboy has been listed on the New York Stock Exchange for years, where its stock certificates are always in demand. A German sex shop chain, run by 80-year-old Beate Uhse, went public in one of the most talked about Neuer Markt IPOs of 2000.

Regulators will look for the following:

- Experienced management and directors in place.
- Conflicts of interest between the business and its shareholders.
- Conflicts of interest with directors' private affairs.
- Plans for the future and strategy.
- Recently audited financial statements.

The financial advisors assist companies to prepare for flotations by making recommendations for non-executive directors, sorting out any internal conflicts of interest, aiding in the development of future strategy, and putting management in contact with other professional advisors. If a company is uncertain whether it is ready, it should first consult its financial advisors. If there is still some doubt, the company would be advised to have an informal meeting with the regulators.

## Corporate issues

While a firm's directors and shareholders are considering a flotation, they need to turn their minds to how to get the company in condition for the public markets. Many companies require a good deal of corporate housekeeping before they can go public. For corporates, the process may begin a year or more prior to the issue, while privatizations can take several years of work. For example, Merrill Lynch was mandated with the Joint Global Coordinator role for the privatization of ENEL, the Italian electricity company, in 1993. The record-setting €18 billion IPO finally took place in late 1999.

When growing companies first start thinking about their IPO, they often discuss corporate structure and organizational issues with their accountants and lawyers. Potential issuers may find it useful to involve an investment bank or stockbroker at this early stage. The bankers can provide input on what the market prefers in terms of structure and organization. This input could enhance the company's valuation, speed the IPO process, or even mean the difference between going public at a specific time.

*The corporate structure and domicile will need to be determined.* In some cases, private companies are domiciled in offshore tax havens to benefit the private owners. Public shareholders generally prefer a domicile in the same country as the main stock listing. There are exceptions of course. For example, a number of South African companies have their primary listing on the London Stock Exchange.

Determining the corporate structure is straightforward in most cases, but in privatizations, turning a department into a corporate entity is an early requirement, both in a legal and an operational sense.

Similarly in privatizations, it can be extremely difficult to get at financials in order to provide a three-year history in accordance with local GAAP for the prospectus. Spin-offs, equity carve-outs and demergers face similar issues, although they don't have the added burden of transforming civil servants into red-blooded capitalists. The legal organization of a unit or division must be designed to meet the approval of investors – not for group corporate or tax purposes. In both situations it is often necessary to upgrade the financial accounting and control function. In addition, the senior financial officer must have or develop the skills of a CFO or finance director.

*Determining the timetable is also important.* No issuer wants to be ready to come to market in August or in late December and find all investors on holiday. The IPO process will take a minimum of three months, and often much, much longer. A marketed secondary offering will take from two weeks to two months, depending on the jurisdiction(s) in which the shares are being offered. An accelerated bookbuilding will take from three hours to three days, while from the selling shareholders' perspective, a bought deal takes the ten minutes required to sign the documents. From the investment bank's perspective, a bought deal can take much, much longer, if they get it wrong.

*Determining membership of the board of directors.* It is important to include several independent directors and preferably ensure that the non-executive directors are in the majority. It is useful to have as independent directors people who have been directors or senior officers of other public companies and who are known to the main institutional investors. The company's financial advisors often help with the selection of outside directors, but there are also headhunting firms that specialize in searches for independent directors.

Although it regularly happens, a company should not wait until immediately before its flotation to appoint the outside directors. If someone is a director at the time of the offering, he will be responsible for the contents of the prospectus. It is unreasonable to bring a new director on board two weeks prior to an offering and expect him to sign off on the document.

*Employee participation.* Some offerings, particularly large privatizations, include a separate tranche of shares offered to the company's employees. The shares are usually priced at a discount to the price paid by investors, with 5 per cent being a common discount. Depending on the jurisdiction, employees may be offered loans to purchase the shares. In other offerings, employees place orders for shares like any retail investor, but receive a preferential allocation.

*Shareholder agreements and lockups.* This is particularly important in situations where the issuer has venture capital or other corporate backing. Investors generally prefer to see IPOs raise funds for the company, not provide an exit route for all of the existing shareholders. Lockup agreements are now standard practice and are discussed in more detail in Chapter 11.

## Offering structure

For most companies that are about to go public, the decision of where to sell its shares and which stock exchange(s) to list upon is straightforward. If the company is large, well-established, profitable and part of the old economy, it will list on its home country's main stock exchange and sell shares to domestic investors. If it is *very* large it will list on its home exchange and may sell shares internationally.

The main listing choices that face a company are:

- Which local exchange should it choose?
- Should the company bypass the local market entirely?

- Should the issuer consider multiple listings: in its home market and on an international exchange such as London or New York?

Younger, smaller, more speculative companies tend to list on the home country's second market – stock markets that have been specially developed for such companies. In either case, the company will be subject to its home jurisdiction rules and regulations as administered by local securities regulators.

In certain circumstances the listing decision will be more difficult and/or more complex, such as when a firm lists on a foreign stock exchange only or when it makes concurrent public offerings in two or more markets.

The typical offer structure is dictated first by the planned size of the offering and second by the objectives of the issuer. Small issues of up to, say, €25 million will almost always be sold exclusively in one local market. Offers of up to €125 million or possibly more will stay domestic if the home market is large enough.

Larger offerings generally will require a broader marketing effort – possibly extending to several markets. The first step would be to include foreign institutions in the offering, by way of a private placement. If an offering is sufficiently large, or the issuer has operations in many countries, a second public offering might be contemplated in a major market such as the USA, or where it has its operations.

## *Domestic public offer*

As noted, the domestic public offer is the first step. For the smallest offerings, say less than $15 million, distribution will tend to focus on retail investors and possibly specialist small cap investment funds. Larger, mainstream institutional investors shun the very small offerings as trading tends to be illiquid after the offering.

In some countries it is possible to do an IPO without selling any shares to individual investors. In a UK Placing, shares are sold only to institutional investors, excluding retail investors.

Larger offerings will be distributed more evenly between institutional and retail investors. On average, institutions will account for two-thirds of the allocations of shares, while individuals will receive the other third. The cap on the size of an exclusively domestic offering will vary with the capacity of the domestic market. An American company could raise more than $1 billion without difficulty in its home market, but a Swedish company would struggle to raise that much from its domestic investors.

## *Junior vs. senior stock exchange*

Over 90 per cent of companies list on their home stock exchanges only. Once a domestic listing has been decided, the issuer may need to consider whether to list on the 'senior' vs. 'junior' exchange. This decision is usually straightforward and a question of fact. That is, either a company meets the listing requirements of the senior exchange or it does not. In general, the second markets are 'easier' places to obtain a listing, as they do not have the same requirements regarding length of operations, profitability or net assets.

| | Second market |
|---|---|
| France | Nouveau Marché |
| Germany | Neuer Markt |
| Italy | Neuvo Mercato |
| Spain | Neuvo Mercado |
| Switzerland | SWX New Market |
| UK | Alternative Investment Market (AIM) |
| Pan-European | EASDAQ (European Association of Securities Dealers Automated Quotation system) |

**Table 3.1** European second markets

In Europe, most major markets have developed 'second markets' in the hope of emulating the Nasdaq's success. Now companies wishing to list on a junior exchange for high growth companies have a variety of national and pan-European choices (see Table 3.1).

The UK's AIM was established in 1995, as a second market for those companies that did not meet the requirements of the LSE's main market. The AIM has no minimum limits on capitalization and less onerous regulations than the senior exchange. Between 1997 and 2001, 738 companies (including investment trusts) launched offerings on the AIM.

Germany's Neuer Markt played an important role in the development of an equity culture among German retail investors. It quickly grew to be the largest second market in Europe, with 300 IPOs between 1997 and 2001. Neuer Markt deals ranged in size from €10 million to more than €3 billion (T-Online). France, Italy and Spain all set up second markets in the late 1990s.

By the end of 2001, the junior markets had grown substantially, with the exception of Nasdaq Europe.

| Exchange | Market capitalization (€m) | Turnover (€m) |
|---|---|---|
| Neuer Markt | 53 190 | 4142 |
| Nasdaq Europe | 7733 | 83 |
| Neuvo Mercato | 15 354 | 3620 |
| Nouveau Marché | 16 000 | 770 |
| AIM | 17 999 | 637 |

*Source:* Deutsche Borse, Facts and Figures, January 2002.

**Table 3.2** European 'second' stock markets

## *Combining domestic and international offerings*

Once the decision has been made to extend the marketing to non-domestic investors, the lead bank will have two main decisions. Should the company make public offerings in foreign market(s), and in particular, should it consider a US public offering? The second decision is how to organize the marketing of the issue, by deciding on the number of tranches to include. A tranche is a distinct offering that covers one country or a group of countries.

During the 1980s, it was common for large IPOs to have as many as eight to 10 'ring-fenced' tranches. Banks in each tranche were limited to selling to investors in the tranche's geographic region. As the larger investment banks developed global distribution capabilities, the number of tranches, and banks taking part, declined.

The number of tranches and banks involved will usually be larger for IPOs than for secondary offerings, as both the breadth and depth of distribution are important in an IPO. Many secondary offerings conducted as accelerated bookbuilds or bought deals will have only one or two banks involved. One head of equity capital markets was quoted as saying: 'Ring-fenced tranching means that analysts' research and sales people focus on their region, leaving no stone unturned. This way, the vendor gets maximum placing. With a single global syndicate, everyone will be trying to talk to the top 100 accounts' (Dean, 1997).

The following subsections consider five different offering structures. There are many more combinations:

- Domestic public offer + international private placement
- Domestic public offer + international private placement + Rule 144a placement in the USA
- Domestic public offer + international private placement + US public offering
- Multiple public offers (including domestic market) + international private placement
- International public offering.

If a multi-tranche offering is considered, the lead manager is entitled to call itself the global coordinator, a grandiose title that means nothing except in the compilation of league tables. Syndicate structure and nomenclature are covered in Chapter 10.

### Domestic public offer + international private placement

In the simplest extension to foreign investors, a domestic public offering will be combined with an international private placement – an offering directed at institutional investors. For a European issuer, international may mean the UK and Switzerland, or it could be the entire world. It depends on the size of the deal and whether it is an IPO or secondary offering.

Most US equity offerings follow this structure. US deals regularly allocate between 10 and 20 per cent of the offering to non-US investors. The distribution of this portion of the offering is usually managed out of the London office of the bookrunner, but sales of shares are made throughout Europe, the Middle East and Asia.

### Domestic public offer + international private placement + Rule 144a placement in the USA

Research indicates that the presence of US investors in offerings leads to less underpricing (Ljungqvist, Jenkinson and Wilhelm (LJW)). The easiest method of reaching a broad range of American institutional investors is through a Rule 144a private placement. Using Rule 144a means that the issuer is not required to file its prospectus with the SEC, nor does it have to reconcile its financial statements to US GAAP.

Approximately 14 per cent of non-US offerings during the period 1992–1999 made use of Rule 144a to reach American institutional investors (LJW). Rule 144a is discussed in detail in Chapter 8.

### Domestic public offer + international private placement + US public offering

The next stage of complexity teams a domestic offer with a US public offer and an international private placement. Again international may take a limited meaning or a broad one. When a US public offering is included, the issuer will usually be abrogating the timetable to the US bankers and lawyers. Because the disclosure requirements for US public offers are so strict, the US lawyers typically take the lead in drafting the prospectus – both home and American.

Between 1992 and 1999, approximately 18 per cent of non-US IPOs (381 companies) included a US public offering (LJW).

### Multiple public offers + international private placement

Finally, the issuer may decide to launch multiple public offers when the anticipated demand will justify the expense. For example, Deutsche Post's $15 billion IPO in 2001 included a public offer in all EU countries – the first time it had been done for an IPO. Deutsche Telekom had completed a $14.8 billion follow-on pan-European public offering the previous year.

When France Telecom took its mobile telephone subsidiary, Orange, public in early 2001, it opted for public offers in France, Germany, Italy and the UK and listings in both Paris and London. Institutions outside the four countries participated in a private placement including a Rule 144a offering in the USA. The choice of public offerings was driven in part by where Orange had built significant operations, and the bankers hoped to tap into demand from the company's customers.

You should note that companies that do list on more than one stock exchange must designate one exchange as their primary listing. It will then be subject to that exchange's rules and regulations as well as those of the host securities commission.

For Orange, the primary jurisdiction was France, where the deal was conducted as an 'offre à prix ouvert' (OPA) or open-priced offer, via a bookbuilding process. Dresdner Kleinwort Benson, Morgan Stanley and Société Générale managed the offering.

### International public offering and listing

Sometimes circumstances dictate that a company should list on an exchange outside its home market, ignoring its home stock exchange, at least initially. This is usually when the firm involved is in an industry that does not have any other representatives listed in the home market.

During the 1990s, approximately 13 per cent of IPOs from non-US and Canadian issuers were from companies that chose to bypass their home market entirely. Of the companies that did so, 58 per cent chose to go to the American market, a further 10 per cent chose the American market and another stock exchange, and the final third chose a non-American exchange for the initial listing (Ljungqvist et al., 2001).

Two recent examples include MTS and Wimm Bill Dann, Russian companies that chose to raise funds through a US public offering and listing on the New York Stock Exchange.

### *Common factors in selecting a stock exchange*

At an early stage, the issuer has to decide which stock exchange to list on. As noted above, for most companies it is simply a choice between their domestic main market and junior market. However, some companies find that it is advantageous to have their primary listing on a foreign stock exchange.

When companies have a choice between or among exchanges, whether domestic or foreign, they will consider the following criteria when selecting the exchange on which to list their shares:

1 Listing requirements
2 Number of related firms already listed (investor familiarity)
3 Continuing requirements
4 Liquidity and future financing
5 Initial fees and annual listing fees.

#### Listing requirements

In most countries the differences in listing requirements tend to relate to the size of the company, age (particularly a minimum number of years of audited financial statements) and profitability. Second markets have less exacting standards than those of the primary market. Notwithstanding, most countries have made it difficult for extremely speculative ventures to receive public financing via an IPO.

#### Number of related firms already listed

Related firm listings are an important factor in the choice of a listing venue. The more companies of a certain type already listed on a certain stock exchange, the more likely businesses contemplating an IPO will be to join them.

Investors who are familiar with a particular market segment, e.g. biotech or microelectronics, will be able to place more accurate valuations on companies coming to the market for the first time. If the company is breaking open a new sector in its home market, it may find that investors are less willing to pay a full price for the shares as a result of unfamiliarity with the industry and its prospects.

Numerous European technology companies launched their IPOs on America's Nasdaq stock market during the 1990s boom – bypassing their home stock exchanges. They argued that investors on Nasdaq understood companies at an early stage of development and would willingly invest in them. Several obtained home market listings after they had become established on Nasdaq.

### Continuing requirements

Reporting requirements tend to be driven by a country's securities commission, so the disclosure required of companies listed on the first or second market will likely be very similar.

Stock exchanges do have requirements over minimum trading volumes, minimum share prices, etc. If a firm's share price drops below a minimum threshold for a preset period of time, its shares may be delisted.

### Liquidity and future financing

The last thing a newly public company wants is for liquidity in its shares to dry up. Some believe that exchanges that operate with market makers will be more likely to guarantee liquidity.

### Initial fees and annual listing fees

With all the other costs of an IPO, companies may try to minimize the amount of fees that they have to pay to the stock exchange on issue as well as in the years following the IPO. Second markets tend to have lower listing fees and continuing fees. Research indicates that initial fees and ongoing listing fees are not important considerations in the initial listing decision (Corwin and Harris, 2001).

Once the structural issues have been worked out, the IPO timetable kicks in. Table 3.3 provides a stylized offering timetable.

## Regulators and documentation

Once the primary listing location has been determined, the issuer and its advisors must begin to think about the documentation that will be required to be produced – both for potential investors and for the regulators.

The main documents to be drafted are the listing particulars (Europe) or registration statement (USA). Listing particulars and registration statements both contain a prospectus – the document that is distributed to potential investors. The prospectus contains all the financial and non-financial information that potential investors require in order to make an investment decision. It must be both a selling document as well as meeting the disclosure requirements of the local regulator (a 'liability document').

In most countries, when shares are being offered to retail investors, the local securities regulator or stock exchange has to approve the contents of the prospectus before the offering can take place. In markets where a public offering is not taking place, the document may be called an offering memorandum, offering circular or private placement memorandum. The information contained in a private placement document is not proscribed by the regulator, but will be similar to, although perhaps not as extensive as, that required for a public offering.

Different national securities regulators take widely varying amounts of time to review a company's IPO prospectus: 'There are varying timetables for prospectus

| | Pre-work | −12 | −11 | −10 | −9 | −8 | −7 | −6 | −5 | −4 | −3 | −2 | −1 | Pricing | +1 | Beyond |
|---|---|---|---|---|---|---|---|---|---|---|---|---|---|---|---|---|
| Organizational and structural issues | | | | | | | | | | | | | | | | |
| Appoint advisors | | | | | | | | | | | | | | | | |
| Due diligence | | | | | | | | | | | | | | | | |
| Prospectus drafting | | | | | | | | | | | | | | | | |
| Regulatory review of prospectus | | | | | | | | | | | | | | | | |
| Draft other documents | | | | | | | | | | | | | | | | |
| Syndicate presentation | | | | | | | | | | | | | | | | |
| Pre-marketing | | | | | | | | | | | | | | | | |
| Research released | | | | | | | | | | | | | | | | |
| Marketing | | | | | | | | | | | | | | | | |
| Roadshow | | | | | | | | | | | | | | | | |
| Bookbuilding | | | | | | | | | | | | | | | | |
| Final regulatory approval | | | | | | | | | | | | | | | | |
| Pricing | | | | | | | | | | | | | | | | |
| Allocation | | | | | | | | | | | | | | | | |
| Stabilization | | | | | | | | | | | | | | | | |
| Research published | | | | | | | | | | | | | | | | |
| Investor relations activity | | | | | | | | | | | | | | | | |
| End of lock-up | | | | | | | | | | | | | | | | |

'Pre-work' can begin anywhere from a few weeks to years before the start of this timetable.
Areas in light grey are legal, regulatory and documentary, areas with vertical stripes are marketing activities, and areas in black are post-pricing activities.

**Table 3.3** Indicative timetable for Initial Public Offering. This table gives an indication of the sequence and amount of time various activities take. It is not a definitive timetable. Every deal is different.

publication and marketing and differing content requirements' (Caplen et al., 2000).

In the USA (generally regarded as the most stringent jurisdiction), the average length of time between filing an IPO registration statement and the offering was 11 weeks during the last three years of the 1990s (Loughran and Ritter, 2001).

In most markets, follow-on equity offerings require the preparation of a prospectus as well. The same information is required, but because the original prospectus has been done, it is generally easier and less time consuming to prepare.

While preparing the prospectus, investment bankers and their lawyers conduct a due diligence investigation. Due diligence is the process of investigating the issuer's commercial, financial and legal status and condition. Matters uncovered during due diligence must be disclosed in the prospectus. The due diligence investigation mitigates the potential liability of the issuer's officers and directors and its advisors. In the UK market, the bankers and advisors also conduct a verification exercise, which authenticates every factual statement contained in the prospectus.

## Marketing

While the documentation is being prepared and the due diligence investigation conducted, the research, sales and syndicate groups at the lead banks begin preparation for marketing and distributing the shares. Differing degrees of restriction are placed on the marketing activities of banks involved in the offering by local regulators.

The US SEC is the most harsh – stating that the only (written) marketing materials that can be used are the preliminary prospectus and prospectus. In addition, marketing to US investors can only commence on filing of the preliminary prospectus. Other countries are wide open and place few restrictions on the marketing activities supporting IPOs. Many European countries distinguish between offerings made only to institutional investors and those that include individual investors. Institutional offerings are regulated with a much lighter touch.

Depending on the size and complexity of an offering, the marketing period can last from four weeks to four months and even longer. Marketing for a secondary offering can last from two hours to two or three weeks, depending on the structure and size of the offering. The marketing process contains three main segments, each with several subsegments, as shown in Table 3.4.

The pre-marketing period is the most variable in length. Some privatizations see the marketing campaign begin more than a year before the launch of the issue. When the deal does come to market, investors are already familiar with the company.

Companies planning a flotation may increase or commence corporate advertising, aimed at either institutional or retail investors, depending on who is expected to provide the strongest demand in the offering. Most companies being privatized start a retail-oriented information advertising campaign months before they start advertising the offering.

The second stage – the formal marketing period – is more finite. The shortest might be five days to two weeks during a hot new issues market, while the longest might range up to six weeks for a multi-billion dollar global offering of shares with an

| | |
|---|---|
| Pre-marketing | 1. Developing the investment case<br>2. Preparing the market<br>3. Preparing the management<br>4. Initial research published (where permitted) |
| Marketing | 1. Setting the price range<br>2. Filing the preliminary prospectus<br>3. Sales briefing<br>4. Roadshow and 'one-on-ones'<br>5. Sales/research follow-up<br>6. Bookbuilding |
| Pricing and allocation | 1. Setting the price<br>2. Allocation<br>3. Stabilization |

**Table 3.4** Marketing process

extensive roadshow. The start of the formal marketing period is usually driven by the documentation teams – as soon as they are ready to file a preliminary (pathfinder) prospectus, the marketing team cranks up.

Telephone calls and visits by the syndicate's research analysts to potential investors precede a 'roadshow' by the company. The roadshow is the centrepiece of new issue marketing, where the company gets a chance to tell its story and investors get to size up the senior management face-to-face. Marketing is covered in detail in Chapter 9.

## Pricing and allocation

On completion of at least some of the marketing, the company and its advisors must set the price of the new issue. There are three approaches to the pricing of an offering:

1 **Bookbuilding** – a price range is established and salesmen solicit expressions of interest from investors. There is complete flexibility over the price of the shares and number to be issued right up until the last moment. Bookbuilding takes place in almost all domestic American and Canadian new issues and the majority of large international offerings.
2 **Fixed price** – the price and number of shares offered are fixed at an early stage of the marketing. The banks guarantee the proceeds to the issuer, but have the risk of any unsold shares after a selling period that lasts from three days to three weeks. Traditionally, European and Asian equity offerings employed the fixed price process. Now, the fixed price offer tends to be restricted to smaller domestic offers, while larger deals are done using bookbuilding.

3 **Auction/tender offer** – investors submit bids for the number of shares they want at a particular price. The issue price is set at a clearing price, where all the shares are spoken for. Auctions have been out of favour in most countries since the late 1980s.

When offers are oversubscribed, allocations of shares to potential investors can be either non-discretionary or discretionary, where the issuer and its bankers have considerable latitude in determining which investors receive shares. There are two main non-discretionary approaches: allocation on a pro rata basis and by lot (picking out of a hat). Most international offerings run under the bookbuilding approach use a discretionary allocation procedure based upon criteria that will vary deal by deal. We discuss the price-setting mechanisms in detail in the following chapter.

## Aftermarket

The period immediately after pricing and listing of the shares is vital. If a company does not get off to a good start, its shares may languish on the stock exchange and a company that requires further equity financing may find it difficult. Jegadeesh et al. (1993) found that firms that made follow-on offerings tended to have had higher short-term returns than companies that did not return to the market.

Most US and international offerings undertake to stabilize the share price in the immediate aftermarket, using something called the 'greenshoe' or overallotment option. So if demand is weak and the share price drops below the offer price, the lead manager can stop, or slow, the price decline by buying shares in the market.

Existing shareholders in IPO companies are almost always subject to a 'lockup period': the length of time during which they are not permitted to sell any shares. The lockup period is typically six months in length, and can be shortened with the permission of the lead manager of the IPO.

All jurisdictions require companies who have floated on their stock exchanges to commit to providing ongoing information. At a minimum this includes an interim and annual report and announcements to the market whenever anything happens that might have an impact on the price of its shares or its prospects.

In recent years regulators in many countries have tightened the rules surrounding 'selective disclosure' (the situation where a company discloses information to a small group of favoured analysts or investors prior to making public the information). In the USA, Regulation FD (for fair disclosure) is the applicable piece of legislation.

# 4 The offering process, part 2

This chapter explores in greater detail, two of the issues introduced in the previous chapter.

First, should a company extend its marketing effort outside its home market? Going international adds to the cost and complexity of the IPO, but delivers clear benefits. Companies have long offered shares outside their home market. For example, North and South American railroads would never have been built were it not for the funds raised from European investors in the 19th century. However, the phenomenon of international offerings – where a company offers shares domestically and internationally simultaneously, is relatively new. Most observers date the first international offerings to late 1983, when UBS led European tranches for secondary offerings by two large Canadian companies, Bell Canada and Alcan.

International equity offerings received a significant boost the following year from the UK Government's privatization of British Telecom. Shares were offered in simultaneous public offers in the UK, Canada and the USA. BT shares were also distributed to investors in the rest of Europe and the Middle East. The Government took the decision to launch an international offering because it believed that the UK equity market was too small to absorb such a large issue without seriously affecting the price the Government received.

Second, what price-setting mechanism will be used: bookbuilding, fixed price or an auction? In some countries the choice is dictated by local regulators or business practice. In other countries issuers have a choice. Most international deals use bookbuilding. We will examine the procedures of each type of offering.

## Rationale for international offerings

An issuer can sell shares exclusively to domestic investors, or it may decide upon an international offering. The domestic offering is the route chosen for most smaller (i.e. under $100 million) flotations. It is cheaper and simpler to complete. International offerings can achieve incredible size, as illustrated in Table 4.1.

There are many reasons for an issuer to contemplate accessing international investors in its initial public offering:

- Limited size of domestic market
- Broader investor base
- Differential valuations
- Mergers and acquisitions.

| Rank | Date | Company | Country | Amount ($m) | IPO/SEO* |
|---|---|---|---|---|---|
| 1 | Nov-87 | NTT | Japan | 40 260 | SEO |
| 2 | Oct-88 | NTT | Japan | 22 400 | SEO |
| 3 | Nov-99 | ENEL | Italy | 18 900 | IPO |
| 4 | Oct-98 | NTT DoCoMo | Japan | 18 000 | IPO |
| 5 | Oct-97 | Telecom Italia | Italy | 15 500 | SEO |
| 6 | Feb-87 | NTT | Japan | 15 097 | IPO |
| 7 | Nov-99 | NTT | Japan | 15 000 | IPO |
| 8 | Jun-00 | Deutsche Telekom | Germany | 14 760 | SEO |
| 9 | Nov-96 | Deutsche Telekom | Germany | 13 330 | IPO |
| 10 | Oct-87 | British Petroleum | UK | 12 430 | SEO |
| 11 | Apr-00 | ATT Wireless | USA | 10 600 | IPO |
| 12 | Nov-97 | France Telecom | France | 10 530 | SEO |
| 13 | Nov-98 | Telstra | Australia | 10 500 | IPO |
| 14 | Oct-99 | Telstra | Australia | 10 400 | SEO |
| 15 | Jun-99 | Deutsche Telekom | Germany | 10 200 | SEO |
| 16 | Dec-90 | Regional Electricity Companies | UK | 9995 | IPO |
| 17 | Dec-91 | British Telecom | UK | 9927 | SEO |
| 18 | Dec-89 | UK Water Authorities | UK | 8679 | IPO |
| 19 | Dec-86 | British Gas | UK | 8012 | IPO |
| 20 | Jun-98 | Endesa | Spain | 8000 | SEO |
| 21 | Jun-97 | ENI | Italy | 7800 | SEO |
| 22 | Apr-00 | Oracle Japan | Japan | 7500 | IPO |
| 23 | Jul-93 | British Telecom | UK | 7360 | SEO |
| 24 | Oct-93 | Japan Railroad East | Japan | 7312 | IPO |
| 25 | Dec-98 | NTT | Japan | 7300 | SEO |
| 26 | Oct-97 | France Telecom | France | 7080 | IPO |
| 27 | Jul-99 | Crédit Lyonnaise | France | 6960 | IPO |
| 28 | Feb-94 | Elf Aquitaine | France | 6823 | SEO |
| 29 | Jun-97 | Halifax Building Society | UK | 6813 | IPO |
| 30 | Jun-98 | ENI | Italy | 6740 | SEO |

*SEO – Seasoned Equity Offering (follow-on).
*Source:* Megginson, Nash, Netter and Schwartz (2000)

**Table 4.1** Largest international equity offerings (1984–2000)

## *Size of local market*

Issuers often turn to international markets because their home market is too small to supply the funds required. This has occurred often in the smaller European markets and in the emerging markets of Latin America and South East Asia. For example, most emerging markets privatizations, including Telmex, Telkom Malaysia and YPF, require international investors in order to raise sufficient funds. The presence of international investors in privatizations increases demand, allowing the selling government to maximize the proceeds of the offering. Even countries with large and deep equity markets find companies issuing shares internationally. Most US offerings over $250 million include an international tranche, even though the domestic market can easily absorb issues of that size.

Sometimes foreign companies go to another market, bypassing their home market altogether. Since the Russian economic crisis of 1998, several corporate issuers have decided to go public in the USA, ignoring their home market. In June 2000, MTS raised £323 million on the New York Stock Exchange. Eighteen months later, dairy products company Wimm Bill Dann Foods (say it quickly and think tennis) raised $238 million. During the bubble years, many European and Israeli technology companies went directly to Nasdaq. A number of these companies subsequently listed in their home markets.

## *Broader investor base*

A broader shareholder base is likely to increase demand for shares and therefore maximize the value of the offering. A company's international profile will certainly be increased by offering shares outside its home country, which may bring marketing benefits.

During the late 1990s and 2000, the German Government gradually reduced its ownership in Deutsche Telekom through a series of international equity offerings. In November 1996, the company's IPO raised DM19.67 billion ($13.3 billion) from domestic and international investors. Of the funds raised, 67 per cent came from the domestic market, 14 per cent from the rest of Europe, and 19 per cent from the rest of the world. In June 1999, the first follow-on offering was made, raising $10.2 billion from investors in Germany and internationally. The second follow-on offering, one year later, in June 2000, was the largest yet. The $14.8 billion deal involved a public offering of shares in all countries in the EU, the first time that this had been done. The company and the Government were concerned that there would be insufficient institutional support for a third share issue in three and a half years. The pan-European public offering paved the way for Deutsche Post's pan-European initial public offering.

Toyota Motor, one of the world's big three automobile manufacturers, completed a secondary offering in September 1999 that raised Y155 billion (approximately $1.2 billion). The offering coincided with the company's listings on the London and New York Stock Exchanges. The offering and listings were designed to increase its international shareholder base and to commit the company to the internationalization of its business standards (Mullins and Toyama, 1999).

The two main sources of international demand for equities are Britain and the United States. This is supported by a number of international listings on the main stock exchanges of the two countries. Figure 4.1 shows that the London Stock Exchange, Nasdaq and New York Stock Exchange are the most popular exchanges for companies listing outside their home markets.

## *Maximize the proceeds of the issue*

Maximizing proceeds is one of the shared goals of the company, selling shareholders and the lead investment banks. By offering shares in multiple markets, the bankers are

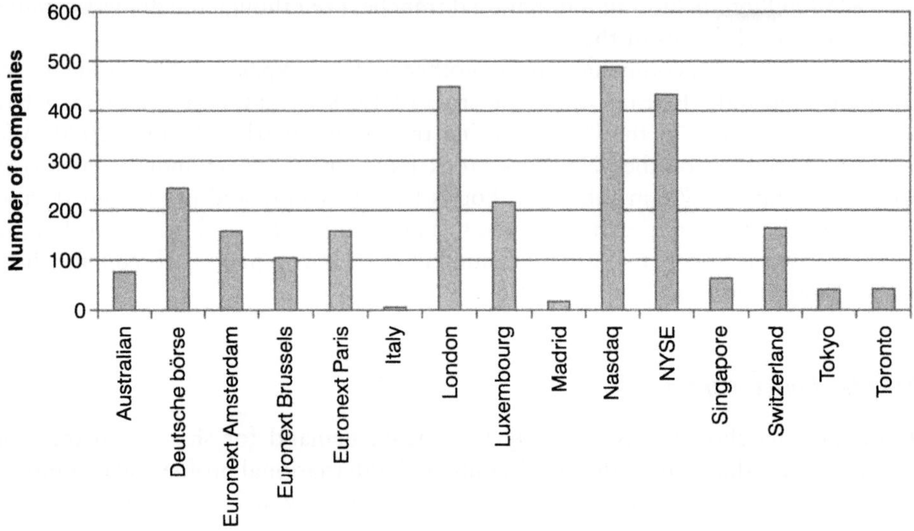


*Source*: FIBV.

**Figure 4.1** Number of foreign companies listed on selected stock exchanges (2000)

able to expose the issuer to a much larger number of potential shareholders than if they were restricted to one market. The maximization of proceeds is based on the creation of price tensions and the ability of the issue managers to play one group of investors off against another.

For example, Ljungqvist et al. (2001) found that non-US issuers reduced the level of underpricing significantly by offering shares in the US market. That is, proceeds were increased over the amount that the company might have raised without marketing to US investors. In their paper, LJW built a model showing that for every 1 per cent increase in allocations to US investors, underpricing was reduced by 2.4 per cent.

Notwithstanding the short-term benefits of the US market on pricing, over the long-term, international companies' shares suffer from underperformance. Foerster and Karolyi (1999) examined 333 global equity offerings that included a US tranche during the period 1982–1996. They found that the issuers underperformed local and global benchmarks by 8 to 39 per cent over the three years following the deal. In particular, deals from emerging market issuers and those companies using Rule 144a private placements were the poorest performers.

### *Mergers and acquisitions*

Another benefit (cited regularly in the late 1980s) was that international distribution of a company's shares was useful in merger and acquisition activity. The theory being that if a company's shares were well known outside its own market, it could use the shares as currency for international acquisitions.

For example, Daimler Benz of Germany listed its shares on the New York Stock Exchange in late 1993, a few years before it acquired Chrysler Corporation in a share swap to create DaimlerChrysler.

In addition, it was believed that widespread international shareholdings of a company's stock would reduce its vulnerability to hostile take-overs. This can work two ways. Some believe that Vodafone's hostile take-over bid for Germany's Mannesmann was successful because of the relatively high proportion of non-German shareholders on Mannesmann's share register. They suggest that the international shareholders supported Vodafone's bid and not Mannesmann's management who initially resisted it.

### *Differential valuations*

In certain industries, companies have found it beneficial to go to the international market, because investors outside their home market value the securities more highly than do domestic investors. This may be because the international market has more experience of a certain industry, or because of temporary anomalies.

One example of this was the dual listing of many British cable television companies in London and on the Nasdaq market in the USA in 1994 and 1995. Investors in America had much more experience of the cable TV industry than did those in the UK, and were prepared to pay a higher price for the shares. In order to maximize the proceeds of the offerings, the lead managers allocated a large proportion of the offerings to US investors who had indicated that they were willing to pay a higher price for the shares than had UK investors.

## Disadvantages of selling shares internationally

However, international equity offerings do not come without a price. Some of the disadvantages of selling to and maintaining an international investor base are:

- Cost and complexity
- Increased disclosure requirements
- Flowback.

### *Cost and complexity*

Additional time must be allowed in order to prepare an offering for multiple markets. This is particularly true if the issuer plans a public offering in more than one country. In most cases, international private placements only require extra marketing time, say one or two weeks. However, when conducting multiple public offerings, more than one prospectus must be prepared and then approved in order to meet the various jurisdictions' disclosure requirements.

The most time-consuming and expensive option is when a company plans a public offering in the USA. It must prepare a registration statement that will satisfy the SEC. A US registration statement can contain significantly more information than required in many markets. Review of the registration statement will take at least six weeks, and during hot new issues markets or for more complicated offerings, will take from 10 to 12 weeks.

### *Increased disclosure*

Not only is there increased disclosure in an American prospectus, but any company whose shares are listed on a US stock market must also provide ongoing disclosure at a level that is often higher than that required in their home markets.

Increased disclosure is a two-way street. Botosan (1997, 2000) found that increased disclosure can reduce the cost of equity capital. As we discuss in Chapter 5, a lower cost of capital increases the value of a company.

### *Flowback*

One of the biggest concerns of companies completing international offerings is that shares placed offshore (with the consequent extra time and effort) are not held by long-term international investors, but return (or flowback) to the domestic market.

Flowback often occurs in large, heavily oversubscribed offerings that open at a substantial premium. Domestic investors may be desperate to get stock, in order to achieve an appropriate weighting. In particular, index-tracking funds will need to buy shares, regardless of the price, until the weighting of the stock in their portfolio matches its weighting in the index. Foreign investors often take advantage of the ability to take 'instant profits' and sell back into the home market.

## International investors

### *Advantages of investing internationally*

While the above section outlines the corporate drivers for international offerings, there is increasing demand from institutional investors. There are several reasons for this, including:

- More securities and industries to choose from – even large markets don't have shares in every sector.
- Greater returns – many emerging markets provide higher rates of return than do more mature markets and some markets may not be as efficient as others, allowing professional investors an advantage.
- Reduction of risk – not all national stock markets advance (or decline) at the same time. Therefore international diversification may reduce risk in an investor's portfolio.
- Liquidity – some institutions demand significant liquidity in their portfolios, which can only be met by investing in the largest global companies.
- Single European currency – many investors now look at the Eurozone as a single country for portfolio purposes. An investor in France, for example, no longer considers France to be his home market; the entire Eurozone is now treated as the domestic market.

### *Disadvantages for international investors*

However, as always, there are some costs. Share ownership, particularly, but not exclusively, in emerging markets can raise significant settlement and custody issues. Smaller institutions and individuals can face costly currency conversions, both on purchase and sale of shares as well as every time a dividend is paid. Poor information flow and unreliable custody services can also add to the headaches of an international portfolio manager.

Depository receipts are a partial solution to these issues and can be the best way of effecting international investment, particularly for individual investors and smaller institutions. A full discussion of depository receipts follows in Chapter 8.

## Price-setting mechanisms

The second major decision involves the choice of a price-setting mechanism for a firm's IPO. Remember that there are three methods by which a company can come to market for the first time:

1 Auction
2 Fixed price offer
  (a) underwritten
  (b) best efforts
3 Bookbuilding.

Auctions, or tenders, are the least common form of price setting, although they continue to be used occasionally in some markets. Investors are invited to bid for shares, and once the offering is covered, shares are allocated at a single, clearing price.

From its origins in the American market, bookbuilding spread through the late 1980s and 1990s, and has largely replaced the fixed price offering, at least for sizeable IPOs. Some markets have retained the fixed price offer, at least for domestic offerings. Of the two forms of fixed price offer, the underwritten variety, is by far the most common. Traditionally, UK offerings have operated on a fixed price basis and many Commonwealth countries continue to do so.

In some cases, more than one type of price-setting mechanism will be used in a single offering. The most common is the situation where a bookbuilding is followed by a fixed price offer. The managers of the offering direct the bookbuilding towards institutional and international investors. Once the price has been set via the bookbuilding, the shares are offered at the same price to the domestic retail investor base in a fixed price offering.

A number of UK privatizations mixed fixed price offers with auctions. The majority of the offering was sold via the traditional fixed price offer, but included a 'back-end' tender, where institutions could bid for shares at prices above the fixed price offer, after the main offer had closed.

Table 4.2 illustrates the types of IPO structures commonly used in a number of markets.

| Country | Offer type | | | |
|---|---|---|---|---|
| | Bookbuilding | Fixed price offer (underwritten) | Fixed price offer (best efforts) | Auction |
| Australia | X | X | | |
| Canada | X | | X | |
| France | X | X | X | X |
| Germany | X | X | | |
| Hong Kong | | X | | |
| Italy | X | X | | |
| Japan | X | | | (1) |
| Singapore | | X | | |
| UK | X | X | X(2) | |
| USA | X | | X | X |

(1) Not used since bookbuilding was permitted in 1997.
(2) Rarely used.

**Table 4.2** Types of offerings used in IPOs in selected markets

### *Auctions or tender offers*

Auctions, or tenders, are the least common form of price setting, although they continue to be used occasionally in some markets (notably France and Israel). Other markets in which auctions have accounted for a significant proportion of IPOs include Belgium, Chile, Japan (until September 1997) and Portugal.

Some auctions set a minimum price and invite investors (both institutional and retail) to bid for shares at, or above, the minimum price. Investors are allowed to make only one bid at one price. The final offering price is the 'clearing price' (i.e. where sufficient orders at decreasing prices cover the number of shares on offer), and all investors are charged the clearing price for their shares. All the shares are sold at the one price, even if an investor was willing to pay a higher price. If there is insufficient demand at the minimum price, the auction can start again with a lower minimum price or the issuer can decide to cancel or postpone the offering.

In other auctions, investors can place multiple bids at different prices – creating their own demand curve. Whatever the nuances, the common aspect of IPO auctions is that all shares are sold at one price. Table 4.3 provides an illustration of an auction and the allocation of shares.

Since all orders are filled at the offer price, the share price is unlikely to rise significantly in the first days of trading because there is no unsatisfied demand from investors who were not allocated all the shares they bid for. By naming their own price, investors pre-empt much of the first-day volatility that occurs as some investors flip their allocations to others desperate to get a piece of the action. The only source of potential demand is from investors who were not canvassed or decided not to bid in the auction.

Willy's Wertberters Inc. is planning an IPO through an auction. The company needs to raise $35 million in order to increase production of wertberters for export to the rapidly growing European wertberter market. Its investment bank suggests a price range of $11.50 to $13.50, with a proposed offer size of three million shares.

After the marketing period, the order book looks as follows:

| Price ($) | No. of shares bid | Cumulative demand | Allocation (%) |
|---|---|---|---|
| 14.25 | 50 000 | 50 000 | 100 |
| 14.00 | 75 000 | 125 000 | 100 |
| 13.75 | 40 000 | 165 000 | 100 |
| 13.50 | 250 000 | 415 000 | 100 |
| 13.25 | 300 000 | 715 000 | 100 |
| 13.00 | 500 000 | 1 215 000 | 100 |
| 12.75 | 1 000 000 | 2 215 000 | 100 |
| *12.50* | *1 250 000* | *3 000 000* | *62.8* |
| 12.25 | 2 000 000 | | 0 |
| 12.00 | 1 750 000 | | 0 |
| 11.75 | 3 000 000 | | 0 |
| 11.50 | 3 750 000 | | 0 |
| 11.25 | 1 000 000 | | 0 |
| 11.00 | 1 500 000 | | 0 |

*Note the trend is for more shares at progressively lower prices, but is not uniformly so. There may be fewer people bidding below the floor of $11.50 because they would think that there was little likelihood of getting shares.*

Bids for a total of 2 215 000 shares were received at prices from $12.75 to $14.25. Willy's received bids for 1 250 000 shares at $12.50 when it needed only 785 000 more shares to clear. In most auctions, each investor who bid above $12.50 would receive all the shares they asked for, at the price of $12.50, while those who bid $12.50 per share would receive a pro rata allocation of 62.8% (785 000 ÷ 1 250 000).

**Table 4.3** The operation of an IPO auction

An auction can be beneficial for the issuer – generally it incurs lower costs (commissions) and it should be able to maximize proceeds. However, the potential lack of aftermarket demand can cause shares offered in this manner to languish in the stock market, which does not bode well for any future offerings it may have planned.

In a study of all 27 Israeli auctions in early 1994, researchers found that the one-day premium (as adjusted for market movements) was 4.5 per cent (Kandel et al., 1999) compared with the 16.6 per cent average cited in Chapter 1.

Kaneko and Pettway (2001) looked at the Japanese experience between 1993 and mid-2001. Between 1993 and 1 September 1997, 481 auction IPOs registered an average one-day gain of 11.4 per cent (standard deviation 15.5 per cent). From

1 September 1997 to 31 July 2001, a further 301 IPOs were launched, all using the bookbuilding price-setting process. The average first-day premium leapt to 49.8 per cent, but the standard deviation increased to 104.9 per cent.

The auction process has traditionally accounted for a large portion of French domestic offerings. The widespread use of auctions in French IPOs, especially prior to the 1990s, may be one factor in the lower first-day premia (4.2 per cent) found in French IPOs compared with the 16.6 per cent average.

## Internet-based auctions

Although not common in the USA, some auctions did appear during the Internet IPO boom. WR Hambrecht, a West Coast investment bank, developed the 'OpenIPO' Dutch auction process in 1998, in which investors set the price of an offering through an open bid process. The investment bank introduced the process in response to complaints by retail investors that they were unable to participate in IPOs because the lead managers of deals would allocate shares to their most important clients first, regardless of how much an investor might be willing to pay. Remember, this process came about during a period when the average one-day premium for US IPOs increased from 20 per cent to 70 per cent above the offering price. Internet IPOs regularly had much higher one-day premia.

In June 1999, WR Hambrecht and Daiwa Securities America used the Dutch auction process in the flotation of Salon.com, an online publisher with low revenues and big losses. The shares were priced at $10.50, at the low end of the proposed $10.50 to $13.50 price range. On June 22, the first day of trading, the shares opened at $10.81 on the Nasdaq stock market. However, by the end of the day, the shares slid nearly 5 per cent below the offer price to $10.00 as a result of weak demand.

## *Fixed price offers*

There are two types of fixed price offers: underwritten and non-underwritten (or best efforts). Underwritten fixed price offerings are most common in the UK, European and Asian markets, while best efforts offerings are infrequently used in Canada and the USA. At the time of writing, usage of underwritten fixed price offerings had been in decline for many years, especially for larger offerings.

In an underwritten fixed price offer, the lead manager(s) canvass institutional investor opinion in a less formal manner than in a bookbuilding. Using the information gathered, the issuer and its bank(s) agree an offering price. When the price is agreed, the bank(s) underwrite the offer – they guarantee that the issuer will receive the full proceeds of the issue (less expenses), regardless of demand. The subsequent offering period can last from just a few days to two or three weeks, depending on the jurisdiction in which the offering is taking place.

During the offering, orders are solicited from institutional and individual investors and advertising (where permitted) encourages retail investors to subscribe for shares. The same pre-marketing and marketing process as used in bookbuilding can be used in a fixed price offer. Documentation is also the same. The big difference is the time at which the price is established for the offer.

Many fixed price offers, particularly smaller ones, rely on limited marketing to a select number of institutions prior to setting the price. Larger fixed price offers will employ a roadshow to sell the issue to investors, prior to setting the price. No formal bookbuilding takes place in such issues, but the lead bank and syndicate keep in close contact with investors to determine what price would be acceptable to make the offer a success.

### Underwritten

Both fixed price and bookbuilt offerings are underwritten. The banking syndicate buys the shares on offer from the selling shareholder and resells the shares to investors. In some jurisdictions, the syndicate does not legally take possession, but just guarantees the offer price. The main difference between fixed price underwritten offers and bookbuilding is the length of time underwriting lasts and the attendant risks.

In fixed price offerings, the underwriting period will vary, but it starts when the price is set (known as Impact Day in the UK) and continues to the close of subscription period (between two days and three weeks). If the issuer is seeking to attract individual investors, it must leave the subscription period open for a sufficient length of time for the investors to respond to the offer. If the offering is unsuccessful, the underwriters are required to take up the unsold shares in proportion to their underwriting commitment.

In a bookbuilt offering, the deal is only underwritten once the syndicate knows there is sufficient demand for the shares on offer. If there is insufficient demand on the planned pricing day, the offering price is reduced or the size of the offer is scaled down.

A fixed price offer is riskier for investment banks – they are exposed to the uncertainty of demand for the offering as well as the vagaries of market conditions for up to three weeks. Investment bankers argue that fixed price offers set the price at a lower level than a company could achieve through bookbuilding. The degree of risk involved is one of the reasons that large equity offerings around the world have moved towards the bookbuilding process, at the prodding of the investment banking community.

### Best efforts

A best efforts fixed price offering involves no underwriting, just the manager's 'best effort' to sell the shares. The price is set after negotiation between manager and issuer, and a minimum and sometimes maximum offer size set. On closing of the subscription period, if there are insufficient orders to reach the minimum size, the offering is abandoned. If there is heavy demand and the maximum offer size is attained, the subscription period may be curtailed.

Best efforts deals tend to be done for smaller enterprises or special purpose vehicles (often providing tax advantages to investors). Depending on the type of transaction a single bank or a syndicate of banks may be involved. Finally, investors in best efforts offerings tend to be individuals, not institutions.

## Bookbuilding

In a bookbuilding IPO, the syndicate undertakes a widespread marketing campaign to canvass institutional investor opinion prior to pricing the shares. Starting with a likely offering price range, syndicate members solicit expressions of interest with respect to both size of order and number of shares the institutional investor is interested in. Thus, a book is built which gives the company, selling shareholders and investment bank a clear picture of demand for shares at different price levels. Bookbuilding is supposed to maximize proceeds for the issuer. Shares are offered to all investors (institutional and individual) at the same price.

Bookbuilding's adherents claim that it gives issuer and lead bank greater control over the distribution of shares. In an auction, the highest bidder is allocated shares, regardless of its long-term intentions. Bookbuilding also allows the manager to retain price flexibility – the price range and size of offering can change and price is only set at the end of the bookbuilding period.

> 'Bookbuilding generates higher expected proceeds and exclusively provides an opportunity to sell additional shares at full value (the greenshoe or over-allotment offering) but, in the process, exposes the issuer to greater risk. In comparison, fixed price offerings . . . guarantee the issuer certain proceeds.'
>
> (Benveniste and Busaba, 1997)

At the close of the bookbuilding period, when the prospectus/registration statement has been approved, the lead bank, or bookrunner, will set the price of the shares and the number of shares to be offered. At this stage, the syndicate 'underwrites' the offering (i.e. guarantees the issuer the proceeds).

The syndicate is at risk for a relatively short period – usually less than 24 hours, which is the time from which the price is set to the time that orders are confirmed with institutional and retail investors. Since the book is closed only when there are sufficient orders at the offer price, there is very little risk indeed. The main risk is a sudden adverse change in market. To protect themselves against this, banks insert a clause in the underwriting agreement called *force majeure* which allows the banks to cancel the transaction under certain conditions. This 'market out' clause features in all underwriting agreements between banks and issuers.

In the USA and Canada, bookbuilding is the standard way of conducting an IPO: the vast majority of IPOs and secondary offerings are conducted and priced in this manner. In international equity offerings and large offerings bookbuilding was used increasingly frequently during the 1990s. Today, most large international equity offerings are run as bookbuilding exercises, regardless of the issuer's traditional domestic market practice.

Bookbuilding has spread as far as markets such as India, where it is operated as a modified auction. In India, even retail investors are invited to submit bids at specified prices, while in other markets, retail investors generally indicate their demand with no price sensitivity. In the early 2002 IPO for Bharti Tele-Ventures (BTVL), investors were asked to submit bids at or above the floor price of Rs45 during a six-day bookbuild period.

## Types of bid

The expressions of interest, or bids, can take the form of the number of shares the investor desires, or a monetary amount (e.g. 100 000 shares or £3.0 million worth of shares, respectively). An investor may also specify a maximum price it is willing to pay.

There are three types of bid:

- **Limit order** – specifies the maximum price the investor is willing to pay for shares.
- **Strike order** – a bid for a specified number of shares (or currency amount) regardless of the issue price.
- **Step bid** – the investor submits a demand schedule as a 'step function' (i.e. a series of limit bids at increasing prices).

A step bid provides the most information to the bookrunner, and is therefore the most valued. However, the vast majority of institutions enter strike orders.

> 'Bidders can submit bids at any time and are kept informed of the impending closing date. They can also revise their bids by changing amounts or limit prices, they can transform bids from limit bids to strike bid (or vice versa), and they can cancel bids. Consequently, the number of shares demanded can change considerably over time.'
>
> (Cornelli and Goldreich, 2001)

The bids are submitted to the bookrunner by syndicate members on a daily basis. An example of a bookbuilding form is given in Chapter 9.

Once the bookbuilding process is concluded, the lead bank aggregates all the bids into a demand curve and chooses the issue price according to its discretion. It does not have to allocate shares to the highest bidders. In fact, it may ignore the highest bids entirely if it thinks that will be in the interests of the deal.

## Bidding strategies

During hot new issues markets, institutions often submit bids at a very early stage. This is because the bookrunner usually favours early orders with preferential allocations. See Chapter 11 for a discussion of allocations. During the bubble, it was not uncommon to find new issues oversubscribed several times on the first day of bookbuilding.

In cold new issues markets, investors play the opposite game – they wait until as late as possible in the process to submit their orders, in the hopes of forcing a reduction in the offering price range.

In hot markets, investors, in addition to bidding early, inflate the size of their orders. If they expect the offering to be oversubscribed, they know that investors won't receive a full allocation of shares. Therefore they increase their order size to increase the chance of getting the number of shares they want.

When there is sufficient demand, the bookrunner can decide to increase the price of the shares on offer (in many markets) and, in conjunction with the issuer and selling shareholders, possibly increase the number of shares to be sold (see Tables 4.4 and 4.5).

## Setting the price

On conclusion of the bookbuilding process, the lead manager constructs a demand curve with all bids and then sets the offering price. For example, an issuer plans to sell seven million shares at a price between €10.00 and €12.00. At the end of bookbuilding Figure 4.2 illustrates the number of orders for shares at price intervals of 25 cents. There is just enough demand for the shares at €11.50 for the offering to be fully subscribed. Above that price, there is insufficient demand, below it there is excess demand.

If the bookrunner (lead bank) sets the price at the maximum of €11.50, there would be little demand in the aftermarket. So the share price will always be set below the maximum price that appears to be possible. To set the final price for this offering, the bookrunner would look at the composition of the book at prices between €10.00 and €11.25 and make a determination of what the most appropriate price is.

The offer price is not mechanistically set where demand equals the supply of shares, as in an auction: the bookrunner has significant discretion in setting the price. Thus, a bookbuilding offering will almost always set a lower price than the clearing price as indicated by institutions' expressions of interest.

Setting the price is the result of discussions/negotiations between the issuer and the bookrunner. The price is set the same way for fixed price offers, but the parties in a bookbuilding have more information. According to Cornelli and Goldreich (2001), the price is set very close to the weighted average of all limit prices. The level of oversubscription also affects the offer price, but to a lesser degree.

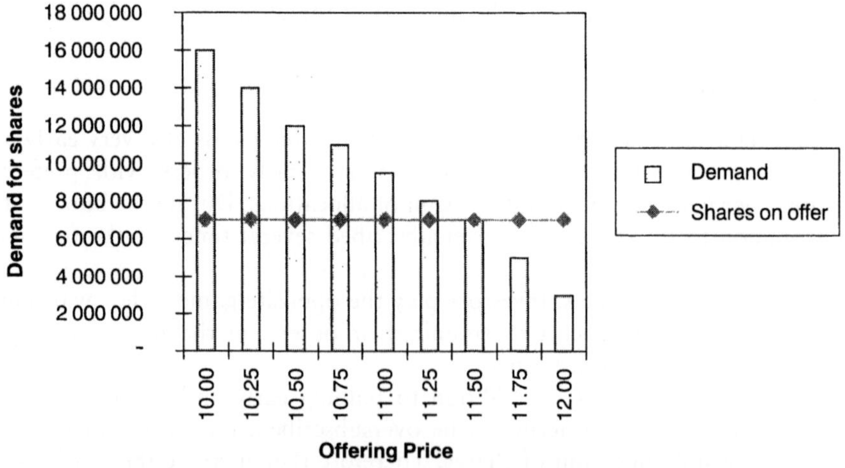


Figure 4.2 Sample demand curve

In setting the price, bookrunners tend to be influenced more by large bids and bids from more frequent investors. Banks often favour input from investors with whom they do significant amounts of secondary business.

## Flexibility of bookbuilding

As noted above, a price range is established at the time of the filing of the preliminary prospectus. During the bookbuilding, the bookrunner can raise or lower the indicative price range and raise or lower the number of shares on offer. Each decision is based on information in the 'book'. The lead manager has significant discretion in setting the price and, in most markets can set the price outside the initial range if there is sufficient/insufficient demand to merit doing so.

In fact, under 50 per cent of US offerings between 1990 and 2001 were priced within the initial price range, as set out in the preliminary prospectus (Ritter, 2001d). In Table 4.4, the column headed 'OP < Lo' indicates deals where the offering price was set below the low point of the initial price range. Similarly, 'OP > Hi' means that the offering price was above the high point of the initial range. Here OP is offering price. Note the leap in proportion of offerings being priced above the high end of the initial price range in 1999 and 2000.

This phenomenon was not limited to the USA. During the bull market, German offerings were also skewed to the high end of the price range. During the period 1998–2001, 71.7 per cent of German deals were priced at the top of the price range, while only 12.9 per cent of offerings were priced at the low point of the price range.

| Year | Number of IPOs | Average one-day premium (%) | OP < Lo (%) | Lo < OP > Hi (%) | OP > Hi (%) |
|---|---|---|---|---|---|
| 1983–1987 | 1430 | | 27.0 | 62.6 | 10.4 |
| 1990 | 89 | 9.46 | 25.8 | 50.6 | 23.6 |
| 1991 | 250 | 11.37 | 19.6 | 55.6 | 24.8 |
| 1992 | 338 | 9.87 | 38.5 | 40.2 | 21.3 |
| 1993 | 437 | 11.64 | 21.5 | 54.2 | 24.3 |
| 1994 | 319 | 8.56 | 37.0 | 49.5 | 13.5 |
| 1995 | 366 | 20.38 | 19.7 | 43.7 | 36.6 |
| 1996 | 571 | 15.99 | 25.2 | 49.6 | 25.2 |
| 1997 | 389 | 13.80 | 30.8 | 45.2 | 23.9 |
| 1998 | 266 | 21.76 | 28.2 | 48.9 | 22.9 |
| 1999 | 446 | 70.89 | 15.0 | 36.3 | 48.7 |
| 2000 | 333 | 57.29 | 22.8 | 36.9 | 40.3 |
| 2001 | 78 | 14.15 | 25.6 | 59.0 | 15.4 |
| | 3885 | 24.30 | 25.4 | 46.3 | 28.3 |

*Sources:* Hanley (1993) for 1983–September 1987 and Ritter (2001d) for 1990–2001.

**Table 4.4** Pricing of US offerings

## Partial adjustment

If the deal is going well, and there is a high demand, the lead manager can revise the offer range upwards to reflect the demand. Similarly, if the deal is in trouble, the price range can be adjusted downwards. In either case, the final offer price can be made above the top or below the bottom of the new price range.

Interestingly, in situations where the price range has been revised upwards and the price has been set at the higher level, IPOs have a higher one-day premium than those that stay within the range, or price below the range: 'Underpricing is positively related to revisions in the offer price from the filing of the preliminary prospectus to the offer date' (Hanley, 1993).

This has been called the partial adjustment phenomenon by Ibbotson, Sindelar and Ritter (1988) and is a condition well recognized in the industry. The press has coined the term 'walk up' to deal with situations where the initial price range is set deliberately low. Bankers build up demand for the shares then increase the price range because of 'substantial' investor interest. The pricing momentum helps to create the appearance of a hot offering. On pricing, the bank 'sets the price just below the maximum point in the range, creating a feel good factor for investors who end up believing they have bought into a popular stock at a discount' (Dovkants, 1999).

The question remains, why don't investment banks increase the offering price by an even greater degree? They cause the issuers and selling shareholders to leave significant amounts of money on the table – to the benefit of investors and the detriment of issuers/selling shareholders.

Hanley (1993: 233) suggests that bankers 'prefer to compensate investors for truthfully revealing information by allocating a smaller number of highly underpriced shares rather than a larger amount of slightly underpriced shares'.

Table 4.5 illustrates that when issues are priced below the initial price range, a reduction in number of shares offered accompanies the offering price reduction. Deals that are going well price above the range and increase the number of shares on offer by approximately 10 per cent.

| | OP < Lo (%) | Lo < OP > Hi (%) | OP > Hi (%) |
|---|---|---|---|
| Change in number of shares offered (1983–1987)[1] | | | |
| Average | –10.0 | 1.4 | 10.0 |
| Median | 0.0 | 0.0 | 5.3 |
| Change in number of shares offered (1990–1996)[2] | –4 | +5 | +9 |
| Days in registration with SEC | 64 | 56 | 48 |

*Source:* [1]Hanley (1993); [2]Logue et al. (1999).

**Table 4.5** Changes in shares offered

To illustrate, in late 2001 Goldman Sachs brought a rare technology offering to an unwelcoming market. Netscreen Technologies filed its preliminary prospectus with the SEC in October 2001 for an offering of 8 million shares to be priced between $9.00 and $11.00 per share. Two days prior to the offering, the company raised the price range to $12.00 to $14.00 per share in response to heavier than expected demand. When the books closed and the deal was priced on December 11, the company sold 10 million shares at $16.00 each – two dollars per share higher than the top of the revised range. The offering raised $160 million (before expenses), twice as much as the company would have had if it sold 8 million shares at the mid-point of the original price range. At the close of the first day of trading, the offering's momentum had continued. The share price surged to $13.72, a 48 per cent increase.

The downside of the partial adjustment phenomenon is illustrated by Crown Castle's IPO. Crown Castle, which is an American wireless communications company, decided to go public during the hot new issues market. When the company filed its 31.25 million share IPO with the SEC, it was confident that it could achieve a price of between $17.00 and $19.00 per share. Conducting its roadshow during a weak market (the Dow dropped by 10 per cent while the company was in registration) led Crown Castle to cut the issue in half to 14 million shares and reduce the price range to $14.00–$16.00. In the event, Lehman Brothers, manager of the offering, priced the deal at $13.00. During the first week of trading the price hovered around $13.00 – between $12.87 and $13.19. The company raised $182 million, not the $563 million it had originally anticipated.

# 5 Determining the value of an IPO company

One of the most important aspects of the IPO process is building the investment case. The investment case is comprised of the four or five most compelling reasons for a potential investor to buy the shares. Underpinning the investment case is the price or value of the company being sold. Investors don't want to overpay – they want to buy companies that are valued at a discount to companies that are already trading in the market.

In delivering this crucial component of the investment case, the banks involved in the flotation must provide an indicative valuation (price range) at the beginning of the offering process. In fact the first valuation analysis is usually done when investment banks are pitching for the lead manager mandate. To help win the business they will present the company or selling shareholder with a preliminary valuation. The valuation will be refined as the bankers learn more about the company during due diligence.

Ultimately the price of an IPO is set through negotiation between the vendor and the investment banks involved. In a fixed price offer, the lead manager has resort to limited assessment of investor demand and valuation. In a bookbuilding offering, the managers of the deal undertake extensive marketing to canvass investor opinion regarding price and demand.

Before bookbuilding commences, the managers set a price range to give investors an idea of what value they consider reasonable. The price range is indicative only and may be adjusted, sometimes dramatically, during the marketing of the offering, as Orange's experience illustrates.

Orange is the cellular telecommunications subsidiary of France Telecom, formed when France Telecom merged its cellular operations with those of Orange, which it acquired from Vodafone in 2000. At the time, senior France Telecom executives suggested that the value of the combined businesses was more than €100 billion. However, by the time the company was preparing Orange for flotation, the bankers involved said that an appropriate valuation range was between €70 billion and €80 billion. The value dropped even more by the time the preliminary prospectus was published, with a price range of €11.50 to €13.50 per share, or an aggregate equity value of €55.2 billion to €64.8 billion. During marketing in February 2001, lead banks Dresdner Kleinwort Benson, Morgan Stanley and Société Générale scaled back the price even further given weak investor demand. The final price range used to market to investors was €9.50 to €11.00 (€45.6 billion to €52.8 billion).

## Types of valuation

When bankers are pitching to win the mandate to lead an IPO, or when they first think about the value of the business, they look at the valuation question in two ways:

- What is the value of this company based on the value of similar publicly traded companies?
- What is the company's intrinsic value?

The answer to the former should give a rough idea as to the price the shares will trade at following the issue. The answer to the second is the value a purchaser of 100 per cent of the shares might place on the business.

A peer group or relative valuation takes various investment ratios from comparable companies to determine a likely trading value of the potential issuer. An intrinsic valuation is done by forecasting the firm's free cash flows and discounting them at the firm's cost of capital to arrive at a present value. This is called a 'discounted cash flow' valuation. In either case, valuation involves making a great number of assumptions. The ability to construct complex spreadsheets is but one part of the process. Different industries make use of different valuation techniques. The stage of a company's development will have an impact on the choice of valuation method. In situations where there is no peer group or the company is at a very early stage of development, it may be necessary to rely entirely on a discounted cash flow (DCF) valuation.

This chapter examines these two most widespread corporate valuation techniques. The technique or techniques chosen and their relative importance will vary from one deal to another. Senior bankers use their experience and judgment when determining the most appropriate valuation method to use. But they will always use more than one technique in valuing a company's shares.

This is not a book on valuation. There are numerous texts that cover valuation in great detail. A good one is Copeland, Koller and Murrin's *Valuation*, 3rd edn, published by John Wiley & Sons.

## Relative valuations

The most common, and in many ways the easiest to complete, method of valuing a company's shares is by comparing a number of financial and investment ratios (multiples) with those of the firm's peer group that are already listed on a stock exchange. In general, it is easy to calculate multiples for other companies, and this method is particularly useful when there are several truly comparable firms and the market is pricing these firms correctly. However, the determination of what is a 'comparable' company is not always straightforward, and often open to interpretation. When selecting companies to use in peer group analysis, bankers look for similar:

- Size and future growth prospects
- Riskiness of the business
- Scope of product offering

- Customer base
- Geographic reach
- Current and future profitability.

All these variables have an impact on the valuation of the comparable companies and judgment needs to be used in drawing conclusions as to the appropriate multiples to be used for the value range.

There are numerous ratios that can be used in comparing value. We will look at five of the most popular:

- Capitalization of earnings (or price/earnings (P/E) multiples)
- Price/EBIT (earnings before interest and tax)
- Price/book value (i.e. market value/book value)
- Enterprise value/EBITDA (earnings before interest, tax, depreciation and amortization)
- Enterprise value/revenues (sales).

The first three give an estimate of the equity value (market capitalization) of the firm. The latter two, based on enterprise value, give an estimate of the equity value plus the value of the company's debt. There are, of course, a number of other investment ratios that can be used. Some are more applicable to certain industries than others. The five that we look at are some of the most widely applicable and widely used.

To help with the discussion of relative valuations, we will use an example. Blockade Limited is currently considering an IPO. As part of its decision-making process, it will ask a number of investment banks to provide an estimate of value. Table 5.1 is a

| 1<br>Company | 2<br>Price | 3<br>Market Cap. ($m) | 4<br>P/E 2002 | 5<br>P/E 2003 | 6<br>Price/ EBIT | 7<br>MV/ BV | 8<br>EV/ EBITDA | 9<br>EV/ Revenues |
|---|---|---|---|---|---|---|---|---|
| Bay | 47.9 | 534 | 18.7 | 14.3 | 7.4 | 1.00 | 6.9 | 1.24 |
| Bloor | 21.6 | 287 | 14.4 | 13.5 | 6.9 | 0.16 | 7.3 | 0.64 |
| Front | 37.8 | 900 | 7.6 | 7.1 | 4.0 | 0.55 | 4.5 | 0.70 |
| Spadina | 5.3 | 456 | 11.8 | 7.3 | 6.0 | 0.25 | 3.9 | 0.51 |
| Yonge | 77.3 | 175 | 13.8 | 12.7 | 7.1 | 0.79 | 6.6 | 1.01 |
| Average | | | 13.3 | 11.0 | 6.3 | 0.55 | 5.8 | 0.82 |
| Median | | | 13.8 | 12.7 | 6.9 | 0.55 | 6.6 | 0.70 |

Market cap. = market capitalization (# shares × share price).
P/E = price/earnings ratio (for 2002 and 2003).
MV = market value (market capitalization).
BV = book value of shareholders' equity.
EV = enterprise value.
EBITDA = earnings before interest, tax, depreciation and amortization.

**Table 5.1** Selected comparable companies

typical 'comparables table', as constructed by an investment banking analyst. The analyst, a recent graduate from a top university, has looked at a much larger group of companies in Blockade's industry and narrowed down the initial group of companies to five that have the most similar characteristics (as listed above). Price can refer to either price per share or market capitalization, depending on the denominator in the ratio. Note that the mean (average) and median (middle value) statistics are reasonably close for most ratios. This indicates there are few 'outliers' that might skew the valuation range. An analyst will usually eliminate outliers from his calculation of the mean used in determining the average value for the peer group.

Table 5.2 presents summary financial statements for Blockade Limited for the year ended 31 December 2002. The company's net income is expected to grow to £20 million in the following year (2003) from £17 million.

| **Income statement (£)** | 2002 | **Balance sheet (£)** | 2002 |
|---|---|---|---|
| Revenues | 300 | Fixed assets | 400 |
| Cost of sales | (250) | Current assets | 100 |
| EBITDA | 50 | Current liabilities | 60 |
| Depreciation | (14) | | |
| EBIT | 36 | Long-term debt | 80 |
| Interest expenses | (12) | Shareholders' funds | 360 |
| Earnings before tax | 24 | | |
| Income tax | (7) | | |
| Profit after tax | 17 | | |

**Table 5.2** Summary financial statements (£ million)

We will now work through a comparables valuation based on the five main ratios mentioned above.

## *Capitalization of earnings or price/earnings ratio basis*

The most common earnings valuations method used is the price/earnings ratio (PER or P/E ratio). To determine value, annual maintainable (or sustainable) earnings are multiplied by the average P/E ratio of the sector or group of comparable companies. Sometimes this method is called the 'capitalization of earnings' approach and is stated as:

$$\text{Sustainable earnings per share} \times \text{price/earnings multiple} = \text{share price}$$

or

$$\text{Sustainable net profit} \times \text{price/earnings multiple} = \text{market capitalization}$$

The maintainable earnings approach is very common in some markets, such as Malaysia, as the following excerpts from IPO prospectuses illustrate:

> 'The IPO price of RM2.70 per Share was determined and agreed upon by the Company and Arab-Malaysian Bank as Advisor and Managing Underwriter based on various factors including the following:
>
> (i) The pro forma forecast net PE multiple of approximately 8.55 times based on the pro forma forecast net eps of 31.59 sen . . .'
>
> *Top Glove Corporation, 16 February 2001*
>
> 'The IPO price of RM1.60 per DeGem ordinary share has been determined and arrived at after taking into consideration, *inter alia*, the following factors:
>
> (i) The forecast net PE multiple of 6.11 times based on the forecast net EPS of 26.2 sen computed using the enlarged issued share capital of 42 000 000 ordinary shares of RM1.00 each . . .'
>
> *DeGem Berhad, 27 August 2001*

Note that both valuations looked at forecast PE multiples. Future-oriented information is more useful than historic.

The first step is to identify sustainable earnings (net profit or net income) attributable to common (ordinary) shareholders. In coming to a figure, bankers and investors will look at:

- Historic earnings growth
- Quality of earnings (i.e. stability or resilience)
- Potential accounting adjustments
- External factors that may have an impact on future earnings.

Aside from estimating sustainable earnings, which in itself involves several assumptions, the determination of the appropriate multiple is equally uncertain. Investors will look to the industry average, or more appropriately, the average multiple of those companies that are most comparable to the company being valued.

As a simple example, consider a company with estimated sustainable earnings attributable to ordinary shareholders of $5 million. An analyst who believes that a capitalization rate of between eight and 12 times is appropriate would value the company at between £40 million and £60 million. If the company had 10 million shares outstanding, the estimated share price would be between 400p and 600p per share. Alternatively, bankers can look at the trailing (last year), estimated (for the remainder of the current year) and forecast (next year) earnings (net profit) of the company and compare them to the estimated and forecast P/E ratios of the peer group. In the Blockade example, we see that the average trailing (2002) P/E multiple for the five companies is 13.3 times, while the average forecast P/E multiple comes in at 11 times 2003 earnings.

Applying industry averages to Blockade would see its market capitalization estimated at between £220 million and £230 million:

| | Multiple | × | Net profit | = | Market capitalization |
|---|---|---|---|---|---|
| 2002 | 13.3 | × | £17m | = | £226.1m |
| 2003 | 11.0 | × | £20m | = | £220.0m |

While using the price/earnings multiple or sustainable earnings approach is one of the most straightforward of the relative valuation methods, it is not perfect. According to the *Financial Times* Lex Column (10 March 1997): 'The biggest weakness is the unscientific way growth is valued.'

Other difficulties arise because the ratio does not take account of:

- Differences in accounting approaches (domestic and international) (e.g. amortization of goodwill)
- Differences in debt levels
- Differences in tax rates.

Consider a research report issued prior to the flotation of IPSOS, a French market research company in June 1999. At the time there were no other market research companies listed in France, so the research analysts had to look abroad to find suitable comparable companies. They were able to identify five companies (one in the UK and four in the USA) with which to compare IPSOS. However, the analysts wrote: 'Owing to our desire to be consistent, we have not valued IPSOS using the P/E multiple derived from our sample. This is because in the case of most groups in the sample, the information needed to restate the data for goodwill amortization is not available.'

Despite its shortcomings, the P/E approach to valuation continues to be one of the most widely used methods. It is relatively simple to calculate and use and is understood by all market participants, including individual investors. However, no responsible banker would stop at the capitalization of earnings approach. She will look to other comparable ratios in order to confirm the figure produced using P/Es.

### *Price/EBIT*

An alternative earnings valuation method is to use a multiple of a business's earnings before interest and tax (EBIT). The same procedure is used as that for the capitalization of earnings, except EBIT is substituted for net income. The multiple is particularly useful for valuing companies that are currently making net losses or are highly levered. It also removes the impact of differing tax rates.

EBIT multiples are not commonly quoted for public companies, but can easily be calculated by the analyst. In situations where gearing wipes out net profit, EBIT can substitute. When Fairchild Semiconductor went public in 1999, it had made a net loss in each of the two prior years, meaning that a P/E valuation based on historic figures was impossible.

The average P/EBIT for Blockade's peer group is 6.3 times. Applying this figure to Blockade's EBIT, or £36 million, leads to an estimated value of £227 million, right in line with the two figures produced using the P/E approach.

### *Market value to book value*

The market to book value ratio, also called the price to book value ratio, is another frequently examined investment figure. The market value of a company's shares (i.e. price) is divided by its book value per share (i.e. shareholders' funds divided by number of shares outstanding); alternatively, the market capitalization is divided by shareholders' funds. Its importance is greater in some sectors (e.g. financial services) than others (e.g. high-tech, software).

Some analysts favour the ratio because the book value is a relative constant that eases comparability over time or across companies. The ratio can be calculated for loss-making companies and companies whose EBIT is negative.

However, the book value does not reflect a firm's earnings power or projected cash flows; it reflects the original cost of a firm's assets and is affected by accounting decisions on depreciation. The ratio may not be useful in valuing firms which do not have significant fixed assets. Finally, highly geared companies may sustain net losses for several years, cutting into shareholders' funds dramatically. For example, stockholders' equity at Fairchild Semiconductor was negative $240.4 million in the company's final balance sheet prior to its IPO.

The book value of Blockade's shareholders' equity was £360 million at its most recent year end. Applying a multiple of 0.55 gives a suggested equity value of £198 million.

### *Enterprise value/EBITDA*

This ratio first gained widespread use in the mid-1990s. Enterprise value is calculated as the firm's equity market capitalization (number of shares outstanding times share price) plus the market value of its outstanding debt. The multiple compares the enterprise value to the firm's EBITDA, which is a reasonably close proxy for its cash flow.

EBITDA is a useful figure, particularly for companies or industries that are growing rapidly and may not yet have achieved profitability. The benefits of the ratio are numerous. It may be computed for firms that have net losses and can be more appropriate for industries that require substantial investment in infrastructure and long gestation periods. For leveraged buy-outs, EBITDA multiples capture the ability of the firm to generate cash flows that may be used to support debt payments in the short term. Finally, the EBITDA multiple allows for comparisons of firms with different capital structures.

Looking to Blockade, we see that its EBITDA in 2002 was £50 million. The average EV/EBITDA ratio among the five peer group companies was 5.8 times. Applying that multiple to Blockade's EBITDA results in an estimated enterprise value of £290 million. Subtracting the company's £80 million in debt leaves us with an equity value of £210 million, slightly below (but still in line with) the figures provided using the P/E multiples.

### *Enterprise value/revenues (sales)*

The EV/sales ratio is most useful in cyclical industries where earnings and EBIT are frequently negative during the down part of the industry cycle. One strength of the ratio is that in most industries, the measurement of revenues is straightforward and not subject to differing accounting treatments in the way that expenses can be.

While the EV/sales ratio can be more consistent than other ratios discussed above, it suffers from the fact that it is unable to distinguish between companies with good or poor margins. Nor does it explicitly deal with growth or risk.

In Blockade's industry, the average EV/sales ratio is 0.82 times, giving the company a suggested enterprise value of £246 million, based on annual revenues of £300 million. When debt is subtracted, the equity value of Blockade is estimated to be £166 million, significantly below the value provided by other ratios.

When a ratio turns up a 'rogue' value, the analyst needs to dig deeper, not simply accept the figure and throw it into an average of values. Looking back to Table 5.1, we can see that the EV/revenues column has the widest variation, ranging from 0.51 times to 1.24 times. It may be that the ratio is not appropriate for Blockade's industry. If this were the case, the analyst would eliminate the ratio from her calculations.

### *Summary valuation of Blockade*

Table 5.3 contains the workings of the summary comparable valuation for Blockade. The reader should note that we have made the simplifying assumption that the simple

| Ratio | Suggested equity value (£m) |
|---|---|
| P/E (2002) | 226 |
| P/E (2003) | 220 |
| P/EBIT | 227 |
| P/book value | 198 |
| EV/EBITDA | 210* |
| Range | 198–227 |
| Average | 216 |

*Equity value based on enterprise value of £290 million less £80 million debt.

**Table 5.3** Summary comparable valuation

average of the five companies is the appropriate figure for the four ratios that we have deemed suitable for the valuation of Blockade.

Given a simple average of £216 million and a fairly tight valuation range, a reasonable estimate of value would be £205 million to £225 million. In a real situation, an analyst with in-depth knowledge of Blockade's industry might place a heavier weight on the results of one or two of the valuation ratios. Note that this final range is called 'reasonable'. It is based on the author's judgment: something that is important in all valuations. Although the use of formulas and numerical ratios appears to make valuation a science, it remains very much an art.

## Discounted cash flow valuation

> 'In principle, valuing IPOs is no different from valuing other stocks. In practice, because many IPOs are of young growth firms in high technology industries, historical accounting information is of limited use in projecting future profits or cash flows.'
>
> (Ritter, 1998a)

From a theoretical perspective, DCF valuations provide the most reliable indications of corporate value, but their use is often limited in practice by lack of reliable cash flow forecasts and the numerous assumptions required.

The five steps in determining the value of a firm through a DCF valuation are as follows:

- Forecast future cash flows over the next business cycle, or at least five years. If the forecast is derived from the company's financial statements, ensure proper adjustment is made for depreciation and amortization, capital expenditure and changes in working capital.
- Make an estimate of the value of the company beyond the forecast period (this is called the residual or terminal value).
- Using an appropriate discount rate, calculate the present value of all the cash flows.
- Add any excess cash or marketable securities and non-operating assets to determine the firm's enterprise value.
- Adjust for the firm's outstanding debt to determine its equity value.

### *Step 1*

The free cash flow figure computed in a DCF forecast combines information from both income statement and balance sheet (for example, capital expenditures can be a significant use of cash, but do not appear on the firm's income statement). Depreciation and amortization are both recorded as expenses on the income statement, but do not represent any movement in cash.

Typically, a research analyst or corporate financier will make a cash flow forecast for a period of five years. In particularly volatile or uncertain industries, the forecast period may only be for three years, while in more stable industries, or where long-term contracts are in place, cash flows can be forecast for 10 years or more. Although it can be difficult, the financial modeller should attempt to capture one business cycle.

The following sets out the calculations for a firm's free cash flow:

| | |
|---|---|
| | Earnings before interest and tax (EBIT) |
| Less: | Notional taxes on EBIT (i.e. company's highest marginal tax rate times EBIT) |
| Equals: | NOPAT (Net Operating Profit After Tax) |
| Plus: | Non-cash expenses, particularly depreciation and amortization |
| Less: | Capital expenditures<br>Increase (decrease) in non-cash working capital |
| Equals: | Free cash flow |

Starting with the firm's earnings before interest and tax (also called PBIT – profit before interest and tax – or as one wag put it, profit before interesting things), we work down and make the necessary adjustments to arrive at a company's free cash flow. The tax charge represents the income tax the company would pay if it had no debt, marketable securities, non-operating income or expenses. That is, taxes (at the firm's highest marginal rate) are applied to EBIT. Net operating profit after tax (NOPAT) is sometimes called NOPLAT – net operating profit less adjusted taxes. They are the same thing.

| | £ millions | | | | |
|---|---|---|---|---|---|
| | **Year 1** | **Year 2** | **Year 3** | **Year 4** | **Year 5** |
| EBIT | 100 | 106 | 112 | 119 | 126 |
| Notional tax charge (30%) | 30 | 32 | 34 | 36 | 38 |
| NOPAT | 70 | 74 | 78 | 83 | 88 |
| *Plus:* | | | | | |
| Depreciation | 25 | 28 | 30 | 33 | 37 |
| *Less:* | | | | | |
| Capital expenditure | 30 | 32 | 33 | 35 | 36 |
| Increase in working capital | 12 | 15 | 16 | 10 | (5)* |
| **Free cash flow** | 53 | 55 | 59 | 71 | 94 |

*This represents a decrease in working capital, or a freeing up of cash.

**Table 5.4** Sample cash flow forecast

An increase in non-cash working capital (sometimes called working investment) is a use of cash, while a decrease frees up cash and should be added, not subtracted, to the equation.

Free cash flow is the cash that is theoretically available to pay a return to the providers of capital – both debt holders as well as shareholders. From the free cash flow, the corporate financier begins to determine the enterprise value of the firm.

Table 5.4 (page 85) illustrates a simplified five-year forecast of free cash flows for a business whose EBIT is growing at approximately 6 per cent annually. When valuing growing businesses, analysts must also look to the capital expenditures and increases in working investment that will support their growth.

### *Step 2: Determining the terminal (residual) value*

Once the banker or analyst has calculated the present value of the cash flows over the forecast period, he is left with the issue of determining the value to be ascribed to the ongoing operations of the company. In the simplest cases, the final or terminal value of a project is the salvage value of the fixed assets. However, when valuing companies with an indeterminate or indefinite life span, a value must be assigned to the business after the end of the forecast period. Often the terminal value constitutes the largest portion of the valuation.

There are three common approaches for determining the terminal value of projects or firms:

- Asset values
- Relative or comparable investment multiples (the *accounting approach*)
- Valuation of a perpetual cash flow (the *economic approach*).

#### Asset value

In certain, very specific valuations, particularly in the natural resources or extractive industries, the final value of the business is simply the value of the plant and equipment at the end of the life of the mine or well. The value in year 10, say, is then discounted to the present value using the appropriate cost of capital. Remember that the residual value of assets could be negative if, for example, there were significant environmental clean-up costs.

#### Relative valuations (accounting approach)

This approach suggests the use of comparable multiples as described earlier in the chapter. If the analyst is going to use a relative valuation to determine terminal value it should either use EV ratios or be sure to gross up EV ratios by the anticipated debt outstanding.

Thus, a multiple of EBITDA at the end of the fifth year might be estimated (generally using current average EBITDA multiples) and applied to the estimate of the fifth year's EBITDA. The deficiency of this method is in the uncertainty over the choice of multiple to use on the future EBITDA. Multiples expand and contract over time, and it adds a second layer of difficulty to accurately determining future value.

### Discounted cash flow (economic approach)

The economic approach is the most appropriate method of determining residual value according to financial theory. We will look at two possibilities. The first assumes that there is no growth in free cash flows following the final year of the forecast. The second assumes that growth continues.

The first DCF approach assumes that the final year's free cash flow continues at the same level in perpetuity. The discount rate ($r$) to be used in the calculation of a perpetual cash flow is the weighted average cost of capital (see p. 90). The formula for calculated steady cash flows for ever follows:

$$\text{Terminal value} = \text{cash flow}/r$$

In some instances a 'steady-state' approach is not appropriate. Some companies or projects might legitimately be assumed to continue to grow after the explicit forecast period. If the growth is estimated to be a constant, the residual value can be estimated by using the mathematical concept of a growing perpetuity.

The formula for a growing perpetuity is:

$$\text{Terminal value} = [CF_n \times (1 + g)]/(r - g)$$

where $CF_n$ is the cash flow in the final year of the forecast, $g$ is the growth rate and $r$ is the discount rate.

It is generally recommended that the maximum growth rate used in the calculation should not exceed the long-term sustainable growth rate of the economy. For companies operating in EU or North American markets, a perpetual growth rate of 2 to 3 per cent would be the maximum reasonable amount.

| | 0% Growth | 2.5% Growth |
|---|---|---|
| Year 5 cash flow | £94m | £94m |
| Calculation | 94/0.10 | $\frac{(94 \times 1.025)}{(0.10 - 0.025)}$ |
| Terminal value | £940 million | £1205 million |

**Table 5.5** Comparison of terminal values with differing growth rates

For our example, Table 5.5 illustrates the terminal value based on the final year's cash flow of £94 million and two different assumptions of growth: zero and 2.5 per cent. In both instances, we have used a discount rate of 10 per cent. While the differences in growth rates seem small, a 2.5 per cent difference results in a terminal value difference of nearly 30 per cent.

### *Step 3: Discounting the cash flows*

Once the forecast of free cash flows has been developed and a terminal value calculated, the investment analyst must discount the cash flows by an appropriate discount rate in order to arrive at a value of the business. Table 5.6 uses the free cash flows from Table 5.4, assumes no growth in the terminal value calculation, and a discount rate of 10 per cent.

| | Year 1 | Year 2 | Year 3 | Year 4 | Year 5 | Beyond |
|---|---|---|---|---|---|---|
| Free cash flow | 53 | 55 | 59 | 71 | 94 | 940 |
| *Discount factor* | *0.909* | *0.826* | *0.751* | *0.683* | *0.621* | *0.621* |
| Present value | 48 | 45 | 44 | 48 | 58 | 584 |
| PV of FCFs | £827 | | | | | |

**Table 5.6** Discounting the cash flows

Note that the terminal value provides 70 per cent of the total value of the business (£584m/£827m).

### Determining the value of a business

The enterprise value of a business is calculated as the sum of the following items:

Discounted cash flows from forecast period

+ Present value of terminal value
+ Cash on hand (including marketable securities) at date of valuation
+ Redundant assets at date of valuation
= Enterprise value

When cash on hand is valued separately, as above, it is important that the valuer does not include interest income from that cash in the forecast. This would result in double counting. Redundant assets are assets that the business owns, but does not use in the ordinary course of operations. If they have value, the assets should be included in the enterprise value calculation.

The enterprise value for the example company is:

| | |
|---|---|
| Forecast DCFs | £243m |
| Present value of terminal value | £584m |
| Cash on hand* | £10m |
| Redundant assets* | £10m |
| Enterprise value | £847m |

*Assumptions made for illustrative purposes.

Enterprise value refers to the value of the assets of the business. (Here the business can be a division of a company, a privately held company, a stock exchange listed company or other entity.) The assets do not refer to the accounting book value or to the salvage value. It is the present value of the cash flows that assets of the firm are capable of generating. Enterprise value does not concern itself with how the assets are financed.

On the other hand, stock market investors are interested in the equity valuation, which is calculated as shown below:

Enterprise value
*Less market value of:*
Preference shares
Debt (including convertible bonds, bank loans and other outstanding debt)

= Equity value

The value of the equity in the business is simply the enterprise value less the market value of securities that rank ahead of ordinary (common) shares in the event of a winding up or liquidation. Debt holders and preference shareholders have a prior claim on the assets of the company. Therefore the equity value of the business is the residual of the enterprise value after deduction for prior claims.

In practice, it can be difficult to determine the market value of the debt and other securities. When this is the case, bankers and analysts frequently use the book value as reported in the most recent financial statements.

Let's say our example company has £325 million face value in long-term debt, but the market value is £300 million. It is the latter figure that is subtracted from the enterprise value to determine the equity value:

| | |
|---|---|
| Forecast DCFs | £243m |
| Present value of terminal value | 584m |
| Cash on hand* | 10m |
| Redundant assets* | 10m |
| **Enterprise value** | **£847m** |
| *Less market value of:* | |
| Preference shares* | 0m |
| Debt | 300m |
| **Equity value** | **£547m** |

*Assumptions made for illustrative purposes.

The equity value is the estimate of the business's market capitalization. This will be the starting point for analysts and investment bankers in setting the price of an IPO.

Note that while the discounted cash flow valuation approach is the most 'scientific', it does suffer from shortcomings. In particular, there are estimation errors surrounding most cash flow forecasts, the determination of the terminal value and often, most importantly, the choice of discount rate (cost of capital).

## Determining the cost of capital

When discounting forecast cash flows or the terminal value, the analyst should be using the company's (or division's or business unit's) cost of capital; that is the amount (in per cent) that the firm must 'pay' to its providers of debt and equity. Each source of capital has a cost – with the cost of equity typically higher than the cost of debt.

When trying to determine the correct discount rate, an analyst should calculate the weighted average of the cost of each component or source of finance (capital). The weighted average cost of capital (WACC) will equal the opportunity cost of capital (i.e. the amount of return that a rational investor requires for an investment of similar risk).

The WACC must be calculated on an after-tax basis because, when calculating free cash flows, we deduct a notional tax charge from EBIT to determine NOPAT.

The formula for the WACC of a company with two sources of capital (common/ordinary shares and straight debt) is set out below:

$$\text{WACC} = [(K_d \times (1 - t) \times (D/T)] + [K_e \times (E/T)]$$

where $K_d$ is the cost of debt, $t$ is tax rate, $D$ is the total amount of debt at market value, $K_e$ is the cost of equity, $E$ is the total amount of equity at market value and $T$ is debt + equity (both at market values).

There are two key issues to remember:

- *Use market values* – The weightings used in the formula should be based on the market values of outstanding debt and equity, not their book values. The WACC is the expected return on a firm's securities based on their current price. That is the return required by an investor at that time.
- *Use target/optimal weightings* – The proportions used in the weighted average cost of capital may not be the proportions that exist today. They should be the expected or target ratio of debt to equity intended to finance the company during the period in question. The target capital structure should be that which minimizes the WACC, and therefore maximizes the value of the business.

For example, a company has the following component costs of capital:

| | |
|---|---|
| Cost of debt (pre-tax) | 8% |
| Cost of equity | 11% |
| Tax rate | 30% |
| Market value of debt | €5m |
| Book value of debt | €5m |
| Market value of equity | €20m |
| Book value of equity | €10m |

Assume that the company is at its target capital structure. To determine its cost of capital, follow these steps:

- First, determine the after-tax cost of debt:

$$8\% \times (1 - 30\%) = 8\% \times 0.70 = 5.6\%$$

- Second, using market values, determine the total capital outstanding:

€5.0 million + €20.0 million = €25.0 million

- Third, determine the proportions of debt and equity:

Debt €5.0/€25.0 = 0.20

Equity €20.0/€25.0 = 0.80

- Fourth, fill in the WACC equation to determine the result:

$$\begin{aligned} \text{WACC} &= [5.6\% \times 0.20] + [11.0\% \times 0.80] \\ &= 1.12\% + 8.80\% \\ &= 9.92\% \end{aligned}$$

## Cost of debt

The cost of debt to a company is the borrowing cost that the company would incur if it were raising funds today. It must be stated after tax in order to match the cash flows which are also calculated on an after-tax basis.

The cost of debt is not the coupon rate on outstanding debt. It is the current yield to maturity. If a firm has issued bonds with a coupon of 9.0 per cent and the current yield to maturity is 7.5 per cent, the latter figure would be used in calculating the cost of debt, even though the company will continue to pay 9.0 per cent until the debt matures. Remember also, that if the yield to maturity has changed from the initial coupon rate, the market price of the bonds will also have changed. If the yield to maturity has increased, the market price of the debt will be lower than the original book price, while if the yield to maturity has decreased, the market price of the debt will have increased.

## Cost of equity

Remember that a company's cost of capital equals an investor's expected return from investing in the company's assets. Determining the expected return on shares is difficult because there are two components: future dividends and anticipated capital appreciation. Forecasting dividends can be managed, but it is nearly impossible to determine expected capital appreciation with any precision. Financiers have turned to academic models for the calculation of the expected returns on, or the cost of, equity.

## *Capital Asset Pricing Model*

Despite many shortcomings, the Capital Asset Pricing Model (CAPM) is the most popular method of determining the cost of equity (Bruner et al., 1998; Geddes, 1998). The CAPM (pronounced cap-em) is a theory of the relationship between the risk of an asset (company shares) and the rate of return required of the asset.

The opportunity cost of equity equals the return on a risk-free asset plus the company's systematic risk (beta) times the market price of risk (market risk premium), as the following equation sets out:

$$K_e = r_f + \beta(r_m - r_f)$$

where $K_e$ is the cost of equity, $r_f$ is the risk-free rate of return, $\beta$ is the beta, $r_m$ is the (expected) equity market return and $(r_m - r_f)$ is the equity (market) risk premium.

The CAPM begins with the logical premise that investors require a rate of return of at least that which can be earned on the risk-free asset (i.e. the risk-free return). Its next step says that to be attracted to investing in the stock market, an investor requires a premium to compensate him for the additional risk involved. This is represented by $(r_m - r_f)$ and is referred to as the equity risk premium or market risk premium. The major (simplifying) assumption of CAPM is that the only influence on share price movements is the movement of the stock market as a whole (market risk). The CAPM quantifies the risk of an individual company share in its beta factor. Beta is a measurement of a share's riskiness compared with the stock market as a whole.

You should note that the above paragraph is a gross simplification of the theory supporting the CAPM. Those readers who are interested should consult any finance textbook (Brealey and Myers is good).

The following sections briefly describe each component of the CAPM.

### Risk-free rate

The risk-free rate is the return on a security that has no default risk. Theoretically, any government security in the home market (e.g. gilts in the UK) can be used. For company valuation, the yield on medium to long-term (e.g. 10-year) government bonds is usually used as the risk-free rate.

### Equity risk premium/market risk premium

The equity risk premium is the difference between the expected rate of return on the stock market (market portfolio) and the risk-free rate. Historic averages of risk premia are frequently used, as the long-term relationship between the stock market's returns and the risk-free return is relatively stable. Note that the short-term relationship (i.e. for periods of less than 10 years) can vary significantly.

In both the UK and the USA, a premium of between 4 and 6 per cent above the government bond yield is typically used as the equity risk premium. During bull markets there is a tendency towards excessive optimism (or 'irrational exuberance'), and bankers and investors often reduce the required risk premium. During the late 1990s, some bankers reduced the risk premium used in the cost of equity calculation to as low as 2 or 3 per cent.

For those interested, Bradford Cornell has written an entire book on *The Equity Risk Premium* (John Wiley & Sons, 1999).

### Beta

The beta measures the extent to which the returns on a given stock move with the market as a whole. It is a measure of relative risk. A beta of 1.0 means that the company's shares are expected to move exactly in line with the market. A beta of 1.5 means that if the market index changes by 1.0 per cent, the stock price will change by 1.5 per cent in the same direction that the market moves. Companies that are riskier than the overall equity market have a beta greater than 1.0, while those that are less risky have a beta of less than 1.0. This is another gross simplification. Interested readers should refer to a finance textbook.

### Example cost of equity calculation

In October 2000, the 10-year gilt yield (UK Government bond) was approximately 5.15 per cent. Severn Trent, a UK water company, had a beta of 0.95, reflecting the relatively low variability of its shares compared with the market. Assuming that the equity risk premium in the UK was 5.0 per cent, Severn Trent's cost of equity was:

$$\begin{aligned} K_e &= 5.15 + (0.95 \times 5.0) \\ &= 5.15 + 4.75 \\ &= 9.90\% \end{aligned}$$

### *Health warning*

The reader should note that there are significant problems with using the CAPM to determine the cost of equity of a business. Studies in many countries have found that the beta factor is not a good predictor of security returns. However, the formula continues to be widely used by corporate financiers, analysts and investors because of its ease of computation and the lack of any widely accepted substitute.

Those readers interested in the shortcomings of the CAPM and beta can read Fama and French (1992, 1997). Because of these shortcomings, some investment bankers will estimate a company's cost of equity capital by simply adding the risk-free rate to an assumed, company-specific risk premium. There is no 'science' in this approach, but the results are not necessarily incorrect.

## Conclusion

A company valuation is the starting point in setting the price of an IPO. Many dot.coms that were worthless based on a DCF calculation at the time of their flotations achieved billion dollar market capitalizations. Similarly, the market will sometimes undervalue businesses.

Banks involved with the IPO will refine their valuation during the early stages of the offering process. The process of due diligence often reveals useful information relating to the value of the company. But, as noted at the beginning of the chapter, supply and demand have the greatest impact on setting the price of a new issue. The following illustrative paragraphs are excerpted from Fairchild Semiconductor's IPO preliminary prospectus.

> 'Prior to this offering, there has been no public market for our Class A Common Stock. The initial public offering price for the Class A Common Stock will be determined by negotiation between us [Fairchild] and Credit Suisse First Boston Corporation [the lead manager], and does not reflect the market price for Class A Common Stock following the offering.'

This is standard language in US IPO prospectuses. However, Fairchild goes further:

> 'Among the principal factors considered in determining the initial public offering price will be:
>
> - the information set forth in this prospectus and otherwise available to Credit Suisse First Boston Corporation;
> - market conditions for initial public offerings;
> - the history of and prospects for the industry in which we are competing;
> - our past and present operations;
> - our past and present earnings and current financial position;
> - the ability of our management;
> - *the recent market prices of, and the demand for, publicly traded common stock of generally comparable companies*;
> - the general conditions of the securities markets at the time of the offering; and,
> - other relevant factors.'

Italics added.

# 6 Documentation and due diligence

Picture this – it's 2 a.m., a large anonymous meeting room with a board table capable of seating 24. The tabletop is covered with copies of the most recent draft of the prospectus, crumpled pieces of paper with discarded edits, old prospectuses being used as precedents, and a couple of copies of the regulatory requirements. On top of this add several half-empty pizza boxes, innumerable empty soda tins and at one end of the table, six lawyers arguing over the use of the conditional subjunctive case in a sentence on page 123 of the current draft. At the other end, two junior investment bankers toss a cricket/baseball back and forth, while just outside the room, mid-level bankers mumble into their cellphones or check their Blackberries for emails.

While this seems glamorous to final year students and MBAs, the sheen wears off quickly. Notably, because the scene can play out night after night and frequently go through the night when trying to meet a filing deadline. The glamorous side of an IPO, if there is one, is the marketing of the deal. Preparing the disclosure documents and legal agreements is a grind. Perhaps this is why more and more of the documentation drafting has been farmed out to lawyers working on the deal.

Underpinning the documentation is the due diligence investigation of the issuer's financial and business history, as well as its prospects. Because documentation requirements are country-specific, this chapter takes a general view of the prospectus and its contents. It also describes the due diligence process. Chapter 7 examines the UK prospectus and regulation in detail, and Chapter 8 the documentation and SEC regulation involved in an American offering.

## Purposes of documentation

We noted in Chapter 3 that documentation and marketing run in parallel, but the emphasis changes on a week-by-week basis. While drafting of the preliminary prospectus is ongoing, the pre-marketing campaign will be warming up. Once the preliminary prospectus is printed, the formal marketing campaign begins and the documentation team takes a back seat until required to respond to comments made by the securities regulators. They will start working on other documents and agreements such as the underwriting agreement.

The main document delivered to investors in an equity offering, either IPO or subsequent equity offering, is the prospectus. A prospectus contains information about the offering (price, number of shares on offer, subscription procedure), about the business of the company (industry, management, operations) and audited financial statements. Prospectuses are delivered to investors for three reasons. First, in a public offer, it is a legal requirement. Second, it is where the issuer tells its story. Third, the delivery of a prospectus containing comprehensive information about the issuer reduces the risk of liability for misleading potential investors. Getting the balance between the second and third is crucial – too much marketing, and the document may not provide sufficient disclosure, too much legalese in the disclosure, and investors won't get past page three.

Even when the offering is being conducted as a private placement, investors will receive a disclosure document. The contents will be similar to that of a prospectus, and it is delivered for the second and third reasons outlined above. Private placement disclosure documents are called offering memoranda or offering circulars. In international equity offerings, the document provided to private placement investors outside the primary jurisdiction will be substantially the same as the home market prospectus.

So, we can see that the prospectus has a lot of roles to fill. It has to mitigate management liability, therefore it is going to be long and heavy on the facts, but it is also a selling document. In fact, in the USA, the prospectus is the only document that an investment bank is permitted to deliver to potential investors. In most other major markets, with the exceptions of Canada and Japan, research reports written by the syndicate's research teams will circulate before and during the time the prospectus is being reviewed by investors.

An interesting, alternative use for the prospectus is in determining whether the market is 'too' hot. One fund manager stacks all the IPO prospectuses he receives on the corner of his desk. When the pile of prospectuses is so tall that it tips over, the manager views it as a signal of the end of a bull market and stops buying new issues.

### *The preliminary or pathfinder prospectus*

The preliminary prospectus is issued somewhere between two and six weeks prior to the final prospectus. It is also known as the 'red herring' in the USA and Canada, because of the warning printed in red ink on the front cover. The preliminary prospectus is called a Pathfinder in the UK.

The 'prelim' will contain nearly all the information that the final prospectus will contain, with the exception of the price and possibly the number of shares being offered. In US offerings, the prelim is frequently not printed until the SEC has conducted its initial review of the contents and received corrections from the company and its lawyers. In other countries, the preliminary prospectus is often printed when it is delivered to the securities regulator. In these cases, there may be more significant differences between the preliminary and final prospectuses.

### *The 'final' prospectus*

In jurisdictions or offerings that follow the fixed price underwritten offering, only one prospectus is printed and distributed to potential shareholders. The prospectus will have the same corporate and financial information as a preliminary prospectus, but will also include the price and, in Europe, the dates and times by which investors have to place orders.

In the USA, Canada and in bookbuilding offerings elsewhere, the final prospectus is printed when the securities regulators have approved the contents and the price of the shares has been set. Immediately on approval by the regulators, and pricing, allocations of shares to investors will be made, and a copy of the prospectus will be sent to each successful applicant.

### *Prospectus contents*

Each country, securities commission and stock exchange has its own specific requirements regarding the contents of a prospectus. However, all share common characteristics.

In 1998, IOSCO, the International Organization of Securities Commissions, issued 'International Disclosure Standards' in order to facilitate cross-border equity offerings and listings by multinational issuers.[1] The standards are meant to enhance comparability of information and ensure a high level of investor protection. The standards 'provide alternative standards for the preparation of a single disclosure document by foreign issuers, but do not necessarily replace a jurisdiction's existing disclosure requirements for foreign or domestic issuers or preclude foreign issuers from complying with those existing requirements if permitted by the host jurisdiction'.

The IOSCO standards have 10 categories, as set out below. The standards do not state that a prospectus has to be organized this way, just that all topics should be included. The contents and layout of British and American prospectuses will be discussed in detail in the next two chapters.

At the time of writing this book, the European Union has presented a draft directive on prospectuses, which recommends that issuers follow the IOSCO standards.

In general, if the offer is to include multiple tranches, the home market prospectus and its style will dominate. The document used in international tranches will make slight adaptations to meet international requirements, as necessary. However, if there is to be an American public offering, the prospectus will be drafted with the SEC in mind, and the US prospectus will become the de facto 'home market' prospectus, whether or not the issuer is American.

#### Summary of the offering

Many investors admit that if they even open the cover of a prospectus, the summary is the only section that they read. Therefore, much care must be taken to ensure the investment case for the company is compellingly established in no more than three or four paragraphs. Most prospectus summaries include an overview of the issuer's business, details of the shares being offered, use of proceeds, listing information and summary financial data.

The summary financial information will contain key income statement, balance sheet and operating statistics for the last three to five years plus stub periods. Stub periods are partial years (e.g. three months or six months) used to provide the most up-to-date information. Auditing a stub period can add to the time and expense of an offering.

[1] An offering is considered to be cross-border when it is directed to one or more countries other than the issuer's home country (whether or not the offering or listing is also being made concurrently in the company's home country).

I. IDENTITY OF DIRECTORS, SENIOR MANAGEMENT, AND ADVISORS
   a. Directors and senior management
   b. Advisors
   c. Auditors

II. OFFER STATISTICS AND EXPECTED TIMETABLE

III. KEY INFORMATION
   a. Selected financial data
   b. Capitalization and indebtedness
   c. Reasons for the offer and use of proceeds
   d. Risk factors

IV. INFORMATION ON COMPANY
   a. History and development of the company
   b. Business overview
   c. Organizational structure
   d. Property, plant, and equipment

V. OPERATING AND FINANCIAL REVIEW AND PROSPECTS
   a. Operating results
   b. Liquidity and capital resources
   c. Research and development, patents, licenses, etc.
   d. Trend information

VI. DIRECTORS, SENIOR MANAGEMENT, AND EMPLOYEES
   a. Directors and senior management
   b. Compensation
   c. Board practices
   d. Employees
   e. Share ownership

VII. MAJOR SHAREHOLDERS AND RELATED PARTY TRANSACTIONS
   a. Major shareholders
   b. Related party transactions
   c. Interest of experts and counsel

VIII. FINANCIAL INFORMATION
   a. Consolidated statements and other financial information
   b. Significant changes

IX. THE OFFER AND LISTING
   a. Offer and listing details
   b. Plan of distribution
   c. Markets
   d. Selling shareholders
   e. Dilution
   f. Expenses of the issue

X. ADDITIONAL INFORMATION
   a. Share capital
   b. Memorandum and articles of association
   c. Material contracts
   d. Exchange controls
   e. Taxation
   f. Dividends and paying agents
   g. Statement by experts
   h. Documents on display
   i. Subsidiary information

**Figure 6.1** Contents of IOSCO standards

## Description of the business and its industry

Sometimes these are divided into two sections: the business and the industry. Nonetheless, the content provides a description of the business of the company, usually including some key statistics, such as revenues, number of employees or number of customers, countries operated in and the like. The company may choose to identify and highlight its strengths in this section, and it will usually provide a précis of its strategy.

### *Management and current shareholders*

A table of senior operational management and the board of directors is usually contained in a separate section of the prospectus. A brief one-paragraph profile provides information on the managers' positions within the company and what they have done in the recent three to five years.

Current shareholdings together with a chart of shareholdings, both before and after the offering, may be in this section or in an independent section. Investors are always interested in whether insiders are trying to 'cash out'. As noted earlier in the book, investors prefer to see existing management and shareholders not sell in the IPO. They prefer that all the funds from the offering go to the company. They logically think, if this is such a great company, why are existing shareholders or managers selling now?

Table 6.1 is the table of principal shareholders from the June 2000 prospectus for the IPO of Russian mobile telephone company Mobile TeleSystems OJSC. You will note that the existing shareholders of MTS sold no shares in the $322 million offering.

| Name | Beneficial ownership before the offering | | Beneficial ownership after the offering (assuming no exercise of the overallotment option) | |
|---|---|---|---|---|
| | Number | Percentage | Number | Percentage |
| Sistema | 692 523 468 | 42.37 | 692 523 468 | 35.55 |
| DeTeMobil Deutsche Telekom | 721 536 738 | 44.14 | 721 536 738 | 37.03 |
| Invest-Svyaz-Holding | 160 247 802 | 9.80 | 160 247 802 | 8.23 |
| VAST LLP | 60 219 432 | 3.69 | 60 219 432 | 3.09 |
| Directors and officers | * | * | * | * |
| Total | 1 634 527 440 | 100.00 | 1 634 527 440 | 83.90 |

**Table 6.1** Illustrative principal shareholders

## Operating and financial review (management discussion and analysis)

If an investor gets past the prospectus summary, this is the section that he will concentrate on. The 'Operating and Financial Review' (called management discussion and analysis (MD&A) in the USA) is usually preceded by one or two pages of summary financial and operating information. MD&A describes what has been happening to the company's revenues, expenses (usually broken down by marketing and sales, general and administrative, research and development) and capital expenditures, and compares the current (or most recent year) with the two prior years. The section also includes information on liquidity and capital resources. That is, how much cash has the company used in the past year and how much cash does it have on hand to finance future operations?

The IOSCO standards also call for a statement of capitalization and indebtedness (in banker speak, the Cap Table) as of a date no earlier than 60 days prior to the document's date. This is basically the bottom two sections of the right-hand side of an American-style balance sheet, which includes long-term debt (both fixed and floating rate) and shareholders' equity (including preference shares, ordinary or common share capital, retained earnings, etc.).

The Cap Table includes the actual capitalization of the company and as adjusted for the proceeds of the offering. The information in the table allows the reader to more easily calculate the issuer's leverage following the offering. Table 6.2 is a capitalization section extracted from the IPO preliminary prospectus for 7·24 Solutions Inc., an Internet infrastructure company that made a simultaneous public offering in Canada and the USA in early-2000. The middle column of the table describes a pro forma capitalization which gives effect to the issuance of 10 082 066 common shares for aggregate proceeds of $41.1 million in October 1999, just after the balance sheet date of 30 September. The column on the right adjusts the 30 September figures for the issue of $41.1 million in shares in October, as well as the net proceeds of this offering of 6.0 million common shares at the estimated initial public offering price of $21.00.

When the final prospectus was printed, the right-hand column was adjusted for the actual number of shares issued and the offering price. 'Cash and cash equivalents' is included in the capitalization table when it comprises a significant portion of the company's total assets, as in Table 6.2.

| | As of 30 September 1999 (in thousands of US dollars) | | |
|---|---|---|---|
| | **Actual** | **Pro forma** | **Pro forma adjusted** |
| Cash and cash equivalents | 28 044 | 69 134 | 184 064 |
| Shareholders' equity | | | |
| Common shares | 37 907 | 78 997 | 193 927 |
| Deferred stock-based compensation | (15) | (150) | (150) |
| Accumulated deficit | (10 404) | (10 404) | (10 404) |
| Total capitalization | 27 353 | 68 443 | 183 373 |

**Table 6.2** Sample capitalization table

### Financial statements

In most jurisdictions, regulators require three years of audited historical financial statements with full income statement and balance sheet details. Exemptions can be given for start-up companies going public at an early stage in their lives.

The financial statements must be audited by an independent auditor and include:

- balance sheet
- income statement
- statement of changes in shareholders' equity
- cash flow statement
- notes to the accounts.

If the most recent year end is more than nine months past, interim financial statements for the first six months of the current year should be included, together with a comparison to the same period in the prior year (stub periods). Only the current year's stub period needs to be audited.

The accounts must be prepared according to local GAAP, although some exchanges and regulators in Europe will accept International Accounting Standards (IAS) or US GAAP instead of home market GAAP.

### Risk factors

The risk factors section usually immediately follows the prospectus summary in US prospectuses. The section, which is sometimes called 'Investment Considerations' in non-US prospectuses, may appear elsewhere in non-US prospectuses.

In the late 1990s, the section expanded to include just about any risk the company, its bankers and lawyers could dream up, short of 'management may slip on a banana skin on the way to work'. During the financing of the high tech boom at the end of the 1990s, the 'risk factors' sections expanded and expanded to ridiculous lengths. The registration statement for Docent Inc. (an e-learning company) contained 15 pages of risk factors – and this was not a record. The prior year, Fairchild Semiconductor International Inc., a well-established company in a volatile industry, launched its IPO with a mere seven pages of risk factors.

By disclosing risk factors, the issuer is partially protected from investor lawsuits, if it falls prey to any one of the risks disclosed. Even if something that is not disclosed occurs, the issuer and its advisors may rely on the fact that there was extensive disclosure of potential risks to warn investors of the risks of purchasing shares. Companies launching public offerings in the USA tend to have a much longer list of risk factors than prospectuses for European IPOs. The following two boxes illustrate the differences in approach.

### US prospectus risk factors

The following risk factors are extracted from Docent's IPO prospectus. This list of factors does not include the commentary on each risk (they filled 15 pages of text in the prospectus!).

*Risks related to our business*

- Our limited operating history subjects us to risks encountered by early stage companies and some of these risks are increased because we operate in a new and rapidly evolving market.
- We have a history of losses, expect future losses and may never achieve profitability.
- Fluctuations in our quarterly revenue and other operating results may cause our stock price to decline.
- Our direct sales cycle is lengthy and requires considerable investment with no assurance of when we will generate revenue from our efforts, if at all.
- We have generated only limited revenue from content providers; however, we must generate significant revenue from them in the future to be successful and achieve profitability.
- We have generated only limited revenue from resellers; however, we must generate significant revenue from them in the future to be successful and achieve profitability.
- We anticipate that a substantial portion of our future revenue will depend primarily on a small number of large sales. If we fail to complete one or more of these sales, our revenue will decrease.
- If we are unable to develop and maintain relationships with third party hosting services providers, our operating results would be harmed.
- Our revenue may be adversely affected if we fail to change our revenue model from one based on one-time sales to one based on multi-year, royalty-bearing licence and service agreements.
- Our lack of product diversification means that any decline in price or demand for our products and services would seriously harm our business.
- Our eHub strategy is unproven and may not be successful, in which case our business would be seriously harmed.
- If we lose key personnel, or are unable to attract and retain additional management personnel, we may not be able to successfully grow and manage our business.
- We intend to significantly increase the number of our personnel within the next 12 months and failure to find sufficient qualified candidates would significantly impair our ability to continue our rapid growth.
- Difficulties we may encounter in managing our growth could adversely affect our results of operations.
- Intense competition in our market segment could impair our ability to grow and to achieve profitability.
- We have generated only limited revenue from our international operations, and our inability to expand internationally would limit our growth prospects.
- Our market is subject to rapid technological change and if we fail to continually enhance our products and services, our revenue and business could be harmed.
- We must develop relationships with leading content providers that meet the needs of our customers or our business will suffer.

- We do not have exclusive arrangements with our content providers and some of these providers may offer their content to our competitors in addition to, or instead of, offering their content to us.
- Our business strategy and future success is dependent on our ability to develop relationships and enter into agreements with professional communities to promote, use and participate in our eHub solutions.
- If Hewlett-Packard, Andersen Consulting, or SmartForce change the focus of its business or fail to comply with the terms of its agreements with us, our revenues will be harmed.
- Our expansion into new target industries depends on our ability to recruit new eHub members in those industries.
- Our products sometimes contain errors and by releasing products containing defects, our business and reputation may be harmed.
- If third parties claim that we infringe on their patents or other intellectual property rights, it may result in costly litigation or require us to make royalty payments.
- We may not be able to adequately protect our intellectual property, and our competitors may be able to offer similar products and services which would harm our competitive position.
- We do not have a disaster recovery plan or back-up system, and a disaster or break-down could severely damage our operations.
- We rely on third party software incorporated in our product, and errors in this software or our inability to continue to license this software in the future would decrease our revenue and increase our costs.
- Our revenue would decrease and our costs would increase if we fail to adequately integrate acquired businesses.
- Our stock price may fluctuate substantially, and our stock price may decrease.
- An increase in our stock-based compensation expenses will result in an additional charge against our operating results.

*Risks related to our industry*

- Our revenue may decrease if use of the Web in the markets we target does not grow as projected.
- A breach of Internet commerce security measures could reduce demand for our products and services which would in turn result in a reduction in our revenue.
- We may become subject to government regulation and legal uncertainties that could reduce demand for our products and services or increase the cost of doing business.
- A failure to expand and improve the infrastructure of the Web could constrain the functionality of our products and services.
- In an economic downturn, our customers may cut down on spendings [sic] in new products and services, which would adversely affect our revenue.

*Risks related to this offering*

- Investors will be relying on our management's judgment regarding the use of proceeds from this offering, and the manner in which our management chooses to use the proceeds may not result in a net tangible benefit to us, resulting in a decrease in our stock price.
- Our executive officers, directors and large stockholders can exert control over use [sic] to the detriment of minority stockholders.
- Sales of shares eligible for future sale after this offering could cause our stock price to decline.
- The anti-takeover provisions in our charter documents could adversely affect the rights of the holders of our common stock.
- The liquidity of our common stock is uncertain since it has not been publicly traded.
- If we need additional financing, we may not obtain the required financing on favorable terms and conditions.
- Market prices of Internet and technology companies have been highly volatile and the market for our stock may be volatile as well.
- New investors will suffer immediate and substantial dilution in the tangible net book value of their stock.

***European prospectus risk factors***

In May 1999, AGFA-Gevaert NV, a worldwide developer, manufacturer and distributor of a wide range of photographic and electronic imaging systems, particularly for the graphics sector, the medical diagnostic sector and the consumer photography sector, was 'carved out' from German giant Bayer AG. AGFA is slightly different to Docent in that it was established in 1964 and had an impressive track record of growing revenues and profitability. The offering size of €1 540 million (approximately $1.4 billion) was significantly larger than the technology offerings. The final difference between the two sets of IPOs was that AGFA did not register its shares with the SEC, but instead distributed them under the Rule 144a private placement regulations (see Chapter 8 for description).

Lead managers of the offering were Deutsche Bank and Goldman Sachs. Law firms involved for the underwriters were Loeff Claeys Verbeke (Belgium), Bruckhaus Westrick Heller Löber (Germany) and Cravath Swaine Moore (USA). For the company, Belgian law firm De Bandt van Hecke and Lagae (part of Linklaters & Alliance) stepped up. Finally, the selling shareholder relied on Hengeler Mueller Weitzel Wirtz (Germany) and Stibbe Simont Monahan Duhot (Belgium).

The risk factors in the AGFA prospectus occupied five and a half pages and were presented in a different form than in the Docent prospectus. General headings were provided, followed by several paragraphs of descriptive and explanatory language. Topic headings were:

- Cost of Raw Materials; Impact of Changing Silver Prices; Dependence on Suppliers
- Risk Relating to Relationship with the Bayer Group
- Risks Relating to Software/Accounting Systems
- Risks Relating to Significant Shareholdings in the Company
- Risks Relating to Acquisition Strategy
- Risks Associated with Restructuring Measures
- Exchange Rate Fluctuations; Hedging Policy
- Environmental Matters
- Litigation
- Dependence of Proprietary Technology; Risks of Infringement
- Market and Competition
- Risks Related to the Year 2000
- Introduction of the Euro
- Absence of Prior Trading Market; Potential Volatility of Stock Price
- Shares Eligible for Future Sale

Company executives typically roll their eyes at the seemingly endless disclosure required by the lawyers in this section. However, for those with the time and inclination, the 'risk factors' section can provide minutes, if not hours, of amusement. For example, the rough-and-tumble world of Russian capitalism is highlighted by the risk factors section in the Wimm Bill Dann prospectus:

> ***Allegations about certain of our shareholders or directors could adversely affect our reputation***
> Certain of our shareholders and directors, including the Chairman of our Board of Directors, are shareholders in, and directors of, a group of related companies sometimes referred to as 'Trinity'. . . . The Trinity group has been the subject of speculation in the Russian press, including with respect to possible links with organized crime. However, no charges have been brought by governmental authorities against any of our shareholders or directors and, to the best of our knowledge, none has been threatened. In addition, our largest shareholder, who is not a member of our Board of Directors, was convicted of a violent crime in 1980 under the Soviet system and served nine years in a labour camp. Press speculation about these or other matters relating to our shareholders or directors could adversely affect our reputation and the price of our ADSs.

Mind you, the risk didn't seem to harm the performance of the company's shares. From its IPO in early February 2002 to the end of March 2002, the stock price increased by 22 per cent, making it one of the top five performing IPOs in the first quarter of 2002.

The following includes some of the more ludicrous risk factors found by a couple of authors at eCompany.com.

The following risk factors were found in US prospectuses in early 2000 and reported by eCompany.com in its June issue:

1) **2Bridge**, provider of business-to-business portals and software. First filed March 14, scheduled to go public in late May. 'We have not been able to fund our operations from cash generated by our business, and we may not be able to do so in the future.'
2) **Wahoo Capital Ventures**, a company with no defined business, whose principal asset will be its stock exchange listing. First filed March 13, IPO likely in July. 'We have not identified any possible business and cannot identify any specific business risks. You could lose your entire investment.'
   'Wahoo has not identified and has no commitments to enter into or acquire a specific business opportunity and therefore can disclose the risks and hazards of a business or opportunity that it may enter into in only a general manner, and cannot disclose the risks and hazards of any specific business or opportunity that it may enter into. You can expect a potential business opportunity to be quite risky. Wahoo's acquisition of or participation in a business opportunity will likely be highly liquid and could result in a total loss to Wahoo and its stockholders if the business or opportunity proves to be unsuccessful.'
3) **LinuxOne**, developer and provider of open-source software and services. First filed September 22 [1999], should go out in late May. 'Our management team may not be able to successfully implement our business strategies because it has only recently begun to work together.'
   'We arbitrarily established our offering price for shares. . . . The offering price bears no relationship whatsoever to our assets, earnings, book value or other criteria of value. We have no operating revenues or profits and may be unable to continue as a going concern.'
4) **Buy.com**, online retailer of books, videos, and computer hardware. Went public February 8. 'Because we sell a substantial portion of our products at very competitive prices, we have extremely low and sometimes negative gross margins on our product sales.'
5) **Shopping.com**, originally an online retailer and currently a shopping comparison site. First filed Aug. 1, 1998; acquired in March 1999 by Compaq, but now part of Alta Vista. 'In order to continue to implement its business plan, the Company must raise additional funds. There can be no assurance that such financing will be available, if at all, in amounts or on terms acceptable to the Company. In addition, the investigation by the SEC, the pendency of several class action suits against the Company, and the attendant adverse publicity may also make it difficult for the Company to raise additional capital to continue its development. See "Legal Proceedings".'

By: Tom Taulli, Beth Kwon
Issue: June 2000 – eCompany.com

## Profit forecasts

In many countries profit forecasts are always included in a prospectus, while in others forecasts are forbidden. Where forecasts are permitted to be included, they generally must follow certain guidelines:

- The issuer must explain how the projections were calculated and the assumptions made.
- The auditors or sponsors (i.e. lead manager(s)) of the issue must sign off on how the forecast was determined and calculated. *Note:* The accountants or sponsors do not guarantee the forecast, but only state the methodology used to calculate the projections was reasonable.
- Length of time looking to the future. In most countries, a forecast is permissible to the end of the current financial year.

The draft EU Prospectus Directive requires issuers to provide trend information for the current financial year. Other information on projections and forward-looking information is neither required nor forbidden under the Directive.

### Forecast in prospectus for TIMEdotCom

The Malaysian company TIMEdotCom went public in early 2001 after nearly five years of operations. The company has interests in domestic and international fixed line telecommunications services, cellular telephone networks, payphone services, data communications and Internet services. Historic information for the years 1995–1999 and the nine months to 30 September 2000 was provided to investors in the prospectus.

The company presented a forecast consolidated profit and loss statement and consolidated cash flow statements for the period 2000–2014. The first two years, 2000 and 2001, were called cash flow forecasts, while the remaining period, 2002–2014, was projected.

Following the summary projections were 20 footnotes on the principal assumptions made: 14 regarding the profit forecast and a further six for the cash flow statements.

The company's auditors, Deloitte KassimChan, provided letters for inclusion in the prospectus discussing their review of the accounting policies and calculations for the estimates for profit and cash flow and projections of profits and cash flow.

The accuracy of forecasts in countries where they are permitted has been very mixed. A number of studies summarized in Jelic et al. (1998) found that the forecast error was significant (ranging from –92 per cent to +112 per cent). Their study of Malaysian IPOs found that 57 per cent of issuers exceeded the forecast and 43 per cent fell short.

## Due diligence and verification

Under securities legislation in most countries, the issuer and its directors assume absolute responsibility that the information contained in the prospectus is accurate. In addition, the managers of the offering have a separate responsibility to make a reasonable investigation to ensure the accuracy of the offering documents used in an offering. Thus it is customary for the bankers and their counsel to conduct a 'due diligence' investigation of the company's business which might bear on the accuracy or fairness of any statement in the prospectus or might otherwise be of material interest to a potential purchaser.

Due diligence is the process by which information is gathered about an issuer in order to produce a marketing and a disclosure document that provides full disclosure, thus mitigating liability for those potentially at risk. The risks mitigated by due diligence from the marketing perspective include:

- Inadequate/inaccurate disclosure;
- Pricing not reflecting risk;
- Ill-informed decision making by investors;
- Undermining the reputation of the issuer and investment banks involved.

From the legal perspective, due diligence moderates the civil and/or criminal liability of issuers/directors/investment banks/experts/lawyers for failing to make adequate disclosure. The potential liability of parties involved (e.g. bankers, accountants, lawyers, experts) varies by jurisdiction.

The standards of due diligence, while not varying, will be specific to each transaction and dependent on the type of issue, the issuer, investors (institutions vs. retail), external market information currently available and specific jurisdictional requirements and practices. There is no prescribed routine or checklist for such an investigation; rather, its elements are usually discussed and agreed upon in advance by the bankers and the company based on the nature of the particular offering.

### *Forms of due diligence*

Due diligence can be divided into three main areas:

- Commercial
  - Business risks, environmental, market, etc.
- Financial
  - Ensuring audited financials are correct
  - Assumptions for forecasts (if any)
  - Other financial information included in the prospectus
- Legal (documentary)
  - Review of corporate documents (including asset register, loan agreements, etc.)
  - Ensuring board decisions correctly made.

Other areas of due diligence such as environmental, marketing and HR are included in our discussion of commercial due diligence. Commercial due diligence is the purview of the investment bankers, although much or most of the groundwork may be done by the company's accountants. Review of financial statements and forecast assumptions are the responsibility of the accountants and, as you would anticipate, the lawyers conduct the legal or documentary due diligence.

Several issues are common to all three forms of due diligence:

- preliminary review
- access
- time available
- scope of investigation.

A quick preliminary review by the bankers and accountants can save plenty of time later on. An early stage review is key to understanding the organization and its management, understanding the corporate structure (assets and liabilities), assessing its accounting systems and management information, and highlighting any risks and potential black holes.

The ability to gain access to people, places and documents is key to a thorough due diligence. This can be more of an issue when a selling shareholder is driving the transaction without the full support of the company's management, or if the timing and announcement of the transaction are confidential (e.g. a secondary offering).

Those conducting the due diligence will want to make sure that they understand which locations can be visited, who can be spoken to, what internal documentation can be examined, and whether there will be a data room for the advisors.

The investment bank and company should ensure that there is a designated person at the company who is responsible for provision of information to the advisors. This person should be senior enough within the company that s/he is able to ensure delivery of information. However, it is recommended that it not be the CFO/Finance Director or Chief Executive – they have too much else on their plates.

### Commercial due diligence

Commercial and strategic due diligence will help the managers of the offering more fully understand the business of the company and therefore their ability to develop a selling story. For 'younger' companies going public, the due diligence process may be the first time since the firm's inception that the senior management has considered its strategy. A reflection on the company's strategy and position in its markets can be beneficial to the future success of the operation.

The bankers will look at the market and competitive environment, including:

- Key market dynamics – size, trends, value drivers
- Forces driving competition in the firm's markets
- External influences on past and future results
- Sources of competitive advantage/disadvantage
- Quality of implementation
- Sources of risk (industry and company specific)
- Key success factors.

While examining the company's industry and strategy are important, so is an examination of its operations. The bankers will interview key operating personnel as well as visit the issuer's main operating sites.

### Financial due diligence

Financial due diligence looks at both historic and future-oriented numbers. The scope of the review will depend on whether the accountants have been auditing the issuer for a number of years, or whether the company has recently hired a new firm from the 'Big Four' in anticipation of going public. Other issues relating to the scope and time required to conduct financial due diligence are whether the issuer has been a stand-alone company for at least three years or whether it is being spun out of a corporation or is a privatization. In all cases, the accountants will conduct a historical review of the firm's balance sheet and income statement. Accounting policies that are appropriate for privately held companies may not be so for public entities. In many cases, a company is required to adjust its accounting policies and produce audited financial statements using those policies that are acceptable and familiar to the investing public.

The accountants will provide a 'comfort letter', addressed to the issuer and managers. The contents of the comfort letter are now fairly standard and include:

- the accountants' consent to the inclusion of their audit in the prospectus/offering document;
- confirmation of their independence;
- confirmation that any unaudited figures conform to the accounting principles that apply to the audited statements;
- agreed financial data in the offer document with the financial statements or the issuers' internal accounting records.

Once a preliminary prospectus has been printed, a junior banker at the lead manager will go through the document and mark the items the managers want comfort on.

### Legal due diligence

The painstaking review of all the company's legal documentation is left to the hourly paid junior lawyers on behalf of the underwriter and the company itself. In most situations, the two sets of lawyers will agree to split the tasks in half, in order to speed the process. There is nothing more irritating than waiting for the pricing of a new issue that is delayed because someone forgot to ensure that there was a Board of Directors' authorization for a new issue of shares.

The company should set up a data room to help the lawyers with the review of materials required. Some of the most important documents that should be included are:

- accountants' letters
- articles of incorporation and bylaws
- board and shareholder meeting minutes
- debt instruments, indentures and loan documents
- documentation regarding repurchases of shares
- employee benefit plans

- employment and consulting agreements
- insurance policies
- joint venture and partnership agreements
- key licenses and permits
- labour agreements
- leases
- licenses relating to intellectual property
- material contracts
- patents, copyrights, trademarks and other documentation evidencing intangible property
- pending or threatened litigation
- recent press releases
- records of prior issues of securities
- title insurance
- title to real property.

### *Verification*

In many countries, a process known as verification takes place. It is similar to due diligence in that a thorough investigation of the company's operations and financial statements takes place. However, it differs in the level of detail applied to statements in the prospectus. Due diligence is, by and large, an investigation of the company's operations. Verification is a specific, line-by-line examination of the prospectus and the statements contained therein. Each statement in the prospectus is documented as a fact and the source of the information is collected and placed on file. A director or senior member of management at the issuer takes responsibility for every statement.

The completion of a thorough due diligence examination brings two benefits to the lead investment bank: first, it gives the bankers a deeper appreciation and understanding of the business of the company, allowing them to tailor the marketing story for investors; second, by conducting due diligence the managers of the offering are protected from lawsuits by disgruntled shareholders if the price drops dramatically in the market after the launch of the offering.

## Appendix: Sample due diligence outline

The following is a brief outline of the sort of thing that a preliminary due diligence list might start with. As the investigation continues, more and more detailed questions are added.

### *Commercial issues*

1 *Industry analysis*, economic and political factors:
- (a) Growth of industry over past 10 years. Relative stability of growth and profitability of other companies.
- (b) Significant trends within the industry.
- (c) General level of economic activity.

2 *Management and performance*:
- (a) Track record of management; pattern of earnings.
- (b) Accuracy of past operating forecasts.
- (c) Quality of management information systems; information provided in management reports; adequacy of planning or budgeting process.
- (d) Organization of management: by function, by product line. Organization chart, recent changes.
- (e) Key individuals: company dependence on one or two individuals.
- (f) Senior management: time with the company, past work experience and education, age, family members with company, incentive compensation plans, employment agreements.
- (g) Shares held by management.
- (h) Existence of major outside shareholders which could influence management.
- (i) Composition of board of directors; number of independent directors.

3 *Risks to the company*:
- (a) Purchase of raw materials and machinery, export sales, foreign subsidiaries, debt.
- (b) Supply problems: numbers of alternative suppliers, contractual obligations, price fluctuations, financial strength of suppliers.
- (c) Effect on company of change in tax rates, removal of government assistance: tariffs, subsidies, low-cost loans, investment capital.
- (d) Most recent tax audit.
- (e) Threatened litigation or proceedings against company.

4 *Technological factors*:
- (a) Effect of technological developments on company.
- (b) Inventory obsolescence. Inventory valuation.
- (c) Plant and equipment obsolescence: age, extent of use, maintenance policy, down time experience, insurance coverage, quality of plant and equipment used by competitors.
- (d) Extent of integration in manufacturing process. Flexibility of production process.
- (e) Importance of licence agreements, franchises or patents to company's business.

(f) Importance, and method, of accounting for research and development. Amount and type of research and development expenditure relative to other companies in industry and amount recoverable through product or manufacturing improvements.

5 *Market and competitive factors*:
(a) Seasonal factors and cyclical pattern of industry. Effect on sales, receivables, inventories and financing requirements.
(b) Ability of company to pass on cost increases.
(c) Dependence on small group of substantial customers.
(d) Experience in collectability of accounts receivable. Aging of receivables, bad debt experience and size of reserve for doubtful accounts.
(e) Emphasis placed on product quality control. Product returns.
(f) Markets served:
- Current and projected market share.
- Diversity of markets and geographic breakdown of sales; amount of export sales.
- Extent of market facilities and numbers/quality of sales staff.
- Amount and importance of advertising, relative to others in industry.

(g) Competitors: size and number. Trends in competition: price, channels of distribution, technological innovations. Competitive advantages of company.

6 *Foreign operations*:
(a) Size of overseas operations: contribution to sales and earnings; assets held overseas.
(b) Specific political/economic risks incidental to foreign operations. Restrictions on dividends and repatriation of capital.

7 *Labour relations*:
(a) Relationship with employees. Union or non-union.
(b) Current labour contracts: material provisions, expiration date, expected wage and benefit claims.
(c) Unfunded medical and pension costs.
(d) Staff training. Adequacy of skilled employees in local labour markets.
(e) Vulnerability to strikes. Interdependence of different plants.

## Financial due diligence

1 *Accounting matters*, review of policies on which company's financial statements are based:
(a) Differences between existing accounting policies and GAAP.
(b) Major differences between company's accounting policies and those adopted by others in the industry.
(c) Qualified accountants' opinion on any financial statements. Suggestions made by accountants for improving internal accounting procedures. Specific recommendations or analyses prepared for the company by accountants.
(d) Past changes in accounting policies, rationale and effect.

(e) Internal allocation of expenses and overheads.
(f) Availability of debt or equity capital:
- Present liquidity position: cash marketable securities and unused bank lines; projected financial requirements.
- Present and forecast debt to capitalization ratios in comparison with other companies in the industry.
- Reception given by investors (e.g. VCs) to most recent financing.
- Amount of assets pledged and existence of loan covenants, company bylaws or shareholder agreements restricting new financings.
- Past use of short-term debt for long-term funding purposes.
- Off-balance sheet debt: leases, debt of unconsolidated subsidiaries and contingent liabilities.
- Financial strength of principal shareholders.
- Past bankruptcy or loan renegotiations.
- Past difficulties with creditors.

(g) Scope and frequency of interim audit review:
- Review of changes in capital stock and debt since last audit date.
- Review of material dispositions or acquisitions of assets.
- Review of new mortgage or other lines on assets or other developments that might affect the company's financial position and compliance with existing loan covenants.
- Reading of minutes book of board of directors' meetings.
- Investigation of material transactions between company and its unconsolidated subsidiaries and affiliates.

2 *General financing review*, background materials include:
(a) Five years of projected capital expenditure.
(b) General outline of planned financings to fund planned expenditure.
(c) Identification of specific uses to which money raised will be put: disclosure should include the amount of money designated for each class of expenditure.

3 *Capitalization review*:
(a) Most recent balance sheet information detailing present capitalization of the company (also shown on an adjusted basis to reflect impact of new financing).
(b) Separate schedules breaking down short- and long-term debt, including bank lines and indicating currency of borrowing, amount, maturity, interest rate, security provisions, date of issue and amortization. Special disclosure should also be made of any restrictive covenants attached to these borrowings.

4 *Financial statements review.*

# 7 UK offerings

This chapter is the first of two describing the regulatory regimes and documentation requirements of the two largest international markets for IPOs. Chapter 8 will look at the USA. Within this chapter, we first look at the types of offering available to companies wishing to raise money in the UK. In the UK, IPOs are called flotations. We then discuss the main regulatory and documentary requirements.

## The British market

The British stock market is the third largest in the world by market capitalization, and has been so for a number of decades. The 'Official List' is the LSE's main market and home to corporate giants such as BPAmoco, GlaxoSmithKline and HSBC. It also hosts numerous much smaller companies such as Roxspur and World Trade Systems, with market capitalizations as of January 2003 of £640 000 and £260 000, respectively.

Issuers have a choice between the LSE's main market and the Alternative Investment Market (AIM), which was established in 1995, designed for smaller, more risky firms. The admission rules for companies joining AIM are less onerous than those for the LSE, and ongoing regulation is lighter. In addition, the OFEX (off exchange dealing facility), also established in 1995, exists to provide a trading facility for matched bargains. OFEX is run by JP Jenkins Ltd, a London stockbroker, and is generally (but not exclusively) for the smallest companies.

The London Stock Exchange has always been home to a large number of foreign companies, many from the Commonwealth countries, but also from the USA and many European markets, as illustrated in Figure 7.1. This is in part to tap into the large amount of institutional money that is managed in London and Edinburgh, but also funds managed elsewhere in Europe that are active participants in the London market.

Companies can choose to list shares or depository receipts (DRs) on the London Stock Exchange. There is a full description of depository receipts in Chapter 8.

Foreign companies that do not wish a full quotation on the LSE (or AIM) have the option of trading on the over-the-counter market for foreign shares, SEAQ-International. In many cases, companies find there is more liquidity on SEAQ-International than on their home exchange. There are no listing requirements for companies to trade on the market. As long as three market makers agree to quote prices, a company's shares can trade. In fact, a company is required to do nothing at all.

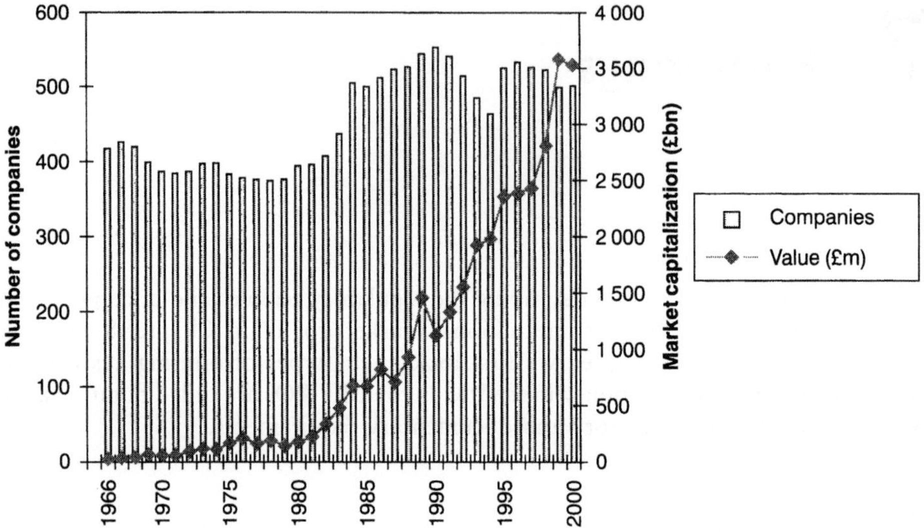


*Source*: London Stock Exchange.

**Figure 7.1** Foreign listings in London (1966–2000)

## UK offer structures

There are a number of different means by which a domestic or foreign company can join the LSE or AIM. Depending on the issuer's requirements, these vary from a placing to institutional investors, through global offerings, to public offers. Indeed on certain flotations, tranches of the offer may be dealt with by each method. Follow-on (secondary) offerings are primarily done by way of rights offerings or placings, as discussed in Chapter 12.

### *Public offers (fixed price)*

In public offers, shares are sold directly to the public through advertisements in the national media. There are two forms: an *Offer for Sale*, where the shares are sold by existing shareholders, and an *Offer for Subscription*, where the company issues new shares and keeps the proceeds. Offers for sale were most commonly seen in privatizations. Other public offers were done for companies with a large or high-profile customer base. Collectively, they are called 'Public Offers'. During the late 1990s and early 2000s, the proportion of public offers has shrunk. In 2000 and 2001, they accounted for just 22.6 per cent and 26 per cent of all IPOs (including investment trusts) on the Official List, respectively. There were no flotations by way of public offering at all on AIM in either year.

In a public offer, the offering price is set prior to any orders being taken. Soundings are taken from institutional investors regarding pricing and the share price is set after negotiation between the bankers, brokers and issuer. Once set, the issue is 'underwritten' and the formal selling period begins. The brokers to the issue contact

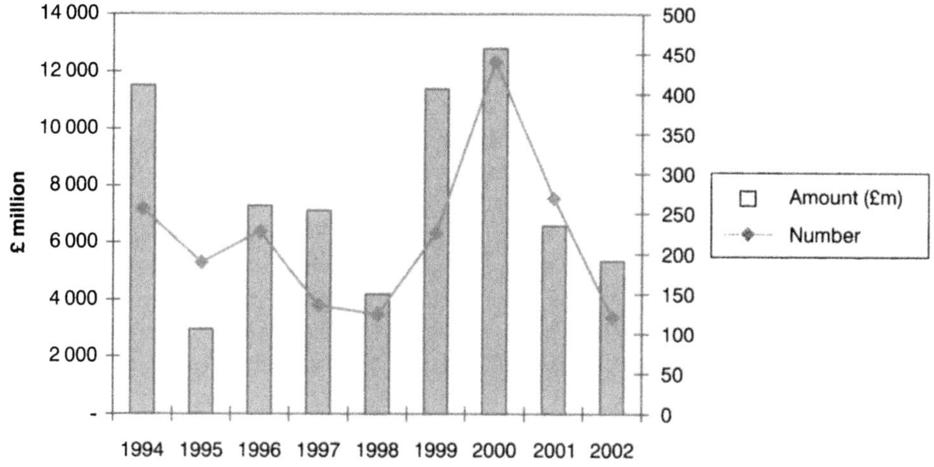


*Source*: London Stock Exchange (includes investment trusts).

**Figure 7.2** IPOs in the UK (both LSE and AIM)

institutional investors and notices are placed in the press to attract retail investors. Investors apply for shares by post, through banks, via 'share shops' or, more recently, over the Internet.

In public offers in 2001, 24 companies raised a total of £1.48 billion compared with the £558 million raised by 37 companies in 2000.

Figure 7.4 is a typical example of a box advertisement used to announce all UK offerings (whether public offer or placing). UK regulations state that the box

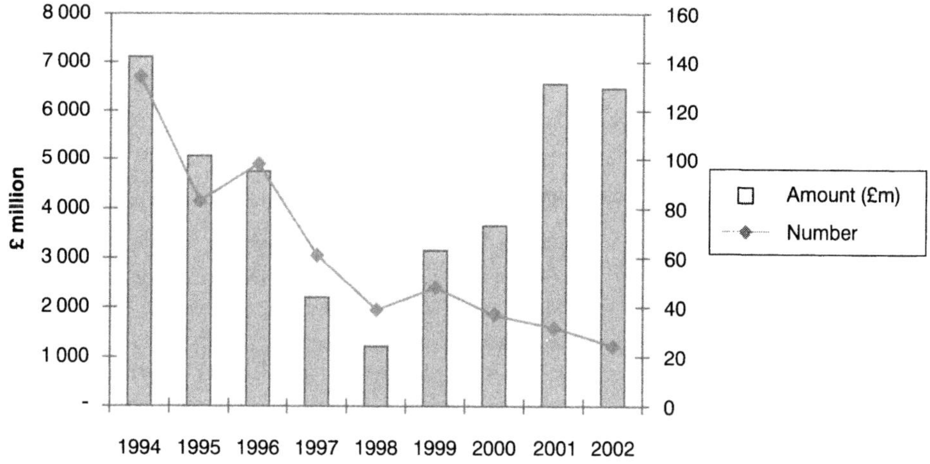


*Source*: London Stock Exchange.

**Figure 7.3** Rights issues in the UK (1994–2001)

advertisement must be placed in at least one national newspaper. Box advertisements form the minimum amount of advertising for a public offering. During the 1980s and early 1990s, issuers had to print the entire prospectus in one of the national newspapers.

Underwriting guarantees the issuing company or selling shareholders the proceeds of the offering (less expenses). If the underwriters (usually the lead bank(s)) are not able to sell the shares to investors (whether as a result of mispricing, adverse market conditions or any other reason), they must purchase the shares not sold at the issue price. The underwriting period will vary, but it starts when the price is set (known as 'Impact Day') and continues to the close of the subscription period (between one and three weeks). If the issuer is seeking to attract individual investors, it must leave the subscription period open for a sufficient length of time for the investors to respond to the offer.

To spread risk, it is common for the sponsor (who is usually the primary underwriter) to 'sub-underwrite' among a group of banks, brokers and investing institutions in order to spread the risk of failure. The sub-underwriting takes place immediately after the price has been set. Each sub-underwriter agrees to guarantee the sale of a small portion of the amount being raised, generally between 1 and 2 per cent.

To illustrate sub-underwriting, assume that an offering of 30 million shares is set at 250p per share. Of the aggregate £75 million on offer, Institution A might be asked to sub-underwrite 2 per cent of the offer, or £1.5 million. To compensate Institution A for the risk of having to purchase the shares, it receives a commission, generally 1.25 per cent of the amount it underwrites. In this instance, Institution A will receive payment of £18 750.

Let's say that Institution A likes the look of the company on offer and places an order for one million shares. If there are orders for more than 30 million shares, Institution A pays for the shares that it is allocated and receives a cheque for £18 750. However, if there was demand for less than 30 million shares, the primary and sub-underwriters will be required to purchase the shortfall. If the shortfall was five million shares, Institution A will be required to step up and purchase 100 000 shares (2 per cent of five million) in addition to the one million shares that it had ordered. Thus it will end up with 1.1 million shares. It will also receive £18 750 in sub-underwriting fees.

### Placings (generally bookbuilding)

When a *placing* is used, the company's shares are sold to specific investors, typically institutions, but on smaller issues, private individuals. Most placings are run as bookbuildings, although 10 years ago, most were fixed price offers. The marketing of the issue is handled by the sponsor or broker who decides on the target investors. The marketing is supported by the issue of a pathfinder (preliminary) prospectus and presentations to potential investors. Individual (private) investors do not apply directly for shares as in an offer, but must place an order through a stockbroker that is participating in the offering in order to receive shares.

Since 1996, placings have become the preferred method of IPO in the UK. In 2000, 44 per cent of UK IPOs were placings, while the proportion decreased to 30 per cent

This notice is issued in compliance with the requirements of the Financial Services Authority (the "FSA") and appears as a matter of record only. It does not constitute an offer or invitation to any person to subscribe for, or purchase, any securities of Detica Group plc in the United States or any other jurisdiction. The shares in Detica Group plc are not being registered under the US Securities Act of 1933, as amended (the "Securities Act") and may not be offered or sold in the United States unless registered under the Securities Act or pursuant to an exemption from such registration. No public offer of shares in Detica Group plc will be made into the United States.

Application has been made to the FSA for the whole of the ordinary share capital of Detica Group plc, issued and to be issued, to be admitted to the Official List of the UK Listing Authority ("admission") and to the London Stock Exchange plc (the "London Stock Exchange") for such shares to be admitted to trading on the London Stock Exchange's market for listed securities. It is expected that admission of the ordinary shares of 2p each of Detica Group plc (the "Shares") will become effective, and that dealings in the Shares will commence on 30 April 2002.

**Detica Group plc**

(incorporated and registered in England and Wales under the Companies Act 1985
with registered number 3328242)

Global offer of up to 9,050,389 ordinary shares of 2p each (the "Global Offer")
at a price expected to be between 440p and 510p per ordinary share

Admission to the Official List of the UK Listing Authority and
to trading on the London Stock Exchange's market for listed securities

Sponsored by UBS Warburg Ltd.

Expected share capital immediately following admission
(assuming no exercise of the over-allotment option and an offer price of 475 pence, being the mid-point of the price range)

| Authorised | | | Issued and fully paid up | |
|---|---|---|---|---|
| Number | Nominal Value | Ordinary shares of 2p | Number | Nominal Value |
| 35,000,000 | £700,000 | each | 21,429,321 | £428,586 |

Detica Group plc is an established UK information technology (IT) services company that provides consultancy and systems implementation services primarily to two markets: the Customer Relationship Management (CRM) market and the UK national security market.

Listing particulars relating to the Global Offer, which have been approved by the FSA as required by the Listing Rules made under section 74 of the Financial Services and Markets Act 2000, were published on 8 April 2002. UBS Warburg Ltd is acting for Detica Group plc in connection with the Global Offer and no-one else and will not be responsible to anyone other than Detica Group plc for providing the protections afforded to clients of UBS Warburg Ltd. or for providing advice in relation to the Global Offer. Copies of the Listing Particulars are available for inspection at the Document Viewing Facility of the Financial Services Authority, 25 North Colonnade, London E14 5HS and may be collected free of charge during normal business hours on any weekday (Saturdays, Sundays and public holidays excepted) from the date of this notice up to and including 23 April 2002 from:

| | | |
|---|---|---|
| Linklaters | Detica Group plc | UBS Warburg Ltd. |
| One Silk Street | Surrey Research Park | 1 Finsbury Avenue |
| London | Guildford | London |
| EC2Y 8HQ | Surrey GU2 7YP | EC2M 2PP |

9 April 2002

**Figure 7.4** Typical box advertisement

in 2001. In order to ensure that there is some retail distribution, placings are often combined with 'Intermediaries Offers' (10 per cent of offers in 2000 and 13 per cent in 2001).

### Intermediaries offers

In intermediaries offerings stockbrokers and banks (intermediaries) apply for shares on behalf of their individual or retail clients. This is similar to the process followed in the USA, where stockbrokers contact their clients with news of a new issue and solicit orders. An intermediaries offer allows individual investors to participate in offerings that they normally would have no access to. Intermediaries offers are always made in conjunction with another form of offer.

Both placings and intermediaries offers can be supported by advertising in the financial press, and general media, if the offer is large enough.

### Introductions

Introductions are not, strictly speaking, new issues, as no money is raised. Typically UK introductions result from companies moving their listing from AIM to the Official List, or demutualizations of building societies or insurance companies. Another source of introductions is the listing of foreign companies that do not raise funds on the LSE. There were 38 introductions in 2000, and 28 in 2001.

## UK new issue regulations

The regulatory process for IPOs in the UK has two components, similar to the USA, Canada and many other countries. There is a securities regulator (the Financial Services Authority (FSA) in the UK or SEC in the USA), which has overriding authority, and the stock exchanges (LSE, NYSE), that have their own rules and regulations regarding whether a company is suitable for listing. In almost all cases, if the company passes muster with the regulator it will pass muster with the stock exchange.

Prior to 2001, issuers dealt solely with the LSE. Now, a company's shares need to be *admitted to the Official List* by the UK Listing Authority (part of the FSA) and *admitted to trading* by the London Stock Exchange. Once both processes are complete, the shares are officially listed and can trade on the Stock Exchange.

The FSA is Britain's financial regulator of securities firms, banks, building societies, insurance companies and other financial institutions. Over time the FSA has assumed regulatory responsibilities from the Bank of England, various self-regulatory organizations and the London Stock Exchange.

The main governing laws are the Financial Services Markets Act 2000 ('FSMA'), the Public Offer of Securities Regulations 1995 ('POS Regulations') and the Companies Act 1985, which have applied various pieces of relevant European legislation including: the Admissions Directive (79/279/EEC); Listing Particulars Directive (80/390/EEC as amended); Prospectus Directive (89/298/EEC); and

Interim Reports Directive (1982/121/EEC). These directives were consolidated into Directive 2001/34/EC, which came into effect in July 2001. At the time of writing (2002), a proposed directive on 'the prospectus to be published when securities are offered to the public or admitted to trading' (the 'Prospectus Directive') is under consideration.

In the UK, if a public offer of shares is made (i.e. sold to individual investors in addition to institutional investors), the provisions of the POS Regulations apply and a prospectus must be approved and distributed. If no public offering is made, the issuers must prepare documentation in the form of Listing Particulars. In practice, the documents seen by investors are very similar.

## *Financial Services and Markets Act 2000 (FSMA)*

The Financial Services and Markets Act 2000 is currently the primary legislation that governs the new issue of shares. It supersedes the *Financial Services Act 1986*. The FSMA is a wide-ranging act: the section that most concerns us is 'Part VI – Official Listing'. In this section, the act sets out the duties and functions of the 'competent authority'; rules on listing and delisting securities; listing particulars, prospectuses and disclosure; sponsors; advertising; and other general provisions. Documentation is discussed in a separate section below.

The competent authority for the regulation of new issues of securities (IPOs and rights offerings) is now the UK Listing Authority (UKLA). It has taken on the role, and most of the staff, of the London Stock Exchange, which had previously acted as regulator of new issues. This has resulted in a minor change to the way companies seek to become publicly listed in the UK. A company that wishes to have shares 'officially listed on a stock exchange' must apply to the UKLA for its securities to be admitted to the Official List and to the LSE for its securities to be 'admitted to trading'.

### Advertisements

One of the key aspects of the FSMA relates to advertisements in connection with listing applications. In the UK, as in most European markets, issuers can make use of a wide range of advertising media. Large issues will even make television advertisements to drum up demand. In the USA, no advertising of new issues is permissible.

The listing rules specify the type of advertisements that are acceptable. If uncertain, the issuer should submit the contents of the advert (or other information) to the UKLA for its approval or authorization that the advertisement is acceptable under the listing rules. When an offering is directed at professional investors only, any advertisements must carry the following legend:

> 'This communication is directed only at persons who (i) are outside the United Kingdom or (ii) have professional experience in matters relating to investments or (iii) are persons falling within Article 49(2)(a) to (d) ("high net worth companies, unincorporated associations etc") of The Financial Services and

Markets Act 2000 (Financial Promotion) Order 2001 (all such persons together being referred to as "relevant persons"). This communication must not be acted on or relied on by persons who are not relevant persons. Any investment or investment activity to which this communication relates is available only to relevant persons and will be engaged in only with relevant persons.'

## Sponsors and brokers

All listed companies must have retained advisors. Companies with a full LSE listing must have an appointed financial advisor and stockbroker. AIM listed companies must have a 'Nominated Advisor' and a 'Nominated Broker'. If a company's sponsors or brokers resign, the company must appoint a new sponsor within a specified period, or face delisting. In 2001, Huntington Life Sciences was delisted after its brokers resigned after facing pressure, including death threats from animal rights activists, opposed to the company's business.

Each of the financial advisors and stockbrokers will receive a retainer from the listed company in addition to being the company's first port of call (generally) when considering a new issue or merger or acquisition. Table 7.1 lists the top financial advisors and stockbrokers at the end of 2001.

Since the deregulation of the UK securities industry in 1986 ('Big Bang'), the sponsor and broker to an issue (and afterwards) may be the same firm. Most merchant banks merged with stockbrokers at the time of deregulation in order to create integrated securities houses along the lines of American investment banks.

| Financial advisors | Number of clients | Stockbrokers | Number of clients |
|---|---|---|---|
| UBS Warburg | 143.5 | Cazenove | 197.0 |
| Dresdner Kleinwort Wasserstein | 82.5 | UBS Warburg | 140.0 |
| HSBC | 77.5 | HSBC | 122.5 |
| Beeson Gregory | 65.5 | Brewin Dolphin | 113.5 |
| Close Brothers | 62.0 | Hoare Govett | 96.5 |
| Investec Henderson Crosthwaite | 61.5 | Beeson Gregory | 91.0 |
| NM Rothschild | 59.0 | Old Mutual | 91.0 |
| Brewin Dolphin | 58.5 | Teather & Greenwood | 79.5 |
| Seymour Pierce | 55.0 | Peel Hunt | 79.5 |
| Old Mutual | 54.5 | Collins Stewart | 79.0 |

*Source:* The Lehman Communications Company Guide (November Quarter 2001).
*Note:* A bank or broker receives 0.5 credit when it shares with another.

**Table 7.1** Top financial advisors and stockbrokers

### *Public Offer of Securities 1995 (POS)*

The other main regulation in the UK is the Public Offer of Securities law of 1995, which sets out the guidelines as to what constitutes a public offer requiring a prospectus and full disclosure, and what constitutes a private placement with no statutory disclosure requirements. The POS law implements the European Commission's Public Offers Directive (89/298/EEC).

One of the most important parts of the POS law is what does not constitute a public offer. It contains a range of safe harbours within which offers of securities are deemed not to be offers to the public and these are expressed in largely similar terms whether the securities are listed or unlisted and include:

- Offers to professionals (i.e. to persons whose ordinary business involves acquiring, holding, managing or disposing of investments (as principal or agent) or to persons in the context of their trades, professions or occupations.
- Offers to no more than 50 persons.
- Offers to a restricted circle of persons who the offeror reasonably believes to be sufficiently knowledgeable to understand the risks involved in accepting the offer.
- Offers involving a high minimum subscription of at least €40 000 or its equivalent.
- Offers of Euro-securities, which include investments that:
  - are to be underwritten and distributed by a syndicate of which at least two of its members have their registered offices in different countries or territories;
  - are to be offered on a significant scale in one or more countries or territories other than the country or territory in which the issuer has its registered office; and
  - may be acquired pursuant to the offer only through a credit institution or other financial institution.[1]

Nearly all non-UK offerings are sold to UK professional investors using the exemptions available in the POS regulations.

### *UK Listing Authority*

On 1 May 2000, the FSA assumed responsibility for the regulation and approval of IPOs and secondary offerings of shares from the London Stock Exchange. In the jargon, the FSA became the 'Competent Authority' for securities issues. The role has not changed as a result of the transfer from the LSE to the FSA, in fact, most of the LSE's regulatory staff are now employed by the FSA.

The regulatory objectives of the FSA in its capacity as the UK Listing Authority are to formulate and enforce listing rules that:

1 Provide an appropriate level of protection for investors in listed securities.
2 Facilitate access to listed markets for a broad range of enterprises.

[1] *The Euromarket – ISSA Handbook*, The International Society of Securities Administrators (ISSA), 1996.

3 Seek to maintain the integrity and competitiveness of UK markets for listed securities.

The duties of the UKLA are set out in Part VI, Section 73(1) of the Financial Services and Markets Act 2000.

When an issuer submits a prospectus for review, it is forwarded to the appropriate industry group within the UKLA. The groups are comprised of full-time employees of the FSA and secondees from stockbrokers, investment banks and law firms. The organization endeavours to provide initial comments on a set of listing particulars within 10 working days of receipt. Subsequent comments on resubmissions of the document are dealt with in five business days.

## London Stock Exchange requirements

In most instances (except if the company is transferring from AIM or is an overseas company), the LSE will want to meet with company management and its advisors. This meeting would take place around the time that the company is approaching the UKLA regarding its application to join the Official List.

The initial meeting between the Exchange and the company allows the Exchange to get an understanding of the business, collect information for the 'New Issues List', explain to the company its continuing responsibilities once it is listed, and start to develop a relationship among the company, its advisors and the Exchange. Since the Stock Exchange has lost its regulatory role, the contact with the Exchange after the initial meeting will be limited, until just prior to the offering. At that stage, the lead manager (sponsor) will have to provide a package of documents to the Exchange, known as the '48-hour documents'.

The 48-hour documents must be submitted to the Exchange by no later than 12:00 at least two business days prior to the day on which the issuer is requesting that the Exchange consider the application for admission to trading. Hence their name. The documents include:

- An application for admission to trading in the appropriate form issued by the Exchange and signed by a duly authorized officer of the issuer.
- Two copies of any listing particulars, circular, announcement or other document relating to the issue, together with copies of any notice of meeting referred to in the documents.
- A copy of the board resolution allotting the securities or authorizing the issue. Where a copy of the board resolution is not available for lodging at this time, written confirmation from the issuer's contact or its nominated representative that the securities have been allotted must be received by the Exchange no later than 07:30 on the day that admission is expected to become effective.[2]

## UK documentation

In the UK, the main document that is submitted to the UKLA is referred to as the 'Listing Particulars'. These contain all the information in the prospectus as well as

[2] *Admission and Disclosure Standards*, London Stock Exchange, May 2001.

some additional information of a more technical nature that does not have a bearing on an investor's investment decision. The contents of the listing particulars are proscribed in the 'Purple Book'.

When the LSE was the primary regulator the listing requirements were contained within a bright yellow binder – hence it was called the 'Yellow Book'. For those who are interested, the UK Take-over Code is contained in a blue binder, and is known as the 'Blue Book'.

In the UK, the offering document must:

> 'contain all such information as investors and their professional advisers would reasonably require, and reasonably expect to find there, for the purpose of making an informed assessment of the assets and liabilities, financial position, profit and losses, and prospects of the issuer of the securities.'
>
> (*s9 POS Regulations, s80 FSMA*)

The listing rules require that the offering document contain the following information. It is in line with that required under European legislation and the IOSCO recommendations described in the previous chapter.

### Contents of UK prospectus

The following information must be included in a UK prospectus:

- **The persons responsible for listing particulars, the auditors and other advisors (banks, brokers and solicitors)**
  This section includes the following declaration:

  > 'The directors of [the issuer], whose names appear on page [ ], accept responsibility for the information contained in this document. To the best of the knowledge and belief of the directors (who have taken all reasonable care to ensure that such is the case) the information contained in this document is in accordance with the facts and does not omit anything likely to affect the import of such information.'

- **The shares for which application is being made**
  Including a description of the characteristics of the shares (e.g. voting rights), the number being offered, names of stock exchanges where listing is being sought.
- **The issuer and its capital**
  Name, registered office and head office of issuer. Description of share capital and any changes in prior three years. Controlling shareholders and any other holder of at least 3 per cent of the capital.
- **The group's activities**
  Description of the business of the company, including breakdown of divisional turnover, number of employees, R&D, main investments, etc.

- **The issuer's assets and liabilities, financial position and profits and losses**
  Three years' of financial results in a comparable table (balance sheet, income statement and cash flow statement together with the notes to the accounts); 'working capital statement' (see below).
- **The management**
  Directors of the issuer with details of previous work; aggregate remuneration paid to directors.
- **The recent development and prospects of the group**
  General information on the trend of the group's business since the end of the financial year to which the last published annual accounts relate; this may include a profit forecast or estimate and the supporting grounds for the forecast or estimate (including sponsor's statement).

### Long form report

At the start of the offering process, the company's accountants will typically begin collecting all relevant information on the issuer. This is distilled into a 'long form report', which forms the basis of the prospectus.

### Working capital statement

Companies listing in the UK must produce a working capital statement attesting to the directors' belief that the company will have sufficient working capital for 12 months following the publication of the prospectus. The working capital statement contained in mm$O_2$'s listing prospectus follows:

> 'In the opinion of the company, following the Proposals [demerger from BT plc] becoming effective and taking account of the mm$O_2$ Group's existing bank facilities, the working capital available to the mm$O_2$ Group is sufficient for the mm$O_2$ Group's present requirements, that is for the next 12 months following the date of this document.'
>
> (Note 11, p. 106, summary listing particulars)

Although the company directors are legally liable for the statement, they will rely on a 'working capital report' produced by the company's accountants.

### Forecasts

Forecasts are optional in UK prospectuses. Most companies include a forecast of earnings to the end of the fiscal year in which the prospectus is published. They will also include an anticipated dividend and calculate the anticipated dividend yield based on the new issue price and the anticipated dividend.

### Ongoing disclosure

Once listed on the LSE, companies are required by the UKLA and the LSE to provide 'timely information so that investors can make well informed investment decisions'.

As a general rule, companies have an obligation to publish price-sensitive information without delay.

The following list indicates the main occasions when public announcements are required:

- Major developments in the company's business activities, such as new products, contracts or customers
- Significant acquisitions or disposals
- A change in directors, or a change in the functions or executive responsibilities of a director
- Decisions to pay dividends
- Half-yearly results, and preliminary statements of annual and half-yearly results
- Changes in the interests of major shareholders and directors
- Further issues of securities and changes in the company's capital structure.

Investors in UK companies must disclose to the Stock Exchange when they reach a shareholding of 3 per cent.

# 8 US offers and American depository receipts

US equity markets are the largest, most liquid, and in many ways the most advanced in the world. They show a well-diversified base; some of the largest investing institutions are US-based and over 50 per cent of US residents own shares or equity-based investments.

This chapter introduces the salient details of offering shares in the largest capital market in the world. The focus is on non-US issuers selling shares into the US markets and is weighted towards the documentation and process issues. Specific issues relating to marketing, syndication, allocations or stabilization are dealt with in the chapters devoted to those topics.

A later section covers depository receipts (DRs), securities representing foreign shares but traded on a local stock exchange. The main DRs are American depository receipts (ADRs), which trade on one of the US exchanges, but global depository receipts (GDRs) also exist, issued primarily by Asian companies and traded primarily on European stock exchanges. The London and Luxembourg Stock Exchanges are the main homes for GDR listings.

The realization by US investors that there were opportunities beyond America's borders drove some of the biggest changes to international equity offerings in the 1990s. Estimates at the beginning of the decade put US institutional ownership of foreign assets at less than 2 per cent of total assets. By the end of the decade, international assets were believed to be between 12 and 14 per cent of total assets. In comparison, UK institutional investors held approximately 24 per cent of their portfolios in overseas equities at the end of 1999.

The 1990s witnessed the emergence of US investors as one of the driving forces behind international offerings. This was caused by two factors: the reallocation of

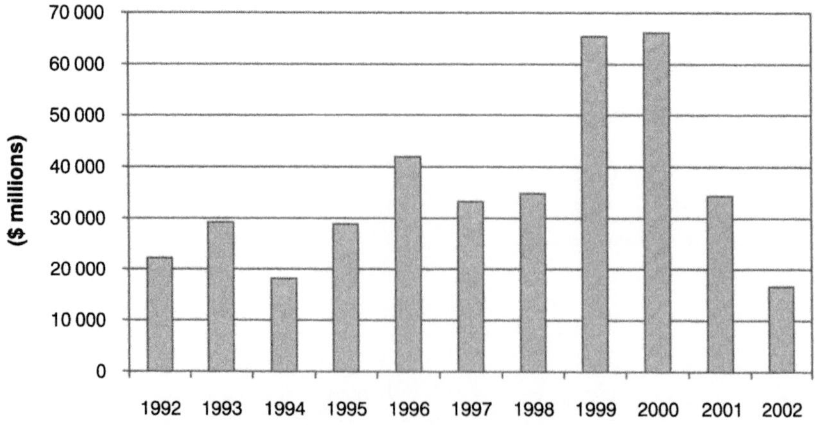


**Figure 8.1** IPOs by US companies

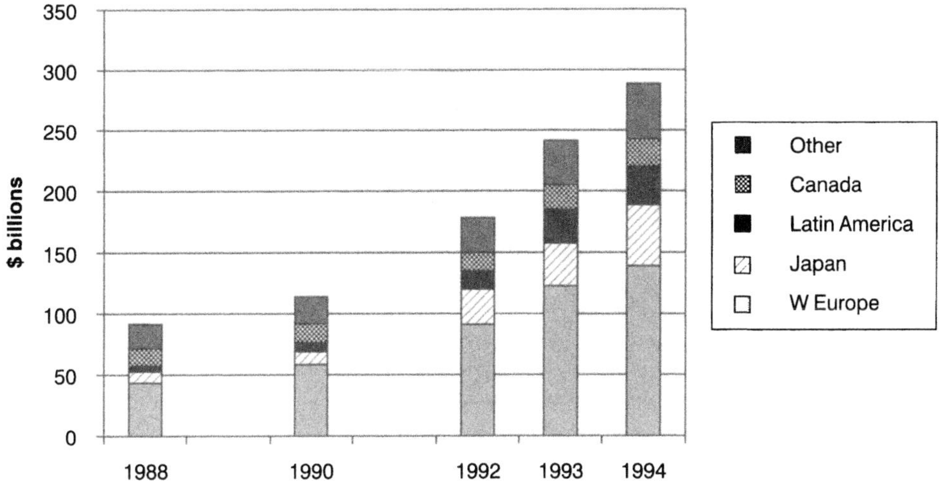


*Source*: Brancato (1996).

**Figure 8.2** US equity holdings of foreign companies (1988–1994)

assets from domestic to international investments on the part of US institutional investors; and an easing of new issues regulation by the US securities regulators.

Non-US issuers made full use of the asset allocation shift by including US investors in approximately 30 per cent of IPOs (Ljungqvist and Wilhelm, 2001). In the 10-year period ending December 2001, international issuers came to the US markets a total of 565 times, raising an aggregate $118.2 billion. In 2000, the peak year, over $28 billion was raised from US investors in both IPOs and secondary offerings.

Foreign issuers can sell shares to US investors in public offerings or private placements. Public offers are full-blown affairs, which allow both institutional and individual participation and require registration with the SEC. Private placements trade off lower regulatory requirements with a reduced investor base. Private placements are directed exclusively at institutional investors, take less time to complete and do not require registration with the SEC. Almost all non-US companies use ADRs to reach American investors. The exception is Canadian issuers that offer common shares in both their home market and the USA.

Figures 8.3 and 8.4 illustrate the growth of offerings in the USA by foreign issuers, until the end of the bubble in 2000. Both charts slightly understate the actual figures, as Canadian companies that sold shares in the USA are not included. In each chart, the left-hand scale represents the value of the offerings and the right-hand scale the number of issues. Both charts include IPOs and secondary offerings.

## Securities regulation in the USA

The SEC regulates US public offerings through the Securities Act of 1933 (the '1933 Act') while rules regarding the general operations of the markets and reporting are set out in the Securities Exchange Act of 1934 (the '1934 Act').

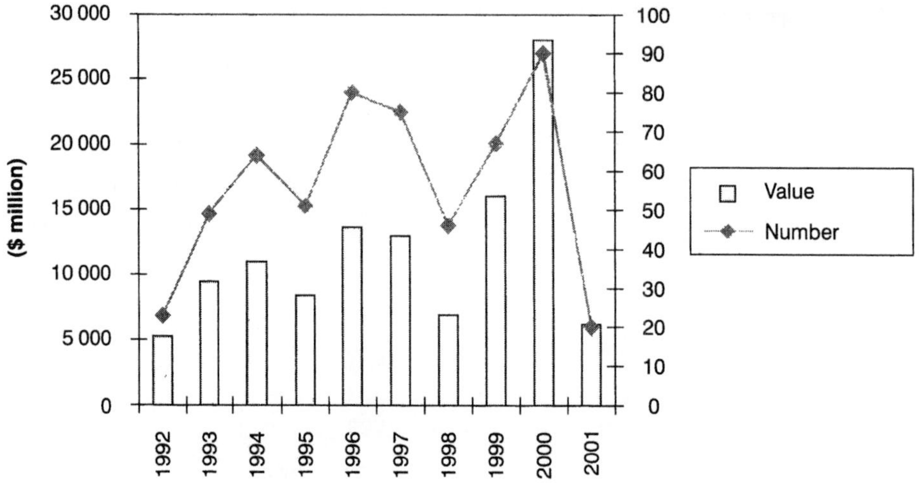


*Source*: Bank of New York.

**Figure 8.3** Foreign public offerings (1992–2001)

## *Securities Act of 1933*

Companies contemplating an IPO or other equity offering in the USA will be most concerned with the 1933 Act. Its two basic objectives are:

- To ensure that investors receive all significant information (including financial information) regarding the securities being offered for sale to the public.
- To prohibit deceit, misrepresentations and other fraud in the sale of securities.

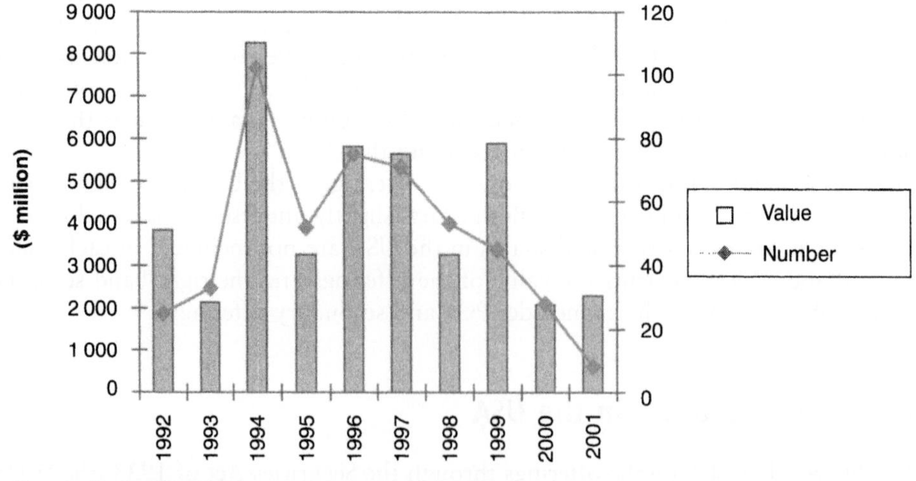


*Source*: Bank of New York.

**Figure 8.4** Private placement depository receipt offerings (1992–2001)

In order to ensure that these objectives are met, the SEC requires that issuers (whether domestic or foreign) file a registration statement (which includes a prospectus) for review by its Corporate Finance group. The information contained in the registration statement must be sufficient to enable an investor to make an informed judgment about whether to purchase a company's shares. Financial reporting presentation is governed by Regulation S-X, which sets out the form and content of financial statements in prospectuses and registration documents. We will discuss the contents of the registration statement soon.

The SEC is always quick to point out that it reviews the registration statement to ensure that all required information necessary to make an investment decision is included, but it does not make any representations about the quality of the issue or the issuer or the price of the securities.

The 1933 Act also covers the behaviour of the issuer and the bankers and underwriters during the offering period. The term underwriter is defined in the Act and 'encompasses persons who act as participants with an issuer in distributing the issuer's securities to the public' (Cramer et al., 2001: 2). The term underwriter is synonymous with the term manager, which we have been using, and is not to be confused with the 'underwriter' of a UK-style offering.

Not all new issues must be registered with the SEC. The main exemptions are private placements to a limited number of individuals or institutions and very small offerings (under $1 million). We will discuss private placements in the next section.

At the time of writing, the full text of the 1933 Act is available at: www.law.uc.edu/CCL/sldtoc.html (the reader should note that the SEC does not control or maintain this site). A summary of the Act can also be found at www.rrdfin.com.

### *Securities Exchange Act of 1934*

The 1934 Act created the Securities and Exchange Commission, giving it broad authority over all aspects of the industry. The main powers granted to the SEC under the 1934 Act include the power to register, regulate and oversee brokerage firms, transfer agents and clearing agencies as well as the stock exchanges and other self-regulatory organizations. The 1934 Act contains the periodic reporting requirements of publicly listed companies and other foundations of corporate governance.

Thus, while the 1933 Act is primarily about new issues, the 1934 Act governs the secondary market but there are parts of the 1934 Act (notably Rule 10b-5) that have an impact on new issues.

The full text of the 1934 Act can also be found at www.law.uc.edu/CCL/sldtoc.html (the SEC does not control or maintain this site) or www.rrdfin.com.

## Private placements vs. public offerings

Foreign issuers have the choice of private placements or public offerings in the USA. Public offers are fully 'registered' with the SEC and may be sold to anyone in the USA who has been provided with the offering prospectus as reviewed and approved by the SEC. An issuer is able to generate greater demand for a public offering of shares, as they will be listed on a US stock exchange, thereby providing liquidity for investors following the issue.

While the average size of a private placement is lower than a public offering, substantial size can be accommodated. During the period 1992–2001, the average private placement from non-US issuers raised $107.3 million. But during 2001, the average private placement by a non-US issuer raised $287.6 million, compared with public offerings' 10-year average size of $212 million and $312 million in 2001 (Bank of New York, 2002).

If the issuer does not want to go to the effort or make the disclosure required by a public offer, it can make a private placement. There are two forms of private placement available to foreign issuers in the USA: both exempt the issuer from the SEC's disclosure requirements and ongoing reporting regulations. The traditional private placement is governed by Rule 144 of the 1933 Act. It is most often used for the distribution of debt securities.

Since its introduction in 1991, the most frequently used private placement exemption for equity offerings is Rule 144a. Of 2143 non-US offerings from 1992 to mid-1999 examined by Ljungqvist and Wilhelm (2001), 17.8 per cent made US public offers, while a further 13.6 per cent offered shares under Rule 144a.

The rest of this section will cover first, regulations surrounding private placements, followed by the upfront and ongoing regulation of public offers and public companies in the USA.

## *Private placements*

The simplest way to tap US demand is via a private placement of shares. There are no registration statements to be filed, no changes in accounting to meet US GAAP, and ongoing reporting requirements are limited to that which is made in the issuer's home market. A US private placement can easily fit into the marketing schedule of all but the most rushed of offerings.

### Traditional private placements (Rule 144)

The 'traditional' private placement market in the USA is dominated by the issuance of fixed-term debt securities by both US and foreign issuers. The main purchasers of private placement debt have traditionally been insurance companies that held the bonds to maturity. In any case, they have to agree to hold the securities for at least one year and there is a legend on the front of the stock certificate that states the shares cannot be distributed to the public.

The documentation for a private placement is relatively simple, comprising two parts: the disclosure part, called a private placement memorandum, and a purchase agreement between the issuer and the purchaser or purchasers. The degree of disclosure will vary with the type of security being offered and the issuer, but must meet the standards of the anti-fraud provisions of the 1934 Act (i.e. Rule 10b-5). The purchase agreement contains the terms of the offering, details of the securities and a statement by each purchaser that it is a sizeable financial institution and does not intend to sell on the purchased securities.

### Rule 144a

Since 1991, the most common form of private placement used by international issuers is the Rule 144a private placement. The main difference between Rule 144 and Rule 144a private placements is that the latter can be traded in a limited secondary market, as described below.

Any offering under Rule 144a may not be of securities that are fungible with securities already listed on a US exchange (including Nasdaq). Thus GlaxoSmith-Kline, the British pharmaceuticals group, whose ADRs are listed on the NYSE, could not make an issue of its ordinary shares or ADRs to institutional investors in the US relying on Rule 144a. If GSK issues new shares, it must either do a public offering in the USA or avoid the US market entirely.

### Buyers of Rule 144a offerings

Rule 144a offerings are sold to 'Qualified Institutional Investors' in the USA, or US investors located offshore (under Regulation S). Qualified Institutional Buyers (QIBs, pronounced kwibs) are institutional investors of sufficient size and sophistication to make informed investment decisions who do not need the protection of the SEC's disclosure requirements.

The strict definition of a QIB is, as with most US securities laws issues, quite complicated, but in summary a QIB is one of the following:

- Any institutional investor registered under the Investment Company Act that owns or manages on a discretionary basis at least $100 million.
- Certain banks and savings and loan associations meeting the requirement of having an audited net worth of $25 million.
- Any broker or dealer registered under the Exchange Act, acting for its own account or the account of QIBs, that in aggregate owns or manages on a discretionary basis at least $10 million.
- Any entity, all of the owners of which are QIBs, if it acts for its own account or the account of another QIB.

### Regulation S

Regulation S was introduced at the same time as the Rule 144a regulation. It limits the long arm of the SEC to offerings made to 'US persons' resident in the USA. US persons can be either citizens or residents in the USA. (Previously, the SEC claimed jurisdiction over offerings made to US citizens outside the USA.)

In order to take advantage of the 'safe harbours' allowed by Regulation S, issuers, their advisors and investment bankers must fulfil two general conditions. The first is that the offering must be an 'offshore transaction', meaning that the issuer and bankers must reasonably believe that the purchaser of shares is offshore (i.e. not in the USA) at the time of the transaction. The second condition forbids directed selling efforts in the USA at the time of the offering.

The SEC's main concern is the protection of individual investors. Thus, an issuer is allowed to make a Rule 144a private placement concurrently with an offshore new issue that qualifies under Regulation S, without being accused of making directed selling efforts in the USA. This is now the approach that most international offerings using the Rule 144a private placement rules take.

## Documents

Potential investors receive a copy of an offering memorandum, which is often the home market prospectus with additional information of interest to US investors added. The two most frequently added sections are a description of the ADRs that are on offer and taxation of US investors.

The SEC receives a copy of the offering memorandum, but does not review it or comment on it. However, the issuer and its agents are not exempt from all SEC regulations. In particular, Rule 10b-5 of the 1934 Act is deemed applicable. In legalese, the rule 'prohibits the use of any device, scheme or artifice to defraud; the making of any untrue statement of a material fact or the admission of a material fact necessary to make the statements made not misleading; or the engaging in "any act, practice or course of business" that would operate to deceive any person in connection with the purchase or sale of any securities. Information is "material" if a reasonable investor would consider it important, in the total mix of facts, to an investment decision . . .' (Cramer et al., 2001: 16).

The rule, which is one of the most wide-ranging of all US securities rules, applies to: both foreign and domestic issuers; both public offerings and private placements; both formal (prospectus and offering memorandum) and informal (press releases) disclosure; and both initial and continuing (i.e. post-offering) disclosure.

## Resale restrictions

There are some restrictions on the resale of securities purchased under reliance of Rule 144a. QIBs must agree to resell the securities only: (a) to the issuer; (b) to a person whom the seller reasonably believes is a QIB in accordance with Rule 144a and to whom the seller has delivered a notice of its reliance on Rule 144a; (c) through PORTAL (a market where QIBs can buy and sell securities); or (d) pursuant to Regulation S, to non-American investors or American investors based offshore, for example on the home stock exchange of the issuer.

The main liquidity for a company's shares is almost always its home market. PORTAL has proved a disappointment in establishing an alternative source of liquidity.

## Ongoing disclosure

In the years following the private placement, a foreign issuer has limited ongoing reporting requirements. In the eyes of the SEC and the 1934 Act, a private placement issuer becomes a 'registrant', subject to all the reporting requirements of publicly listed companies *unless* it applies for an exemption under Rule 12g3-2(b):

> 'Rule 12g3-2(b) exempts securities of "foreign private issuers" from Exchange Act registration and reporting if the issuer furnishes, and agrees to furnish in the future, to the SEC

information, such as annual reports that it (a) makes public pursuant to the law of the country of its domicile, (b) files with a stock exchange on which its securities are traded or (c) distributes to its security-holders. Only information "material to an investment decision" need be furnished. Obtaining a Rule 12g3-2(b) is relatively simple and inexpensive. To apply for the exemption, the issuer must send to the SEC an exemption request letter, to which is appended a list of documents that the company is required to make available each year and the documents it in fact made public during its last fiscal year. Materials furnished to the SEC pursuant to the Rule are not considered "filed", including for the purposes of establishing liability for violation of the anti-fraud provisions of the securities laws.'

(Joyce et al., 1991: 96)

## *Public offerings in the USA*

The perceived onerous disclosure requirements of the SEC in the USA and US investors' love of litigation serves to keep many foreign issuers from making public offerings. However, the size and depth of the market can make it worthwhile, particularly for issuers undertaking very large offerings or who have direct comparables in the USA, but not their home market.

### The offering process

As in other markets, the SEC requires that the issuer prepare and file a prospectus (describing the company and the offering) that is distributed to potential purchasers. In the USA, the prospectus is part of the 'registration statement', which includes additional information not necessarily relevant to making an investment decision, but nonetheless possibly useful. The registration statement is a public document and anyone interested in the offering can obtain a copy. The easiest way to do so is to look at the SEC's website (www.sec.gov) or www.freeedgar.com.

This section examines: the process of getting a prospectus approved by the SEC; the disclosure required in the prospectus; the time involved; legal risks; and ongoing reporting.

Once the company, the bankers, the lawyers, accountants and other interested parties are satisfied with the prospectus/registration statement, it is signed by senior company executives and at least a majority of the board of directors. It must also be signed by an authorized representative of the issuer in the USA.

The documents are then shipped to Washington. (Domestic US issuers file electronically, using EDGAR (Electronic Data Gathering and Retrieval system). Foreign issuers may file electronically if they so desire.) On receipt of the document, an SEC industry team takes responsibility for processing the documentation through to 'effectiveness', and the ability to sell shares. The review process at the SEC generally takes between four and six weeks, depending on the workload of the examiners and the complexity of the offering document.

For complex international privatizations, the company and its lawyers can 'pre-file' the document to get comments on areas that might be of concern to the SEC, while work continues on the prospectus. Only when these issues have been resolved does the company formally file the registration statement.

During the late 1990s bull market the average length of time a prospectus was in registration with the SEC was 78 days – that's right, 11 weeks. With a private placement, there is no review delay.

When the prospectus is filed, the issuer can expect the SEC to thoroughly review the contents and ask for clarification and additional information in a 'comment letter'. Generally, the prospectus will go through one or two rounds of comments and responses before copies of the preliminary prospectus are printed for the public.

The preliminary prospectus that is printed is widely referred to as the 'red herring', because there is cautionary language, printed in red, on the cover of the prospectus. The cautionary language states that the registration statement that has been filed with the SEC is preliminary in nature and is subject to completion and that sales may not be completed until the registration statement is effective. An example of red herring language follows:

> 'The information contained in this prospectus is not complete and may be changed. We may not sell these securities until the registration statement filed with the Securities and Exchange Commission is effective. This preliminary prospectus is not an offer to sell these securities, and we are not soliciting offers to buy these securities in any jurisdiction where the offer or sale is not permitted.'

Once the preliminary prospectus has been published, marketing can begin in earnest, as described in Chapter 9.

## Timetable

It is not unusual for the regulators in the USA to drive the timetable in an international offering. In many markets, the documentation and regulatory review requirements can be dealt with quickly.

When the prelim has been filed, the issuer is said to be in the 'waiting' or 'quiet' period. During this time the investment bankers may not take orders for shares. They may only 'solicit expressions of interest'. When the SEC has approved the registration statement, saying that it contains all the necessary information to make an investment decision, the prospectus is declared to be 'effective'. The shares may only be sold once the registration statement is declared effective.

If the SEC indicates that its review is expected to take longer than four to five weeks, the issuer may delay printing a preliminary prospectus until some of the review has taken place. It is important to coordinate the marketing process with the review process. The last thing managers want is to be sitting on a full order book, but delayed from 'going effective' because the SEC has not completed its review.

In soliciting offers, the syndicate cannot use any written material other than the prospectus. This includes research reports for IPOs.

In the case of secondary (or follow-on) offerings, syndicate members are permitted to 'publish information, opinions, or recommendations about the issuer and any securities of the issuer, so long as they are contained in a publication which is "distributed with reasonable regularity in the normal course of business" and among other things, doesn't contain a higher rating or recommendation than was published in the last report' (Joyce et al., 1991: 31). The SEC is relatively more relaxed about ongoing research when the issuer is large and widely covered by financial analysts.

Thus, a monthly report on the European food retailing sector is fine, but an initial report with a buy recommendation on a company about to make a secondary offering is not.

## Documentation and disclosure

The registration statement Form F-1 for international companies that must be filed with the SEC is similar to the UK's Listing Particulars, in that it contains a prospectus that is sent to potential investors as well as additional information for the regulators. The home market prospectus and US registration statement will have substantially identical content if not identical form. It is imperative that investors in all markets receive the same information.

SEC regulations require the registration statement to include a consolidated balance sheet, a three-year consolidated income statement, and a three-year consolidated cash flow statement each certified by an independent accountant and prepared in accordance with US GAAP. This process can be very expensive and time consuming as companies comply with the financial disclosure requirements.

Compliance with US accounting rules can also throw up anomalies, such as when Daimler Benz listed its shares on the New York Stock Exchange. According to US GAAP, the company lost nearly $1 billion in the year prior to listing, but according to German accounting standards, it had been profitable.

A registration statement on Form F-1 (as its domestic counterpart, Form S-1) is divided into two sections: the prospectus and additional information. The prospectus portion of the F-1 contains the following information:

1 Front cover
   - Gives general information such as the issuer's name, type and amount of securities being offered and whether existing shareholders are selling any shares. If an IPO, it will state that there has been no public market up to now. It will also name the managers of the offering and the amount of their compensation and expenses of the issue.

2 Summary of the offering
   - Information regarding the company that is repeated elsewhere, details of the offering and expected timetable.

3 Key information
   - Selected financial data, capitalization and indebtedness, and use of proceeds. This information is often included as part of the summary and again immediately prior to management's discussion and analysis.

4 Company information
   - Detailed disclosure of the company's history, business plan, organizational structure, operations and competition.

5 Management discussion and analysis
  - Operating results, liquidity and capital resources, and trend information.

6 Directors and senior management
  - Including details of their compensation, employees and share ownership.

7 Major shareholders and related party transactions

8 The offer and listing
  - Offer and listing details, plan of distribution, markets, selling shareholders, dilution and expenses of the issue.

9 Risk factors or investment considerations
  - Generally appears near the front of the prospectus. Each risk factor mentioned will also be disclosed and discussed in more detail in the rest of the prospectus.

10 Description of securities other than equity securities
  - Debt securities, warrants and rights, ADRs, etc.

11 Financial information
  - Audited consolidated statements and notes to financial statements.

The registration statement also includes additional information that is not included in the prospectus:

1 A summary of all the sales of securities not registered under the 1933 Act by the issuer within the last three years and the bases for exemption from the registration requirements of the 1933 Act.

2 As exhibits, various documents and other items including:
  - The underwriting agreement with the underwriters.
  - The issuer's memorandum or articles of association and bylaws.
  - The deposit agreement pursuant to which the ADRs are to be issued.
  - All outstanding long-term debt instruments of the issuer under which indebtedness exceeds 10 per cent of total assets.
  - An opinion of counsel as to the legality of the securities being registered.
  - Consent of attorneys, accountants and other experts referenced in the prospectus as to the use of their names in the prospectus.
  - Certain material contracts not made in the ordinary course of business or referred to in the prospectus.

This supplemental information is on file and publicly available at the SEC, but is not included in the prospectus document that is sent to investors. Exhibits that are not in English must be filed together with an English translation or summary of material provisions.

### Financial statement requirements

The company must include financial information for the last five fiscal years (if it has been in existence that long) together with audited balance sheets for the two most recent years and audited income statements and cash flow statements for the three most recent years. Note that if the home market requires three years' audited balance sheet figures, so does the SEC.

Issuers are generally required to disclose industry and geographic segmented information for (i) revenues and sales, (ii) operating profit or loss, and (iii) assets.

*US GAAP*

The financial statements must either be presented:

1 In conformity to US GAAP (generally accepted accounting principles), or
2 In the home jurisdiction's GAAP with a reconciliation of the material differences (usually net profit and shareholders' equity) between the home GAAP and US GAAP as well as a narrative discussion of the material differences between the accounting principles followed and US GAAP.

The first time a company reconciles to US GAAP can be very time consuming and expensive, but in subsequent years should cause only minor time and expense.

Figure 8.5 illustrates a common form of reconciliation to US GAAP. It is excerpted from the $mmO_2$ prospectus.

UK GAAP differs in certain material respects from US GAAP. US GAAP unaudited pro forma reconciling income and net asset items have been determined as if the acquisitions and proposed Reorganization and Demerger Transaction had occurred on 1 April 2000 and 31 March 2001, respectively. The calculation of unaudited pro forma combined net income and owners' net investment under US GAAP is as follows:'

| | *Year ended 31 March 2001 (£ millions)* |
|---|---|
| **Pro forma loss for the financial year under UK GAAP** | (3926) |
| US GAAP adjustments: | |
| Capitalization of interest, net of related depreciation | 9 |
| Goodwill amortization | 27 |
| Mobile licences, software and other intangible assets | (112) |
| Software impairment | 12 |
| Employee share plans | (8) |
| Other employee compensation expense | (8) |
| Deferred taxation | 19 |
| **Pro forma loss for the financial year under US GAAP** | (3987) |

| | *As at 31 March 2001 (£ millions)* |
|---|---|
| **Pro forma net assets under UK GAAP** | 18 691 |
| US GAAP adjustments: | |
| Capitalization of interest, net of related depreciation | 400 |
| Goodwill amortization | 93 |
| Mobile licences, software and other intangible assets | (167) |
| Employee share plans | (2) |
| Other employee compensation expense | (8) |
| Deferred taxation | (46) |
| **Pro forma net assets under US GAAP** | 18 961 |

**Figure 8.5** Sample reconciliation to US GAAP

*Stub periods*
The SEC requires that if more than nine months have passed since the issuer's year end, the prospectus must also include interim financial statements. If interim statements are required they must cover a period of at least six months, but may be unaudited. The manager(s) of the offering typically require the inclusion of interim financial information more recent than that legally required. So if the offering is made during the fifth month of the issuer's financial year, the first quarter's results will be included. The marketing or pricing of a transaction is often delayed to permit the inclusion of more recent financial information.

*Projections and forward-looking language*
It is unusual for an IPO prospectus in the USA to include financial projections because of liability concerns if the company does not meet its forecasts. However, the 'Management's Discussion and Analysis' (MD&A) section contains information on current trends in the issuer's business and industry as well as anything that might cause the issuer's results to change from the past.

Most US prospectuses now include cautionary language relating to forward-looking statements. Figure 8.6 contains a sample of the language used in $mmO_2$ plc's prospectus.

## Liability and due diligence

Issuers and others involved in US public offerings need to be aware of their potential liability under the two acts which govern the new issue and trading of securities in the USA. Under the provisions of the Securities Act of 1933, all of the following are potentially liable for errors or omissions in the registration statement:

- issuer
- directors of the issuer
- those who sign the registration statement
- underwriters/managers
- experts named with their consent, for the sections they prepared or certified.

Under the law, if at the time the registration statement became effective it contained any untrue statement of a material fact or omitted to state a material fact required to be stated or necessary to make the statements therein not misleading, the above group of individuals and firms could be sued by purchasers of the securities.

The 1934 Act, with its Rule 10b-5, spreads the net wider to 'any person who commits fraud or intentionally or recklessly provides misleading disclosure in connection with the purchase or sale of any security'. The above parties are also a risk according to this rule, as are legal counsel and brokers.

The provisions of the 1933 Act apply only to companies making public offerings, but Rule 10b-5 also applies to private placements, so the managers of a Rule 144a offering must be careful to conduct appropriate due diligence.

Under US law, there is no due diligence defence for the issuer. Other parties (e.g. investment bankers) can rely on due diligence if they can prove: 'after "reasonable investigations", they had reasonable grounds to believe the included information was true and that no material facts were omitted'. What constitutes reasonable investigation increases with the degree of participation in the offering. Thus lead managers are expected to make a greater investigation than someone providing an expert opinion on environmental liability for example.

Pretty much anyone involved can take a hit. This is why the due diligence process as described in Chapter 6 is so important.

In November 2001, British Telecommunications 'de-merged' its mobile phone division $mmO_2$. In doing so, the new company, $mmO_2$, was required to file listing particulars with the UK Listing Authority, and because BT American Depository Shares were listed on the New York Stock Exchange, it was required to file a Form 20-F with the SEC. The Listing Particulars and Form 20-F contained a 'Special Note Regarding Forward-Looking Statements' as reproduced below.

[Page 108 of summary listing particulars]

This document contains certain forward-looking statements. We may also make written or oral forward-looking statements in:

- our periodic reports to the US Securities and Exchange Commission, also known as the SEC, on forms 20-F and 6-K;
- our annual report and accounts and half-yearly reports;
- our press releases and other written materials; and
- oral statements made by our officers, directors or employees to third parties.

We have based these forward-looking statements on our current plans, expectations and projections about future events. These forward-looking statements are subject to risks, uncertainties and assumptions about us. Forward-looking statements speak only as of the date they are made.

Statements that are not historical facts, including statements about our beliefs and expectations, are forward-looking statements. Words like 'believe', 'anticipate', 'expect', 'intend', 'seek', 'will', 'plan', 'could', 'may', 'might', 'project', 'goal', 'target' and similar expressions often identify forward-looking statements but are not the only ways we identify these statements.

These statements may be found in 'Part 1: Key Information', 'Part 3: Business Description', 'Part 5: Relationship with BT', 'Part 6: Operating and Financial Review', 'Part 7: Risk Factors' and in this document generally. Our actual results could differ materially from those anticipated in these forward-looking statements as a result of various factors, including all the risks discussed in the above-mentioned sections.

If any one or more of the foregoing assumptions are ultimately incorrect, our actual results may differ from our expectations based on these assumptions. Also, the sector and markets in which we operate may not grow over the next several years as expected, or at all. The failure of these markets to grow as expected may have a material adverse effect on our business, operating results and financial condition and the market price of our shares and ADSs.

The information on our web site, any web site mentioned in this document or any web site directly or indirectly linked to our or any other web site mentioned in this document is not incorporated by reference into this document and you should not rely on it.

**Figure 8.6** Forward-looking statements: cautionary language

### *Limitation on enforceability of civil liabilities*

While 'anyone can take a hit', in most international offerings into the USA, the majority of the issuer's assets are located outside the USA and therefore beyond the long arm of US law. To warn potential investors of this, most international prospectuses include a section on 'Limitation on Enforceability of Civil Liabilities'.

The following language, which is typical, was extracted from the 29 June 2000 prospectus for Mobile TeleSystems OJSC, a Russian mobile communications group:

> 'Substantially all of our directors and executive officers and the experts named in this prospectus reside outside the United States. All or a substantial portion of their and our assets are located outside the United States, principally in the Russian Federation. As a result, it may not be possible for you to:
>
> - effect service of process within the United States upon substantially all our directors and executive officers and the experts named in this prospectus; or
> - enforce in the United States court judgments obtained against us or substantially all of our directors and executive officers and the experts named in this prospectus in the United States courts in any action, including actions under the civil liability provisions of US securities laws.
>
> In addition, it may be difficult for you to enforce, in original actions brought in courts in jurisdictions located outside the United States, liabilities predicated upon the United States securities laws.'

## Ongoing reporting

Following the IPO, an international company that has listed its shares on the NYSE or Nasdaq must meet ongoing reporting requirements. This section briefly covers the two documents that international issuers are required to file with the SEC in the years following their US public offering.

Companies must file an annual report on Form 20-F (the international equivalent of Form 10-K) within six months of each fiscal year end. The report must be delivered to both the SEC and the US stock exchange on which the company is listed. The Form 20-F requires updates of items 1–11 from the registration statement as described above. The financial statement requirements of Form 20-F are also similar to those for the registration statement Form F-1.

Whenever a material event happens in the company's life it must deliver a Form 6-K to the SEC and the NYSE or Nasdaq. The report is quite simple. It consists of cover and signature pages which sandwich a copy of the document that the firm makes public in either its local market, with any other foreign securities exchange, or is required to distribute to shareholders. There are no precise deadlines for the filing of Form 6-Ks; companies must 'promptly' file the information that has already been made public.

The SEC does not require quarterly interim reports to be filed (as are required of US companies), but most international issuers do so on the advice of their investment banks.

### Listing on a US stock market

The requirements of an international company to list on either the NYSE or Nasdaq are similar, but not identical, to those of American companies. Table 8.1 (page 144) contains the minimum quantitative standards imposed.

## Depository receipts

A depository receipt is a convenient mechanism for transferring ownership, receiving dividends and taking care of other routine transactions in foreign securities. There are two main types of depository receipts: ADRs and GDRs. Of these, ADRs are quoted and traded in US dollars in the US markets (either on an exchange or over-the-counter) while GDRs may be quoted in US dollars but also in pounds sterling and occasionally in another currency, such as the euro. GDRs are often listed in London or Luxembourg. The principles surrounding the operation of each are the same.

Depository receipts are issued by a 'depository bank', which holds the underlying shares in custody. The depository acts as a transfer agent for the DRs, distributes dividends in dollars (or sterling or euros) and distributes corporate information, such as annual reports and accounts to the holders of the DRs. The main banks involved in the business are the Bank of New York (66 per cent market share of sponsored depository receipt programmes as of 2001), Morgan Guaranty (16 per cent), Citibank (15 per cent) and Deutsche Bank (3 per cent).

For example, Nokia, the mobile telephone company whose home market is Finland, has issued ADRs which are listed and traded on the New York Stock Exchange just like US company shares. In fact, in 2001 over 3.5 billion Nokia ADSs worth $88.4 billion changed hands on the NYSE.

The advantages to issuers include the following: ability to access a broader shareholder base and increased liquidity outside the company's home market; enhanced ability to raise new capital in the USA (with respect to ADRs) and internationally (with respect to GDRs).

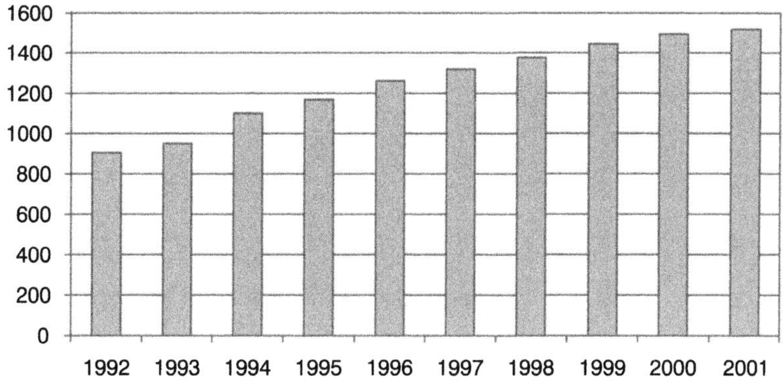


*Source*: Bank of New York.

**Figure 8.7** Number of depository receipt programmes (1992–2001)

| | Nasdaq-NMS Alternative 1 | Nasdaq-NMS Alternative 2 | Nasdaq Small Cap Market | NYSE |
|---|---|---|---|---|
| Aggregate market value of publicly held shares ($m) | 3.0 | 15.0 | | 40.0 |
| Shareholders' equity ($m) | 15.0 | 30.0 | 5.0 | 40.0 |
| Publicly held shares | 500 000 | 1.0m | | 1.1m |
| Number of shareholders* | 800 | 400 | | 2000 |
| Number of market makers | 2 | 2 | | – |

NMS = Nasdaq National Market [system].
*This requirement refers to 2000 round-lot shareholders. Both markets have alternative shareholder requirements for large, actively traded firms. These alternatives do not apply to IPOs.

**Table 8.1** Minimum listing requirements on Nasdaq and NYSE

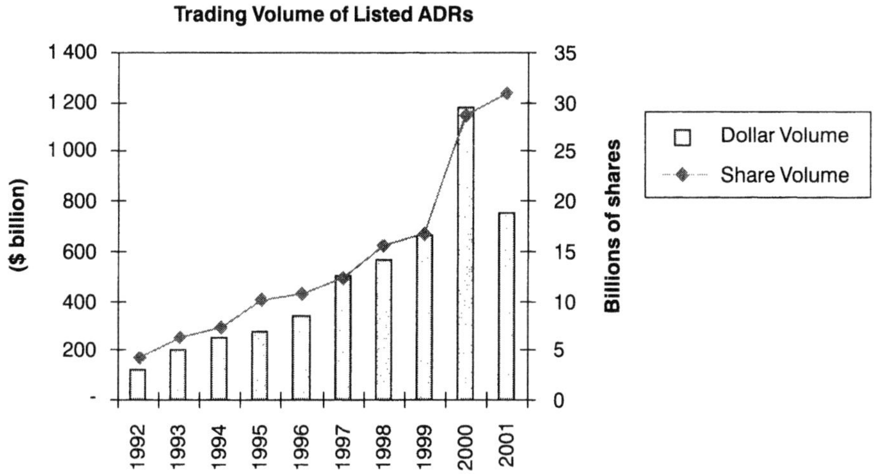


*Source*: Bank of New York.

**Figure 8.8** Trading volume in exchange listed ADRs (1992–2001)

Although the growth of trading in DRs has been impressive during the 1990s, they are not new. JP Morgan established the first ADR, for British retailer Selfridge's in 1927. During the 1990s, demand by investors for DRs grew at an annual rate of between 30 and 40 per cent (Bank of New York). The growth and importance of DRs is illustrated by the fact that for several years during the 1990s, ADR issues from Glaxo and Telefonos de Mexico topped the annual volume charts (including both domestic and non-US equities) of the New York Stock Exchange several times. At the end of 2001, there were over 1500 ADR programmes for companies from over 70 countries.

## *Sponsored or unsponsored*

Depository receipts can be issued with or without the cooperation of the underlying company. Many 'unsponsored' depository receipt programmes were established during the 1970s and 1980s by depository banks responding to investor demand. An unsponsored programme trades on the over-the-counter market and requires no action by the company, either at the time the programme is established or in the following years. Unsponsored programmes are no longer being established due to a lack of control over the facility. Figure 8.9 illustrates the growing proportion of sponsored facilities during the 1990s.

A sponsored facility is established in cooperation with the issuing company and may come in one of many forms:

- Level 1
- Level 2
- Level 3
- Rule 144a (known to some as RADRs, these only exist in the USA)

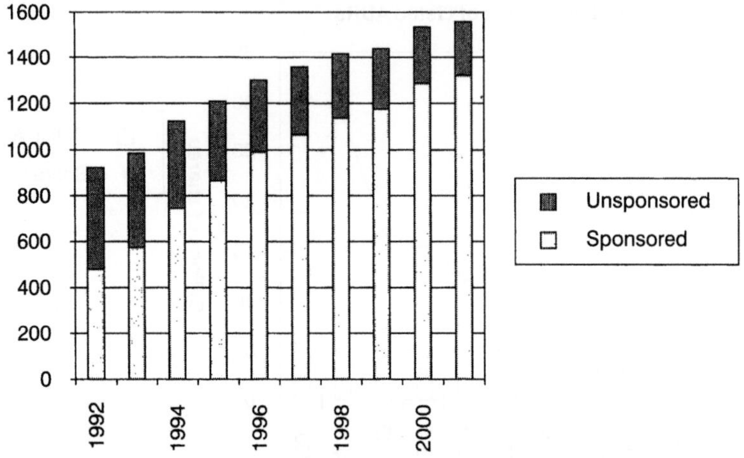


*Source*: Bank of New York.

**Figure 8.9** Total sponsored and unsponsored ADR programmes

which are discussed below. Table 8.2 (page 147) illustrates the different types of DRs that are available. Sponsored depository receipts of any level offer control over the facility, the flexibility to list on a US or European stock exchange and the ability to raise capital, either at the time of establishing the DR or later.

## *Benefits to the issuer*

For over 1300 companies to have issued sponsored ADRs, there must be some pretty significant benefits. And there are. The main one is that the issuer gains access to significant pools of capital – the USA and Europe – allowing it to raise fresh funds. If the DR issuer does not need new capital, a DR programme still allows it exposure to a new group of investors, increasing overall demand for its shares and potentially increasing its share price.

By issuing DRs, the company's employees in that market may be able to more easily partake in option compensation schemes. DRs can increase the profile of the issuer outside its home country at a low incremental cost.

Cross-listing on one of the large international stock exchanges (i.e. London or New York) will significantly increase an issuer's visibility. A company that lists on the NYSE typically adds six research analysts to its following (an increase of 128 per cent). A company adds more analysts if it raises funds simultaneously. Newspaper coverage also increases – in the years following a New York listing, the number of mentions in the *Wall Street Journal* increases by 32 per cent. But coverage does not stop at the US borders, for the same companies listing on the NYSE, *Financial Times* citations increase by 78 per cent and home newspapers run an extra six stories per year (37 per cent increase) (Baker, Nofsinger and Weaver, 1999).

When a foreign company lists its shares or DRs on the London Stock Exchange, it increases its analyst and press coverage as well, although not to the same degree. On average an extra 3.4 research analysts begin commenting on the company, a 48

| | Using existing shares to broaden shareholder base | | Raising capital | | |
|---|---|---|---|---|---|
| | Level 1 ADR | Level 2 ADR | Level 3 ADR | Private placement Rule 144a ADR | Global offering (GDR) |
| Description | Unlisted programme | Listed on a US stock exchange | Public offer in USA and listing on a US stock exchange | Private placement to QIBs | Global offering outside issuer's home market |
| Trading | OTC (pink sheets) | Amex, Nasdaq, NYSE | Amex, Nasdaq, NYSE | PORTAL – US private placement market or outside USA | Non-US exchanges* and occasionally US exchanges |
| SEC registration | Form F-6 | Form F-6 | Forms F-1 (registration statement) and F-6 | None | Varies, depending on structure of US offer |
| US reporting requirements | Exempt under Rule 12g3-2(b) | Form 20-F filed annually | Form 20-F filed annually | Exempt under Rule 12g3-2(b) | Varies, depending on structure of US offer |
| GAAP reconciliation requirements | None | Partial reconciliation of financials | Full reconciliation of financials | No GAAP reconciliation | Depends on structure of US offer |

*Primarily London.

Table 8.2 Types of DR programmes

per cent increase. Companies also see a 49 per cent increase in *Financial Times* citations.

### *Benefits to the investor*

Depository receipts get around many of the difficulties of international investment: settlement issues; currency conversion for receipt of dividends; information flow, among others. These can be particularly onerous for individual investors, but even institutions find that depository receipts can be a very useful tool. DRs are quoted in dollars, pounds sterling, or euros, depending on where they are issued and the investor base the company is trying to attract. DRs follow the trading conventions of the market on which they are listed or where they trade, if over-the-counter.

So, ADRs listed on one of the US stock exchanges have a settlement date of three days following the trade date, known as T + 3 in the jargon. They also trade in decimals, as do stocks listed on the NYSE and traded on Nasdaq. For institutional investors, purchasing ADRs can eliminate international custody charges, which can range from 10 basis points to 40 basis points annually. If an investor wishes to, he may cancel the DRs and take delivery of the underlying shares.

### *Types of DRs*

Depository receipts can be established when a company is making its IPO or at some other date, when it decides that a listing on one of the major exchanges is important.

#### Level 1: Trading ADRs over-the-counter

When a company is simply trying to broaden its shareholder base, without raising equity finance, it may issue what are known as Level 1 or Level 2 ADRs.

Level 1 ADRs provide the simplest method for companies that are trying to attract new shareholders. Level 1 DRs are traded over-the-counter in the USA and can be listed on some non-US stock exchanges. When established in the USA, only minimal regulatory filings with the SEC are required, and the companies do not have to present their financial statements in accordance with US GAAP. Prices of Level 1 ADRs are published in the daily 'Pink Sheets' of all OTC securities traded in the USA.

Since 1998, companies with Level 1 ADR programmes that wish to have prices posted on the OTC Bulletin Board (OTCBB) must register their shares with the SEC under Section 12 of the 1934 Securities Exchange Act. If a company does not wish to post prices on the OTCBB it is able to rely on the SEC's Rule 12g3-2(b) that exempts foreign companies from registering equity securities. These companies' ADRs will trade exclusively on the Pink Sheets.

When a company is establishing its ADR programme it is required to file a Form F-6 registration statement with the SEC. The form is a simple document that is typically completed and filed by the depository bank and its lawyers. The amount of time involved in establishing a Level 1 ADR programme is approximately two months.

It is not uncommon for companies to attract from 5 to 10 per cent of its shareholders from Level 1 programmes. Companies that wish to increase their foreign holdings have the option of stepping up to a Level 2 DR programme, which involves listing their shares on one of the major international stock exchanges.

## Level 2: Listed DRs

Level 2 ADRs are securities that are listed and trade on either Nasdaq or the New York Stock Exchange (almost no foreign companies choose the American Stock Exchange). They require registration and annual filings with the SEC as well as a reconciliation of major financial statement items to US GAAP. There are no restrictions on the buying and selling of Level 2 ADRs, and they trade as regular US stocks do. The number of listed ADRs in the USA increased by about 11 per cent annually during the 1990s.

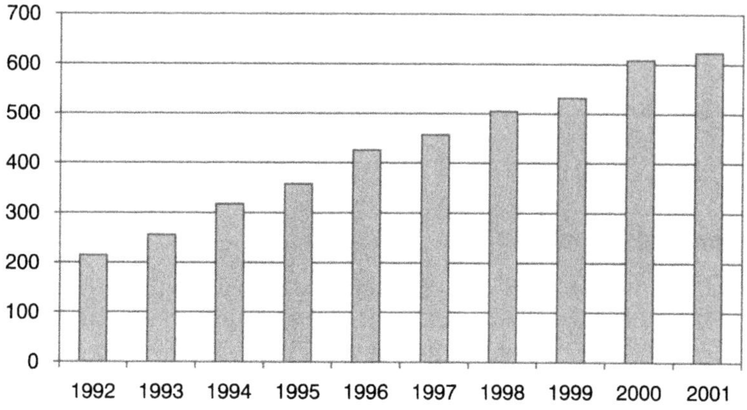


*Source*: Bank of New York.

**Figure 8.10** Number of listed ADR programmes

The main documents involved in establishing and continuing a Level 2 ADR programme are:

- Form F-6 registration statement.
- Annual Form 20-F registration statement which typically includes the issuer's annual report, management discussion and analysis of financial results, financial statements and a reconciliation of financial statements to US GAAP.
- Material event reports as issued in the home market and delivered on Form 6-K to the SEC.

From taking the decision to establish an ADR programme to first day of trading on a US stock market, a Level 2 ADR programme will take about three months to set up. Smart companies setting up a Level 2 programme combine it with a directed marketing programme towards American investors.

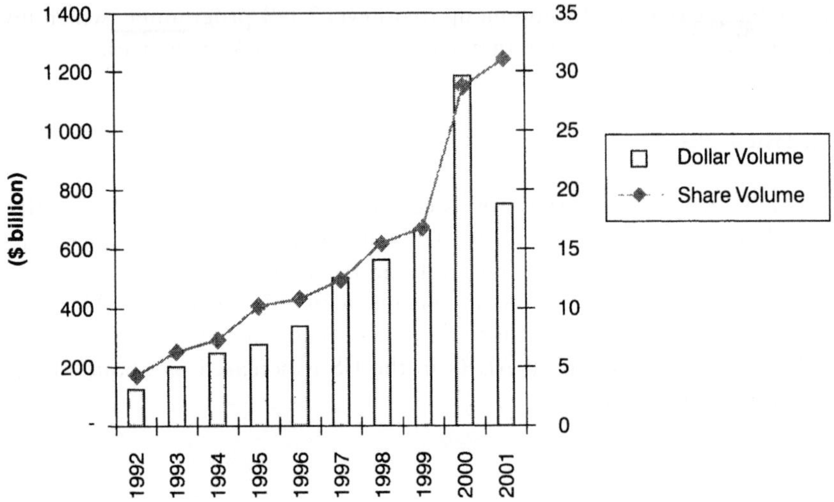


*Source*: Bank of New York.

**Figure 8.11** Number and trading volume of listed DRs (1992–2001)

### Level 3: Capital raising with ADRs

Level 3 ADRs are simply Level 2 ADRs combined with a simultaneous capital raising exercise. This may be a company's IPO or it may be a further issue of shares. Because a company is undergoing a public offering when it establishes a Level 3 programme, it is required to file a registration statement on Form F-1 with the SEC, which qualifies the securities for investment, in addition to Form F-6, which establishes the programme.

When a non-US company completes an offering of new shares, part of which will be sold as DRs in the US or international market, the company delivers shares to the depository bank's local custodian at the time of closing. The depository bank then issues the corresponding depository receipts and delivers them to the members of the underwriting syndicate, who deliver them to investors.

Many international offerings give US investors the choice of purchasing ADRs or ordinary (common) shares.

### Rule 144a ADRs (RADRs)

Companies that don't want to go to the expense and effort of a US public offering may elect to offer shares to institutional investors through a private placement as discussed earlier in this chapter. Rule 144a programmes, or RADRs, provide for raising capital through the private placement of DRs with large institutional investors in the USA. Remember, the SEC's Rule 144a allows issuers to sell shares or ADRs to QIBs. The SEC receives a copy of the prospectus used in a Rule 144a offering, but does not review or pass judgment on it. Rule 144a ADR programmes are the quickest to establish, taking only six to seven weeks from start to finish, compared with up to 12 weeks for Level 2 and Level 3 programmes.

## Global depository receipts

Global depository receipts can trade on multiple foreign stock exchanges (i.e. outside the home market of the issuer). Most GDRs are from African and Asian companies and trade on the London Stock Exchange. The UK Listing Authority and the London Stock Exchange have specialist teams to handle the review and listing of GDRs.

To list on the LSE, a company must be at least three years old. The GDRs must have a market capitalization of at least £700 000 and 25 per cent of the depository receipts (not 25 per cent of the company's shares) must be held by unconnected parties (London Stock Exchange, 1999). For a full listing, a prospectus must be filed and approved by the UKLA, which tends to be accommodating towards foreign issuers.

The disclosure and reporting requirements for GDR issuers listing on the LSE are sometimes seen as a stepping stone to an ADR. The ADR is deemed to be preferable because it is perceived to offer greater liquidity and visibility compared with a London listed GDR (Mullan, 1999).

Companies that wish to list GDRs on the Luxembourg Stock Exchange face slightly less onerous conditions.

## Trading mechanics

An investor who wants to buy a DR approaches his broker in the normal way, whether the broker–dealer is from a full-service firm, discount house, or on-line. Once the order has been placed, the broker–dealer has two choices:

1. Purchase the DRs in the local market.
2. Purchase underlying shares in the home market and have DRs created (issued) for the client.

The choice of whether to purchase existing DRs or have new ones issued will depend upon availability, pricing and market conditions in both markets. When purchasing DRs it is easier to stay in the DR market; but if there are insufficient DRs trading, it may be more efficient (i.e. cheaper) to go to the issuer's home market.

When a broker–dealer decides to follow alternative 2, it sets a chain in motion. Assume that an American client wants to buy 1000 ADRs in Vodafone. The client calls his broker and receives a quote in dollars. When the client agrees the trade his local broker calls either its branch in London or a correspondent broker. The London branch buys 10 000 Vodafone shares in the market and requests that they be delivered to the depository bank's custodian in that country. It buys 10 000 shares, because each Vodafone ADR represents 10 ordinary shares of the company.

When the trade settles, the custodian bank informs the depository bank which then issues ADRs and delivers them to the broker who initiated the trade. The

ADRs then can be physically delivered to the American client, or held in electronic form at his broker's.

The Bank of New York estimates that approximately six months after a company has established a DR programme, approximately 95 per cent of trades are conducted on an intermarket basis that does not require the issuance of new DRs.

# 9 Marketing new issues

The marketing of equity new issues is a sophisticated process which involves three stages: pre-marketing to prepare investors for the issue; formal marketing where direct approaches are made to potential investors; and finally, pricing, allocation and distribution of the shares.

The marketing process runs concurrently and beyond the main documentation process and involves different arms of the lead bank. However, many of the people from the company who are involved in documentation will find themselves also involved with the marketing of the new issue adding to the pressure on management at a critical time. Depending on market conditions, type, size and complexity of the offering, marketing can last from four hours to four months and even longer.

This chapter concentrates on the marketing for offerings using the bookbuilding structure as set out in Table 9.1. Marketing of fixed price offers includes most of the same activities, but the pricing of the offer occurs at an earlier stage.

The initial phase is devoted to educating investors so that they understand the company and the industry in which it operates. Typically a major research document is published by the brokers to the issue and distributed to investing institutions up to eight weeks prior to the anticipated offering date. While the investors study the research report, the lead bank and investor relations consultants work with the company's management to prepare the management for the second phase of marketing – meeting the investors.

| | |
|---|---|
| Pre-marketing | 1. Developing the investment case |
| | 2. Preparing the market |
| | 3. Preparing the management |
| | 4. Research report published |
| Marketing | 1. Setting the price range |
| | 2. Filing the preliminary prospectus |
| | 3. Sales briefing |
| | 4. Roadshow presentations and 'one-on-ones' |
| | 5. Sales/research follow-up |
| | 6. Bookbuilding |
| Pricing and allocation | 1. Setting the price |
| | 2. Allocation |
| | 3. Stabilization |

**Table 9.1** Marketing process for a bookbuilding offering

The pre-marketing period is the most variable in length. The time spent depends on the target investors. If the offering will be directed primarily at institutional investors, a shorter campaign is necessary than if a retail offering is contemplated. Most privatizations have featured large retail components (often in countries where individuals had little history of equity investment), thus requiring more extensive pre-marketing activities. Some potential issuers begin preparing the market more than a year before the IPO.

The second phase commences with the publication of a preliminary prospectus (the pathfinder in the UK). In most large offerings, the preliminary prospectus is published approximately four to five weeks before the issue is priced. The preliminary prospectus includes all the necessary information required to make an investment decision, except the price. Usually the lead bank will indicate a price range at this time, so that investors have an idea of the valuation being contemplated. In some markets, notably the USA, the price range is printed in the preliminary prospectus.

After the preliminary prospectus has been published, company management commences presentations to institutional investors and syndicate salespeople, known as a roadshow. The programme includes a combination of one-on-one meetings with the most important institutions and breakfast, lunch and dinner presentations to selected groups of fund managers and analysts.

During the final one or two weeks of the marketing period in a bookbuilding, institutional investors are canvassed by the banks and brokers involved, for their interest in purchasing shares. As the pricing date approaches, the indicated price range may be adjusted to reflect demand. This allows the sponsors of the issue to more accurately set the issue price. Some banks use computer software to model demand at specific price points and use this to set an 'optimal issue price'.

Pricing a new issue is not an exact science, however. Most flotations are priced in the expectation that the shares will begin trading at approximately 10 to 15 per cent above the issue price. In IPOs of highly risky companies – Internet and biotechnology businesses, for example – the level of underpricing is greater. For example, during the high tech bubble, IPOs in the USA increased by an average of 64 per cent on the first day of trading. At the same time, German IPOs saw their one-day premium peak at 88 per cent in 1998, before dropping to approximately 41 per cent during each of the next two years. In London, the average first-day premium was 60.1 per cent in 2000.

In secondary offerings, where existing shares are already trading in the market, the international offering (bookbuilding) process attempts to price the shares being offered at or marginally below the existing share price.

In a fixed price offer, the bank and company set the offering price based on indications of interest from institutional investors and the bank's knowledge of the market. Once the price has been fixed, the prospectus is published and advertisements printed with information regarding the application process. The offering is underwritten at this stage. The syndicate begins taking firm orders from institutions, and individual investors apply at banks or send their orders to the registrar in the post. Very few countries outside the USA and Canada have the vast retail stockbroker networks that firms such as Merrill Lynch, Morgan Stanley Dean Witter and others have built up.

This chapter focuses on the bookbuilding style offerings, with occasional sections pointing out the differences found in fixed price offers.

## The role of the research analyst

Equity research analysts are integral to the success of IPOs. Table 9.2 outlines the fundamental role played by analysts. They are involved in helping to win the deal, shaping the investment case, and dealing with investors throughout the pre-marketing and marketing periods, as well as providing ongoing research commentary following the IPO.

| Pre-offer phase | Institutional pre-marketing | Marketing | Aftermarket |
|---|---|---|---|
| ■ Help to win the lead manager mandate*<br>■ Publish sector report (optional)<br>■ Raise company profile with investment community<br>■ Background briefings for the media (where permitted) | ■ Presentations to salesmen and selected institutions<br>■ Publish research (where permitted)<br>■ Pre-marketing by research team (institutional visits) | Roadshow<br>■ One-on-ones<br>■ Group meetings<br>■ Press conferences<br>Analyst or salesman follow-up | Ongoing research commitment<br>■ Results announcements<br>■ Occasional longer reports<br>■ Investor feedback to company |

*This role has become somewhat controversial.

**Table 9.2** Schematic of analysts' role in large IPOs

During the 1990s, a trend developed for investors, the big ones anyway, to want to talk to the analyst, not the salesmen. The salesmen are simply passing on the analysts' views, so why not go direct to the source?

Analysts, particularly in the USA, where tens of millions of people are active investors, have also become an important draw for the retail brokers. 'Get analyst X's opinion directly from us – before everyone else hears about it on CNBC' can be a persuasive sales pitch to a retail investor.

During the boom, analysts individually and as a group were profiled in non-business media such as *The New Yorker* and *Vanity Fair.* A new form of royalty was crowned: Mary Meeker was 'Queen of the Net' (*Barron's*, 1998); Jessica Reif Cohen was 'The Queen of all Media' (*Fortune*); and Jack Grubman was promoted from 'guru' to 'almost a demigod' (*Business Week*, May 2000). During the bubble, having a high-profile analyst supporting an IPO was worth millions of dollars on the price (Munk, 2001).

The multifaceted role of the analyst puts him or her in a potential conflict of interest situation – whose interests does the analyst represent: the investor, the issuer or his bank? Secondly, which investors: individuals or institutions? Perceptions of conflicts are particularly noticeable when an analyst publicly changes his opinion on a stock from neutral/hold to buy shortly followed by the analyst's bank appearing in a financing for the company. One example follows:

Jack Grubman, 'almost a demigod', at Salomon Smith Barney had maintained a 'neutral' opinion on AT&T (his former employer as it happens) from 1995 to November 1999, when he changed his rating from neutral to buy. Three months later, Grubman's firm was selected as one of three lead managers of the $10.6 billion equity offering from AT&T Wireless. In that deal alone, Salomon Smith Barney was estimated to have earned $50 million in fees (Smith et al., 2002). In the following year, AT&T shares dropped by 70 per cent. Draw your own conclusions. (Note: Grubman no longer works at SSB.)

At the time of writing, prosecutors in the USA are trying to curtail the analysts' role in winning new corporate finance business for their employers. During the late 1990s and 2000, many research analysts' remuneration was partially based on the fees that they helped to generate from IPOs. In some banks, research analysts were rewarded with 10 per cent of the total fees from deals that they helped to win. Many banks have now ended this practice.

## Pre-marketing

A typical pre-marketing programme will run from about eight weeks before pricing to about three or four weeks before pricing. Some deals will have longer pre-marketing periods because of their size or complexity, while others will run with a shorter period. Transactions that target a high proportion of individual investors require greater pre-marketing. Reaching sufficient individuals to generate $300 million in demand takes significantly more effort than generating aggregate demand of $300 million from institutions.

Pre-marketing is all about preparation. During the time, the company, its advisors and the transaction's managers will:

- Prepare and refine the investment case.
- Prepare and disseminate one or two research reports: the first on the industry (optional) and the second on the company itself.
- Smooth the market through public relations activities such as senior management interviews with the press and presentations to research analysts in the syndicate.
- Prepare the management for the formal marketing period to come.

Pre-marketing helps the managers and company to determine exactly what 'spin' to put on the story for investors. For large offerings, it gets institutional investors thinking about where the shares will fit in their portfolios – and if the offering is a 'must have' – and ensures that sufficient cash will be on hand at the time of the offer.

The publication of a research report is the culmination of the pre-marketing of international offerings. The SEC prohibits publication of research by investment banks involved in the deal prior to the IPO. So in a multi-tranche offering that includes the USA, the managers need to be careful that research reports and other pre-marketing materials are not disseminated in the USA. Similar restrictions are imposed by regulators in Canada and Japan.

Many European regulators do not impose such a blackout period, so research may be published and distributed at any time during the marketing period. Best practice is developing to ensure that research is published four weeks before a deal is priced, or at least two weeks prior to the publication of the preliminary prospectus.

Following the offering, US rules prohibit the publication of research by syndicate members for 25 days.

Best practice regarding research and secondary offerings is evolving as well. Traditionally, when a UK rights offering was announced, the brokers to the issue would publish a research report. Best practice now imposes a research blackout on the day the rights issue is announced, continuing until 25 days following the expiration of the rights.

The issue of research restrictions is complex and evolving. This is an area where legal advice is very important.

### *Developing the investment case*

In order to convince an investment manager to make room in his portfolio for the new offering, the company and its managers must develop and present a compelling investment case. The investment case is the set of the most salient selling points that will persuade an investor to buy the issuer's shares.

In the venture capital industry, there is the concept of the 'elevator pitch', where an entrepreneur has to explain his idea and why a VC should finance it in the time it takes an elevator to go from the ground floor to the VC's office. Basically, it is a 30-second pitch. Public market investors might be a little more patient, but they want to be able to hear what is special about the company in a clear and concise manner.

During the roadshow, company management will have about 25 minutes to present their investment case to investors. Taking longer than 25 minutes risks turning off investors. Prior to the roadshow, research analysts will have a similar amount of time to present their thoughts in visits and telephone calls to major investors. Salesmen will have from 2 to 10 minutes to pitch the company to smaller, less important institutions. The salesmen's pitch is primarily to interest the investors sufficiently that they will attend the roadshow. No-one objects if the institutional investor places an order based solely on the salesman's pitch.

The core investment case will focus on three or four items drawn from the following:

- Market and market growth
- Products and services offered
- Corporate strategy
- Financial position
- Historical financials
- Use of proceeds
- Strength of management.

Each issue will find that its investment case focuses on a unique combination of the above. One of the goals of pre-marketing is matching the investment case with investors who are most likely to be receptive to the particular story.

A major facet of most investment cases is the quality of management. Quality of management is a prerequisite for an investment bank to agree to take on an assignment. It is equally important to the investment case. It is usually presented as the last point in any presentation made by management, but for many investors, the perceived abilities of senior management are paramount in their decision making.

Other points will touch on the market in which the company competes. Its growth, long-term prospects, competition . . . essentially, 'Is this an attractive market or market segment to be in?' Even seemingly unattractive, low-growth industries can be made attractive from some perspective. Knowing the size of the market and potential market share is crucial in building the investment case, particularly for younger companies.

The company's product or service is the next point. Management must be able to describe what the strategy people call its 'sustainable competitive advantage'. Sometimes being first to market is sufficient. Many of the technology companies that went public during 1997–1999 claimed that one of the key reasons to invest was because they had 'first-mover advantage'. This was particularly true in the very crowded e-retailing space, and may have had some validity.

Many privatization offerings made much of the ability of the company to become more efficient after leaving government control. A utility's growth prospects may not be great – national GDP or so – but if it can continue to pump out the same amount of electricity with one-third fewer employees, investors should benefit from increased earnings.

Financial history is important. Showing steadily increasing revenues and profits will attract investors. During hot new issues markets, where extremely young companies are able to float, the business concept or model can be sufficient for investors. However, for old economy companies in normal times, investors will look to historic growth and margins that can be maintained or improved in the future.

The use of proceeds is another important component of most investment cases. A company with a clearly defined use of proceeds will raise money more easily than a company that is going to the market with no clear use in mind.

Finally, most investment cases include a statement regarding the attractive valuation of the new issue. As stated earlier, most IPOs are priced at a 10 to 15 per cent discount to the issuer's peer group. The ability to acquire a sizeable stake in a company with an attractive future, at a discount to the expected market price of the shares, is a convincing factor for many institutions.

For an offering to be successful, the issuer and banking syndicate must ensure that investors receive a consistent message in research reports, telephone calls, roadshow presentations and, to the extent possible, in the prospectus.

### *Preparing the market*

Once the research analysts, bankers and company have worked out the investment case, pre-marketing to investors may commence.

The goal of the pre-marketing period is to increase the awareness of the issuer in the eyes of investors as well as to elicit feedback from selected investors regarding the investment story and possible pricing of the issue. Readers should note that pre-marketing of share offers in the USA is severely curtailed by the SEC, compared with activities that are possible elsewhere in the world.

### *Objectives of pre-marketing*

The main objectives of the pre-marketing phase are to:

- Highlight and discuss investment case with potential investors.
- Create maximum investor awareness of transaction prior to management roadshow.
- Collect and analyse investor feedback.
- Fine tune valuation/price range.
- Fine tune investment case.
- Identify key target investors for one-on-one meetings.

Investor relations and public relations professionals will work the phones to the business editors of the daily press to ensure that press releases describing the company and its business receive prominent placement. In markets where television advertising is possible and the deal is large enough, 15- and 30-second commercials are prepared. The adverts' goal is usually to entice retail investors to register for a prospectus or to tell them where a prospectus may be obtained.

### *Scale of pre-marketing*

The scale of pre-marketing activities will depend on the size of the issue. An IPO worth $100 million in a well-known sector requires much less time and effort than an $8 billion privatization. For most large capitalization IPOs (i.e. market cap following offering greater than $1 billion, offer size greater than $250 million), pre-marketing will cover between 25 and 75 investors, depending on the home market. For billion dollar plus offerings, pre-marketing activity will be cranked up significantly, with calls made to upwards of 150–200 institutions.

During the period each member of the syndicate will try to get its analysts to meet with as many of the top targeted investors as possible. Since all members of the syndicate participate in the pre-marketing, investors can feel deluged by calls regarding the offer. For large offerings, major institutions will often make it known that they wish to talk to only two or three analysts.

If the company going public is one of the first in its industry sector to do so (or the first company to join the market in a long time), the research analysts at the lead bank(s) may publish a sector report two or three months prior to the offering. The sector report will cover the industry structure, statistics regarding industry growth, main players, intensity of competition, industry returns, etc. The client company will be mentioned, but really only in passing, at the same time as its competitors are. The sector report is really a background paper for interested investors to review.

Depending on the size of the offering and the bank the analyst works for, a series of presentations on the sector may follow. This is to get institutional investors warmed up to the idea of investing in a company in the sector. If the sector is really new, the bank may approach two or three of the institutions with which it is closest and discuss the possible offer in greater detail. The institutions that play a part as 'pilot fish' will expect to receive favourable allocations when the deal comes to market.

The use of 'pilot fish' is more prevalent in fixed price offers when the lead bank and brokers are less certain of the valuation to place on the company. As the offer approaches, research analysts from all the senior banks in the syndicate will publish research reports on the company (where permitted). The reports don't have recommendations on them like buy, hold or sell. But you can bet that the only message is buy. This major research piece will discuss the business of the company, its competitive position, strategy, financial performance and future prospects. Depending on the market and the offering, the analyst may also include some fairly detailed valuation work using a variety of methods as described in Chapter 5.

On publication of the detailed company report, the analyst at each syndicate member will make a presentation to his bank's institutional equity sales force. During this presentation, the analyst will present the investment case and supporting details to the sales team. S/he will give to the salesmen a two- to four-page crib sheet with the most important details (such as the timetable for the offer) that should be covered in phone calls to investors. The crib sheet will usually be drafted by the ECM team and reviewed by the research analyst.

Following the presentation, the salesmen will pepper the analyst with questions; questions they expect their clients to ask. The Q&A session is useful preparation for the analyst prior to visiting institutional investors during formal marketing.

After the research report has been distributed to investors, the sales team will follow-up to try to determine initial indications of interest. They will also ask whether the institution would like a call or visit from the analyst, or a one-to-one meeting with the company. In large offerings, this information is transferred to a form, as illustrated in Figures 9.1 and 9.2. In smaller offerings, this information will be fed verbally or electronically to the head of sales and the syndicate desk, eliminating the paperwork.

The elapsed time for the process described above can vary considerably. Large offerings take longer. In small offerings in jurisdictions where there are no research blackouts, the time between issuing research, formal marketing and pricing can be as short as one week to 10 days. Where research blackouts exist, and in larger offerings, the elapsed time will expand, although the pre-marketing rarely lasts more than a month as building and sustaining momentum is important to a deal's success.

### *Pre-marketing feedback*

The most important part of pre-marketing is the feedback provided by investors. Using investor feedback, the lead manager(s) will report back to the issuer and selling shareholders regarding:

- market conditions,
- investor reaction to investment case including attractions and concerns, and
- price range recommendation.

Representative pre-marketing feedback forms are included as Figures 9.1 and 9.2.

| **COMPANY NAME**<br>Pre-marketing Feedback Form | |
|---|---|
| Investor: | Syndicate Member: |
| City: | Date of Call: |
| Fund Manager: | Date of Visit: |
| Fund Type: | |
| PERCEPTIONS OF COMPANY | |
| Positives: | |
| Concerns: | |
| Valuation Views: | |
| Other Comments: | |
| Possible Demand: | Amount (€ million) |

**Figure 9.1** Sample pre-marketing feedback form (1)

### *Management presentations*

For many executives, the presentation that they make on the roadshow is the first public speaking that they've done since primary school. Another part of the pre-marketing process is bringing management's presentation skills up to snuff. No-one expects rhetoric on the level of Winston Churchill, but the importance of the roadshow to a deal's success is such that only a foolish bank would let the chief executive and finance director meet investors without preparation.

The first draft of the 20–25-minute investor presentation will be prepared by management and the investment bankers who have been working on drafting the prospectus. They will use the prospectus contents as a guideline for the content of the presentation. Professional presentation advisors and speech coaches may be hired to polish the presentation.

The executives need to stay focused on the investment case that has been developed and not be diverted by tangential questions.

### *Setting the price range or the price*

The final aspect of pre-marketing in a bookbuilding offering is setting a price range to be used to guide investors during the marketing period. The lead manager(s) will adjust their valuation thoughts based on the feedback received during pre-marketing and on overall market conditions. In US prospectuses, a price range (agreed between the company and issue managers) is included on the cover of the prospectus. This is

Company Name

| | |
|---|---|
| Investor | Interaction |
| City/country | Visited with analyst |
| Fund manager | Called with analyst |

| Assets under management | US$ m | Current weighting |
|---|---|---|
| Total | | |
| Total in equities | | Negative Neutral Positive |
| in <country> equities | | |
| in <sector> stocks | | |

| Investment strategy | |
|---|---|
| Index tracker<br>Asset allocator/top down | Stock picker/bottom up<br>Sector |
| Benchmark | |
| Investment restrictions | |

| Perception of <company> |
|---|
| Major attractions/concerns |
| Comments |
| Follow-up |

| Investor requests one-on-one meeting Yes/No | |
|---|---|
| Possible interest | Valuation views |
| Amount | |
| Bank | Please return continuously, but no later than ..................... to: |
| Tranche | |
| Analyst | <regional bookrunner> |
| Location | <contact> |
| Phone/fax/e-mail | <fax/e-mail> |

**Figure 9.2** Sample pre-marketing feedback form (2)

commonly known as the price talk. In other jurisdictions, the price range may or may not be printed in the prospectus – it may simply be used by the syndicate's sales teams when talking with investors.

Depending on the type of offering, the price range or the price will be set after pre-marketing. In a bookbuilding exercise, a price range is set, while in a fixed priced underwriting, the final price is set.

Most agree that bookbuilding offers the following advantages over a fixed price offer:

- Allows company and investment bank to fine tune the offering price.
- If there is great demand, the price range can be raised.
- If low demand the price range can be lowered.
- If the former, maximize proceeds of the offering, if the latter, ensure that the offer gets away successfully.

A fixed price offer, on the other hand, ensures that the company/selling shareholders will receive a set amount of proceeds and will know the amount several weeks prior to closing.

## Formal marketing

The timing and extent of formal marketing activities varies somewhat, depending on the offer's price-setting mechanism (auction, bookbuilding, fixed price). Formal marketing commences with the printing and distribution of a preliminary or pathfinder prospectus. The prelim includes all the information required for an investor to make a decision, except the price of the shares.

In most fixed price offers and auctions, the pre-marketing and marketing periods are used to determine institutional interest and an appropriate price. Once the price is set, the issue is underwritten, and institutions and individual investors submit their orders during an offering period that usually lasts between three days and three weeks. Most small fixed price offers, say below $50 million in value, use only one 'final' prospectus with the price included. Large fixed price offers may use a preliminary prospectus.

If one of the goals of pre-marketing is to create a 'buzz' around the offering, the formal marketing is meant to intensify the buzz and convert interest into orders. The amount of time given to this depends on the size and complexity of the offering. Table 9.3 sets out the main milestones in the offering process.

Compared with pre-marketing, the formal marketing period is more compressed. The shortest might be five days to two weeks during a hot new issues market, while the longest might range up to six weeks for a global offering of shares with an extensive roadshow. The start of the formal marketing period is usually driven by the documentation teams – as soon as they are ready to file a preliminary (pathfinder) prospectus, the marketing team cranks up.

In the 1998 IPO for Brokat Infosystems, a German technology company launched an extremely successful IPO, using a compressed schedule. Five days of 'pre-marketing' commenced on August 31. Two days after a weekend break, the company began its roadshow. Brokat executives and bankers from Dresdner Kleinwort Benson

| Publication of research | Sales briefings | Analyst pre-marketing | Company roadshow | Analyst follow-up | Retail marketing |
|---|---|---|---|---|---|
| ■ Contents focus on introducing and positioning the company in the market<br>■ Valuation<br>■ Distribution to all target investors | ■ Sales force briefed by lead research analyst<br>■ Briefing enables pre-marketing meetings to be set up and roadshow schedule to be firmed up<br>■ Future briefings address any concerns that arise | ■ Analysts visit major institutions to discuss the investment case and valuation<br>■ Analysts and salesmen provide investor feedback that helps in setting the price range<br>■ Feedback also identifies concerns to be addressed at the roadshow<br>■ Identify potential core investors | ■ Vital – a bad roadshow can kill a deal<br>■ Investors need to meet management before placing order<br>■ Potential core investors meet the company on a one-to-one basis to maximize order conversion<br>■ Smaller investors seen at group meetings and lunches | ■ Analysts and salesmen follow up roadshow meetings<br>■ Analysts to answer any questions, calm any reservations<br>■ Salesmen take orders to submit to bookbuilding | ■ Through bank branch network<br>■ Through stockbroker network (USA and Canada)<br>■ Presentations to retail sales teams in key cities<br>■ Manage the press coverage |

**Table 9.3** The marketing process

and Paribas shuttled between eight European cities during the next five business days. Bookbuilding began on September 10, the day after the roadshow began in Frankfurt and continued until after the final presentation in Zurich. The offering was more than 20 times subscribed, and priced at the top of the DM53–DM64 per share range, raising DM141 million ($83.5 million).

Nearly as short was the marketing period for IPSOS, a French market research company that was floated on the Paris Stock Exchange in 1999. A research report was published by the analysts at SG Securities, the lead manager, on June 4. The IPO was formally announced 10 days later on June 14. Investor meetings were held in major European centres as demand was assessed in the bookbuilding process. Formal marketing complete, the company's management and investment banks agreed to set the final price of the offering on June 25. Shares in IPSOS started trading on July 2, not quite one month following the commencement of formal marketing.

For smallish offerings, one to two weeks will be sufficient to get the message across to investors and collect indicative orders. For the jumbo offerings raising multiple billions, three to six weeks might be necessary. A number of factors will influence the length of the marketing period:

- size of offering (the larger, the longer);
- number of 'tranches' (the more, the longer);
- number of competing offerings in the market;
- hard deadlines (e.g. end of government's financial year for privatizations).

## *Roadshows*

The most time consuming part of formal marketing is the management roadshow. US domestic offerings usually take two weeks to cover the American market alone. They add another week if management is expected to visit key institutions in Europe and/or Asia. Small European offerings will take less than one week, hitting the major European centres, while larger offerings will spend one week in Europe and one week in America. The largest offerings will add a further week to cover the Middle East and Asia.

Three weeks is the maximum length that is desirable, as the issue managers want to keep the deal fresh in the minds of potential investors, and the roadshow will leave the executives physically drained. Where timetables make it impossible to cover all the ground necessary, sometimes two roadshow teams are sent out simultaneously. British privatizations regularly sent two teams to market the shares. The first would cover the UK and Europe, and the second North America and Asia.

The roadshow generally kicks off with a presentation to the lead manager's sales force. Just as the analyst's presentation to the sales force is used to work out bugs and prepare for questions, so does the management presentation.

The roadshow combines presentations to an audience of potential investors at lunch and dinner, with small-group and one-to-one meetings with the most important potential investors. Presentations will be made to audiences that range in size from 5 to 200.

The lead manager of each tranche arranges the timetable, and sets up most of the one-on-ones. In many European offerings, the co-lead managers may be allocated some one-to-one slots, where they are able to invite key clients to meet the issuer.

During the roadshow presentation, the company will try to convey the investment case as persuasively and dynamically as possible. Institutions will ask questions following the presentations – and management must be prepared for all potential questions. Institutions don't like waffle – they want short, precise answers to their questions. Likely areas that investors will query are included in Table 9.4. If they aren't covered in the presentation, be ready to be quizzed.

1. What does the business do and what is its vision (mission statement)?
2. What are the main profit drivers in the business?
3. How is the business doing? What is its recent track record?
4. What is the strategy in terms of technology, products, markets and the delivery of shareholder value?
5. How will the product and market strategies be realized?
6. What is the financial strategy and according to what financial criteria is the business managed and controlled?
7. What are the key management and reporting structures?
8. How does the company compare against its domestic and international peer groups, in terms of products and market penetration as well as financial structure and performance?
9. What is the outlook and what are the key internal and external factors that might affect the business in the future?
10. Why should an investor buy the company's shares?

**Table 9.4** What institutions want to know from company presentations

The standard presentation lasts from 20 to 25 minutes and may include a brief corporate video complete with dramatic images and stirring inspirational music. The role of the presentation is to ensure that the investment case is delivered to an audience that may or may not be familiar with the industry or the company. Not all the points listed in Table 9.4 can be covered in a 20–25-minute presentation. The art lies in touching on the most relevant points for a particular company at a particular point in time.

One potential drawback of the big presentation format of the roadshow is when 'one person has a valid concern and stands up and voices it, all of a sudden 100 people who never would have thought of it are worried' (Bruck, 1988: 179). On the other hand, many investors prefer to ask their questions in the private one-on-ones. They don't want other potential investors to free ride on the information they glean from management.

Despite their name, one-on-ones are never as small as two people. There may be only one investor on his side of the table, but the company's side will be crowded. Either the CEO or CFO or both will be in attendance, together with a research analyst or salesman from one of the banks, and possibly a corporate financier or ECM staffer. The latter are in the room to put a damper on what the issuer's management might say, especially in the USA.

One-on-ones involve a bit of game playing, where the investor tries to extract additional information from management that hasn't appeared in the prospectus. In particular, they are interested in future projections. Giving in to an investor's requests for additional information can be dangerous, as the case of Webvan Group illustrates:

> 'During the Webvan roadshow, the financial press became aware that the story being told in the roadshow included financial projections not included in the preliminary prospectus. According to press reports, the SEC required Webvan to include the financial projections in their registration statement and recirculate the preliminary prospectus to all investors, and further imposed a one-month "cooling off" period before allowing Webvan to go public.'
>
> (Greenstein et al., 2000)

In recent years, 'webcasts' have been broadcast over the Internet. In the USA, the SEC permits webcasts to be viewed on password protected sites by potential 'syndicate members and others who might normally be expected to be invited to a roadshow'.

The choice of roadshow itinerary will vary with the type and size of the offering. The location of the issuer's headquarters will also have an influence. If an issuer is based in Florida, for example, Miami and St Petersburg/Tampa may be added to the cities visited.

Table 9.5 contains cities typically visited by issuers and their bankers. Figure 9.3 illustrates funds under management in major centres. One executive described his

| **Europe** | **USA** | **Asia/RoW** |
|---|---|---|
| *Primary cities* | *Primary cities* | *Primary cities* |
| London | New York | Hong Kong |
| Edinburgh/Glasgow | Boston | Singapore |
| Paris | Chicago | Tokyo |
| Geneva | San Francisco | |
| Zurich | Los Angeles | |
| Frankfurt | Toronto | |
| *Secondary cities* | *Secondary cities* | *Secondary cities* |
| Amsterdam | Atlanta | Abu Dhabi |
| Stockholm | Bahamas | Bahrain |
| Madrid | Baltimore | Sydney |
| | Denver | |
| | Houston | |
| | Kansas City | |
| | Milwaukee | |
| | Minneapolis/St Paul | |
| | Philadelphia | |
| | San Diego | |

**Table 9.5** Roadshow cities

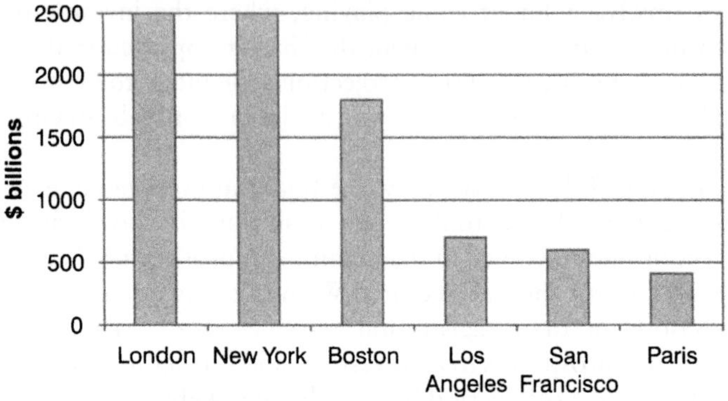


**Figure 9.3** Funds under management

roadshow experience as a 'two week death march' after 60 meetings with over 200 investors across the country. He was lucky, his roadshow only visited US cities. Add in multiple jet lag, air traffic control delays and other impediments to international travel and he really would have felt like death by the end of the roadshow.

The day after the roadshow leaves town, the sales teams will follow-up with investors who had attended the presentation. The call is to determine whether there are any remaining questions, and to take orders. This is the commencement of bookbuilding.

When bookbuilding in a US public offering, salesmen are allowed only to 'solicit expressions of interest'. The formal order may only be taken when the price has been set and the SEC has approved ('declared effective') the prospectus. The orders placed during bookbuilding may be altered at any time that the books are open. An investor can increase or decrease the number of shares he wants, or raise or lower the price he is willing to pay. Members of the syndicate make daily submissions of new orders and any changes to existing orders to the bookrunner. Figure 9.4 contains a sample bookbuilding form.

Date: ______________________

Syndicate member: ______________________

Tranche: ______________________

Name: ______________________

Telephone: ______________________

Fax: ______________________

Email: ______________________

To: <Regional Bookrunner>

Attn: ______________________

Fax: ______________________

| Date | Investor or Fund Manager | Investor Type | Investor Nationality | Investor Quality | N, C, I, D or L | Order Amount (indicate S, A or Currency) | | Price Limit | Delivery S or A | Comments (e.g. aftermarket behaviour, comparable holdings) |
|---|---|---|---|---|---|---|---|---|---|---|
| | | | | | | Previous amount if I/D/L/C | New Total (cumulative) | | | |
| | | | | | | | | | | |
| | | | | | | | | | | |
| | | | | | | | | | | |
| | | | | | | | | | | |
| | | | | | | | | | | |
| | | | | | | | | | | |

*Investor Type:*

MF Mutual Fund
PF Pension Fund
IN Insurance
AM Asset Mgt/Private Bank
CO Corporate
BK Bank
IM Independent Investment Mgr
CH Charity
BD Broker/Dealer
RE Retail
OT Other

Investor Quality:
To be ranked from 1 (highest) to 6

*Delivery Type:*
S = ordinary share, A = ADS

*Share/ADS ratio:* 10 shares = 1 ADS

*Order Type:*
N = new; C = cancelled; I = increase; D = decrease; L = price limit amended

**Figure 9.4** Sample bookbuilding demand form

# 10 Syndication and fees

According to the *Palgrave Dictionary of Money and Finance*, a syndicate is a 'temporary venture that contracts with a seller to place its securities'. Syndication techniques were used by the Bank of England as long ago as 1694, and some features can be traced back to the latter part of the Middle Ages.

In Chapter 2, we quoted Chen and Ritter (2000: 1120): 'Historically, syndicates existed partly for regulatory capital requirement and risk-sharing purposes, and partly to facilitate the distribution of an issue . . . Today, there is little reason to form a syndicate to perform the traditional roles of risk sharing, distribution, and meeting capital requirements.'

While their point is valid, syndicates continue to be formed to market and distribute IPOs. However, perhaps reflecting Chen and Ritter, syndicates for large global offerings are now smaller than they were in the early 1990s. As the investment banking industry has globalized and participants become larger, individual firms have much more capital at hand and far larger distribution networks. To illustrate, in 1991 the Wellcome Trust employed over 50 banks in multiple syndicates for a £2 billion secondary offering of Wellcome plc shares. Ten years later, the Trust hired one bank to place some £1.8 billion of GlaxoSmithKline (the successor company) shares in an accelerated bookbuilding.

In the UK, the traditional triumvirate of sponsor and two brokers, supported by a small army of sub-underwriters, is giving way to international-style syndicates with multiple managers assisting in the distribution.

The first part of this chapter looks at modern syndicate structure, size and composition. The second part examines fees payable by issuers and their distribution among the banks involved in an offering.

## The value of syndication

As Chen and Ritter imply, for most IPOs of moderate size, a single investment bank, or at most two, would be able to take on the risk and be able to distribute the shares to a broad range of investors. However, all but the smallest transactions are sold via a syndicate of banks. IPOs typically have larger syndicates than do secondary offerings, while bought deals and accelerated bookbuildings tend to be limited to one or two banks.

From the issuer's perspective, assembling a syndicate adds value in a number of ways:

- Distribution
- Competition
- Motivation

- Credibility
- Communication.

Employing more than one bank cannot help but increase the distribution. Although all of the top international banks say that they know all the important institutions globally, each bank does not necessarily have strong relationships with all the institutions. Syndicates are usually comprised of firms with global distribution capabilities as well as smaller regional or industry specialist firms. The global firms will be the lead manager/bookrunner/global coordinator, while the regional firms take a less prominent role in the offering.

For example, the 1996 IPO of Danish pharmaceutical firm Neurosearch employed UBS as global coordinator and bookrunner. Carnegie AB (a Nordic region specialist) acted as Scandinavian lead manager and co-lead manager for the rest of the world, a position it shared with Unibank (a Danish bank).[1] This structure ensured coverage of all main Nordic investors, including Danish retail via the two junior syndicate members, while UBS concentrated on the larger European and international investors.

Investment bankers are competitive: inviting a number of banks to participate in a syndicate should, theoretically, lead to a stronger selling effort on everyone's part. In reality, this will vary by deal and can be significantly influenced by the relative number of senior and junior roles in the syndicate, the fee structure and distribution of fees.

Invitation into the IPO or secondary offering syndicate may be necessary to provide banks with the motivation to supply ongoing research coverage. Research analysts are expensive and secondary trading is not lucrative. Fees from financings are necessary to ensure that a bank earns a return on its research effort.

If all members of the syndicate are motivated, the issuer benefits. In recent years, motivation of junior syndicate members has been a concern. Through the mid to late 1990s, the lead managers were increasingly seen to be 'hogging the fees', leaving little monetary reward for those not in control, and therefore little motivation to work the deal. In the latter part of this chapter we will examine how the distribution of fees within a syndicate affects the motivation of syndicate members.

By including high-profile, prestigious investment banks in the syndicate, an issuer provides credibility (or certification in academic jargon) to investors. Many believe that investors prefer to buy offerings from more credible banks. This seems to have been the case during 1980–1998, when IPOs managed by prestigious investment banks were less underpriced than other offerings (see Chapter 2). To put it another way, prestigious banks were able to achieve higher prices for their issuing clients. However, during the Internet bubble, the relationship between prestigious investment banks achieving fuller prices for their issuing clients disappeared. It is unclear how investment bank certification will affect post-bubble IPOs.

A well-organized syndicate will present a consistent message to the investment community, while providing investors with more than one perspective. Communication during the offering and afterwards is two-way. The banks present the selling story to the investment community as well as providing feedback regarding investor response to the bookrunner and the issuer.

[1] *International Financing Review* 1135, 1 June 1996.

## Syndicate selection

The kingpin of the syndicate is the bookrunner. The bank that runs the books is closest to the issuer and controls the allocation of shares to investors. By controlling the allocations, the bookrunner is in a position to favour itself and the orders it has obtained to the detriment of other syndicate members.

Once the bookrunner has been appointed, it and the issuer decide on the rest of the syndicate. The syndicate structure and number of members depend on the size and nature of the transaction and the country of origin. Co-lead and co-managers are not involved in the legal and documentation aspects of the offering. They are invited into the syndicate to add distribution by selling to as many potential investors as possible and to provide a research following for the company after the issue.

Selection for membership in syndicates is based on much the same criteria as for the selection of the lead manager, as described in Chapter 2. The weighting of each factor will differ for each deal, but will be based on the following:

- Research capability
- Distribution capability: global or regional
- Sector expertise
- Track record, credentials
- Client relationship
- Aftermarket commitment.

In many of the largest offerings, the issuer may appoint joint bookrunners. This is particularly the case in privatizations, where the senior local bank and senior international bank are often given joint responsibility.

Several south-east Asian privatizations of the mid-1990s had as many as four joint bookrunners. There is no evidence that the issuer is better served by multiple bookrunners, and in some circumstances multiple bookrunners can damage the success of an issue. In particular, it is not unknown for one bank to withhold information from the other bookrunners and for bankers to spend more time on how they are perceived by the issuer than on the success of the issue. Some believe that the use of multiple bookrunners leads to a loss of accountability. By the end of the decade it was rare to find an offering boasting more than two joint global coordinators.

## Syndicate structure

An international offering is typically divided into tranches: the domestic tranche, where shares are sold to investors in the company's home market, and one or more international tranches.

In the early days of international equity offerings it was not uncommon to have up to a dozen separate international tranches, each devoted to a single country or geographic region. Banks participating in the Italian tranche of an international offering, for example, could sell only to investors in Italy. Current practice is to limit the number of tranches in order to allow the global coordinator more flexibility in allocating shares where demand is greatest (we will discuss the allocation of shares in Chapter 11).

Large European equity offerings now typically have three or four tranches: domestic; United States (either public offer or Rule 144a); and Rest of World (RoW). Some European and Asian offerings establish a separate tranche for UK investors. Occasionally, a separate continental European tranche is included.

Smaller offerings will have but one tranche, with syndicate members concentrating on the domestic market and selected international investors. Most US offerings worth more than $100 million have two tranches: domestic and international, with the domestic tranche taking 80 per cent to 90 per cent of the shares. Other offerings sell to international investors out of a single domestic tranche.

### *Global syndicates*

In recent years, a few offerings have made use of a global syndicate: where there are no separate tranches and the syndicate members sell shares in whatever market they find demand (subject to local regulatory restrictions). This approach was first used in the third British Telecom privatization offering in 1993. Only a handful of international offerings have followed suit. Many bankers believe that global syndicates work better for secondary offerings of companies that already have an investor following.

### *Syndicate terminology*

While the functions of the syndicate and syndicate members are the same in US and international offerings, the names given to the roles differ – sometimes confusingly so. Participants in a syndicate are called managers internationally and underwriters in the USA. Within each international syndicate, there is a hierarchy, adapted from the Eurobond market: lead manager, co-lead manager, co-manager. As you would expect, those at the top of the hierarchy, the lead managers, earn more from the transaction than those at the bottom.

There can be more than one bank at each level of the hierarchy, and this is usually the case. Large syndicates are built like pyramids, with a few banks at the top (lead managers), more banks in the middle (co-lead managers), and many banks at the bottom (co-managers). Small syndicates may do away with the co-manager level altogether.

US syndicates have slightly different names for the different 'brackets' in which an investment bank participates in a domestic offering. In particular, the term co-manager has a different meaning in international offers and US offers. A co-manager in an international syndicate is the most junior tier, while in the US, managers (or collectively, co-managers) comprise the top tier.

Underneath the co-management group come several brackets of underwriters. In order of precedence they are: bulge or special bracket underwriter; major bracket underwriter; sub-major bracket underwriter; and underwriter. The lowest tier of participants in an equity offering syndicate is the selling group. Selling group members do not underwrite any of the offering, but may be included to help distribute the offering.

Each tranche of a multi-tranche offering will have a lead manager. In such cases, an overall lead manager is appointed, called the global coordinator. The global coordinator will normally be part of the syndicate in every tranche where it is licensed

| International | United States |
| --- | --- |
| Bookrunner/global coordinator | Bookrunner/lead manager |
| (Regional) lead manager | Co-managers |
| Co-lead managers* | Underwriting group<br>■ major bracket<br>■ sub-major bracket<br>■ underwriter |
| Co-managers* | Selling group† |

*The co-lead manager and co-manager roles can be subdivided into senior and junior, depending on the underwriting commitment assigned/taken on.
†Selling groups have no part in the management or underwriting of an offering, so do not receive the portion of the commission that is allocated for those purposes.

**Table 10.1** Typical syndicate hierarchy

to sell securities. However, it may not be the lead manager of a particular tranche if its local presence is limited.

In the early days of international offerings, the local lead managers were the bookrunners of their tranche. This allowed a high degree of flexibility in the allocation of shares according to local standards and customs. Over time, the global coordinator has become the overall bookrunner, controlling allocations in each and every tranche.

The bookrunner, or global coordinator, is responsible for the documentation (in conjunction with the lawyers), due diligence, organizing the roadshow and other tasks. It also controls the order book (hence the name), and has the final say on the allocation of shares to investors and therefore is able to favour investors that place orders with it. There is fierce competition among investment banks to be the bookrunner on transactions.

In industry jargon, bankers are fighting to be 'top left' on the prospectus or in the tombstone published after the deal. The bank whose name appears in that position is seen as the most senior bank in the syndicate, whether it has called itself the global coordinator, lead manager or bookrunner. See Figure 10.1.

## *Syndicate size and composition*

As you would expect, the number of syndicate members varies directly with the size of the offering. There are, however, a number of other factors that positively influence the size of a syndicate:

- *IPO:* syndicates are typically larger than syndicates for secondary offerings of similar size. This is done to help ensure a broader distribution and to encourage future research coverage by the banks in the syndicate.

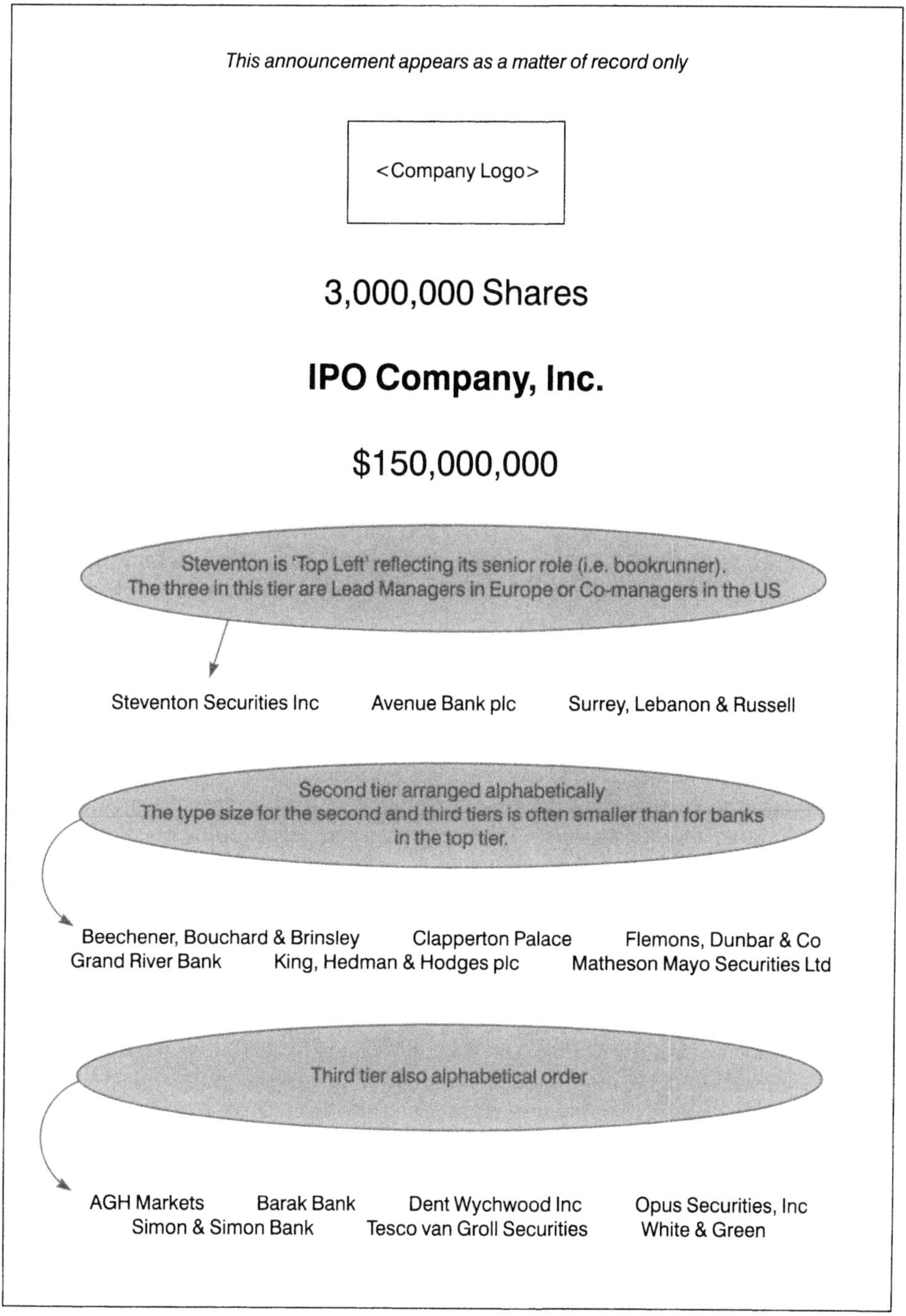


**Figure 10.1** Sample tombstone advertisement

- *Retail orientation:* if an offering is expected to have a large retail investor component, the size of the syndicate will be larger. Because there are a limited number of institutions, the addition of syndicate members will not necessarily increase the number of orders from institutions, because all institutions are covered by numerous banks. Most retail investors, on the other hand, give their business to one financial advisor. The retail-oriented brokers and banks are usually included in lower positions in the syndicate (co-manager internationally or underwriter or selling group in the USA).
- *Broader distribution:* when offering shares internationally, syndicates will be larger. Although the major global investment banks have relationships with most major investing institutions, regional banks and industry specialists will have relationships with those institutions that are too small for the global banks. These institutions can be an important source of incremental demand.
- *Privatizations:* because most privatizations are large, have a retail orientation, are IPOs and require broad distribution, their syndicates are larger than average. Finally, most governments try to include a large number of domestic banks and brokers in privatizations, contributing the larger syndicate sizes.
- *Market conditions:* in turbulent market conditions, syndicates tend to get larger. In the two years following the 1987 market crash, offerings that would previously have been handled by one or two banks were syndicated to include four or five banks in order to spread the risk. At the same time, underwriting risk was spread more widely within the syndicate.
- *Fees and commissions:* if the fee level is low, the lead manager is likely to favour a smaller syndicate, in order to allow all syndicate members to make an adequate return on their effort (see following section for more discussion).
- *Risk of issue:* if the issue is perceived to be particularly risky, the syndicate will be larger than for an issue that is expected to run smoothly.
- *Issuer/selling shareholders' wishes:* ultimately, the vendor or company has the final say in establishing the syndicate. If the company has a large number of banking and financial relationships, it will tend to want to reward those banks with whom it has a relationship and include them in the syndicate.

From the bookrunner's perspective, a small syndicate is easier to control and the information flow is more efficient. As one syndicate manager put it, 'A tighter syndicate works much better than a multi-tranched group. The leads will have greater control over marketing and there's a more efficient information flow. You can confer real responsibility on banks in smaller syndicates. In larger groups, responsibility is more widely spread. There is a real direct relationship between remuneration and effort employed' (Dean, 1997).

Chen and Ritter (2000) looked at the composition of the senior level of US IPO syndicates (co-managers in US jargon). They found that the number of manager syndicates comprising four or more managers doubled from 3 per cent of moderate sized ($20m to $80m) IPOs in 1985–1987 to 6 per cent for the period 1995–1998. For large IPOs (above $80m), the proportion of large syndicates increased from 28 per cent of IPOs in 1985–1987 to 51 per cent of large IPOs in the period 1995–1998.

While the bookrunner and co-lead managers (co-managers in the USA) are selected by the company or selling shareholders, the composition of the remaining syndicate is often left to the discretion of the bookrunner. Privatizations are a notable exception, as governments tend to be closely involved with the appointment of the entire syndicate.

These members of the syndicate are usually invited on an informal basis several weeks before the offering (although the type and size of transaction will have an influence on the timing of the full syndicate composition). For example, in a large transaction that will require significant selling effort on the part of each syndicate member, they may be invited at an early stage in order for their research analysts to have time to investigate the company and issue a report, where permitted.

On the launch of the transaction (i.e. just before the roadshows commence), the bookrunner will send an 'invitation telex' containing details of the offering to all members of the syndicate.

### *Sample syndicate composition*

This section presents two representative syndicates and the proportion of the offering underwritten by each bank. In late 2001, Prudential Financial Inc. 'demutualized' and conducted an IPO that raised approximately $3.5 billion through a syndicate of 47 banks and brokers. Table 10.2 contains the syndicate members of the US tranche.

Agfa-Gevaert's 1999 IPO raised €1.54 billion through the sale of 70 million shares at €22.00 each. The offering employed a syndicate that was 13 members strong (see Table 10.3). Deutsche Bank and Goldman Sachs were appointed joint global coordinators of the offering. There were four co-lead managers and seven co-managers. The co-manager tier was divided in two, with senior co-managers underwriting 2.1 million shares while junior co-managers underwrote 1.4 million shares. The composition of the syndicate was weighted towards European banks, in particular those from Belgium and Germany, where simultaneous public offerings were launched.

In an underwriting syndicate, the shares underwritten are the notional liability of each bank. On signing of the underwriting agreement, each bank and broker must be sure to have sufficient regulatory capital in place to meet the underwriting liability in full. If, in the two examples given, the deals had been complete flops, with not a single share sold to investors, the banks would have had to buy the number of shares that they committed to in the underwriting agreement. So, for example, Dresdner Bank would need to have sufficient capital in place to support a potential liability of €46.2 million (2.1 million shares at €22.00 each) from the time the underwriting agreement was signed (at pricing) to closing.

While the bookbuilding process was developed to minimize underwriting risk, so that the hypothetical situation of a 100 per cent flop would not happen, fixed price offers do fail occasionally, and the managers of the issue are required to take up some or even most of their underwriting commitment.

In such cases, syndicate members do not actually take possession of the shares they are responsible for. The bookrunner will hold the shares until it sees a market opportunity in which it can distribute the remaining shares to investors. This may be

| Bank | Shares underwritten | Role |
|---|---|---|
| Goldman, Sachs & Co. | 19 109 063 | Bookrunner and lead manager |
| Prudential Securities, Inc. | 8 175 000 | Co-lead manager |
| Credit Suisse First Boston Corp. | 6 540 000 | Senior manager |
| Deutsche Banc Alex Brown, Inc. | 6 948 750 | |
| Lehman Brothers, Inc. | 5 722 500 | |
| Merrill Lynch, Pierce, Fenner & Smith, Inc. | 6 540 000 | |
| Morgan Stanley & Co., Inc. | 5 559 000 | |
| Salomon Smith Barney, Inc. | 5 559 000 | |
| The Williams Capital Group, L.P. | 6 131 250 | |
| Banc of America Securities LLC | 2 248 125 | Junior manager |
| Bear, Stearns & Co., Inc. | 2 145 937 | |
| Blaylock & Partners, L.P. | 2 248 125 | |
| First Union Securities, Inc. | 1 635 000 | |
| Ramirez & Co., Inc. | 1 962 000 | |
| UBS Warburg LLC | 1 226 250 | |
| ABN AMRO Rothschild LLC | 500 000 | Major bracket underwriter |
| Allen & Co., Inc. | 500 000 | |
| BNY Capital Markets, Inc. | 500 000 | |
| A.G. Edwards & Sons, Inc. | 500 000 | |
| HSBC Securities (USA), Inc. | 500 000 | |
| Edward D. Jones & Co., L.P. | 500 000 | |
| Keefe, Bruyette & Woods, Inc. | 500 000 | |
| BMO Nesbitt Burns Corp. | 500 000 | |
| Putnam Lovell Securities, Inc. | 500 000 | |
| RBC Dain Rauscher, Inc. | 500 000 | |
| Robertson Stephens, Inc. | 500 000 | |
| Sandler O'Neill & Partners, L.P. | 500 000 | |
| Sturdivant & Co., Inc. | 500 000 | |
| U.S. Bancorp Piper Jaffray, Inc. | 500 000 | |
| Wells Fargo Van Kasper LLC | 500 000 | |
| Advest, Inc. | 250 000 | Underwriter |
| M.R. Beal & Co. | 250 000 | |
| Chatsworth Securities LLC | 250 000 | |
| City National Bank of New Jersey | 250 000 | |
| Doley Securities, Inc. | 250 000 | |
| Gerard Klauer Mattison & Co., Inc. | 250 000 | |
| Guzman & Co. | 250 000 | |
| J.J.B. Hilliard, W.L. Lyons, Inc. | 250 000 | |
| Jackson Securities, Inc. | 250 000 | |
| Legg Mason Wood Walker, Inc. | 250 000 | |
| Loop Capital Markets LLC | 250 000 | |
| The Malachi Group, Inc. | 250 000 | |
| May Davis Group, Inc. | 250 000 | |
| McDonald Investments, Inc. | 250 000 | |
| Ormes Capital Markets, Inc. | 250 000 | |
| Muriel Siebert & Co., Inc. | 250 000 | |
| Utendahl Capital Partners, L.P. | 250 000 | |

**Table 10.2** Prudential's IPO syndicate

| Bank | Shares underwritten | Role |
|---|---|---|
| Deutsche Bank | 23 100 000 | Joint global coordinator |
| Goldman Sachs | 15 400 000 | Joint global coordinator |
| Commerzbank | 4 900 000 | Co-lead manager |
| DG Bank | 4 900 000 | Co-lead manager |
| ING Barings | 4 900 000 | Co-lead manager |
| Salomon Brothers | 4 900 000 | Co-lead manager |
| Banque Nationale de Paris | 1 400 000 | Co-manager |
| BHV | 1 400 000 | Co-manager |
| Credit Suisse First Boston | 2 100 000 | Co-manager |
| Dresdner Bank | 2 100 000 | Co-manager |
| Westdeutsche Landesbank | 2 100 000 | Co-manager |
| Générale Bank | 1 400 000 | Co-manager |
| KBC Securities | 1 400 000 | Co-manager |

**Table 10.3** Underwriting commitments of Agfa-Gevaert's IPO

several weeks after the offering. Any loss on the sale of the shares is apportioned among the syndicate members according to their underwriting commitments.

The number of shares underwritten also forms the basis of the payment of a portion of the commission, as discussed next.

## Fees and commissions

In international offerings commissions of 3 to 6 per cent are common for corporate IPOs. Privatizations typically carry lower commissions, as do secondary offerings of both corporate issuers and privatized companies. Usually, the larger the offering, the lower the percentage commission. In international offerings, it is not uncommon for the managers to pay their own expenses, including legal fees and stabilization costs out of the commissions. In larger offerings, and in privatizations, the issuer may make a contribution to the managers' expenses.

Other costs payable by the issuer include legal and accounting fees, regulatory and stock exchange fees, marketing costs and printing costs. These fees will vary by market, and to some extent by the size of the issue. For example, regulatory and stock exchange listing fees vary directly with the size of the issue, but rarely exceed 0.25 per cent to 0.35 per cent of the proceeds.

In all, the other costs will amount to between $500 000 and $5.0 million. The costs will be at or above the higher end of the range if complex corporate restructuring is required, or if multiple public offerings are undertaken. The greatest costs incurred are when the issuer decides to list its shares on one of the US stock markets. This causes two firms of Wall Street lawyers to be hired (one for the issuer and one for the banking syndicate). The other major incremental costs are the costs involved in the reconciliation of the company's financial statements from local GAAP to US GAAP if a public offering is contemplated.

As competition among investment banks has intensified to win mandates for large international IPOs, so has downward pressure on the level of commissions. The big exception to this pressure is the American market, where the standard commission for small to medium-sized ($20m to $80m) IPOs has remained solid at 7 per cent.

## *'The Seven Percent Solution'*[2]

During the 1990s, as commissions in international offerings, particularly privatizations, fell, the gross commission or spread on US IPOs has tended towards 7 per cent (see Table 10.4). The number of deals with a 7 per cent spread (as the underwriters' commission is called in the USA) increased from approximately 20 per cent of all IPOs in 1985 to 77 per cent of all IPOs in 1998.

| | $20–80m Proceeds | | | $80m+ Proceeds | | | All IPOs | | | Number |
|---|---|---|---|---|---|---|---|---|---|---|
| | <7% | 7% | >7% | <7% | 7% | >7% | <7% | 7% | >7% | |
| 1985–87 | 46% | 26% | 28% | 76% | 12% | 12% | 52% | 23% | 25% | 512 |
| 1988–94 | 14% | 75% | 11% | 90% | 10% | 0% | 31% | 60% | 9% | 1255 |
| 1995–98 | 5% | 91% | 4% | 71% | 28% | 1% | 20% | 77% | 3% | 1436 |

*Source:* Chen and Ritter (2000).

**Table 10.4** Clustering of US underwriting commissions

Incredibly, the number of medium-sized IPOs with the gross spread set at 7 per cent hit 94.6 per cent in 1998. Only nine IPOs raising between $20 million and $80 million in 1998 deviated from 7 per cent: six were lower while three were higher.

The fees for marketed secondary offerings are not nearly so uniform. In the USA, secondary offerings typically attract a spread of 5 per cent, although the fees range from approximately 3.5 per cent to as high as 7 per cent.

Some industry participants have feared that the investment banking arms of commercial banks/universal banks would try to 'buy market share' by reducing fees. This does not appear to be the case, at least in the US market, where commissions for issues between $20 million and $80 million by the securities arms of commercial banks were 6.99 per cent on average, marginally lower than IPO commissions in deals lead managed by investment banks between 1995 and 1999 (Roten and Mullineaux, 2001).

[2] The title and information in this section are taken from Chen and Ritter (2000), The Seven Percent Solution, *Journal of Finance* 59 (3), 1105–1131.

### *Fees outside the USA*

Despite the fact that investment bankers in the USA have maintained such high fees in their domestic market (or maybe because of this), US investment banks have been some of the most aggressive price cutters in the international market. In particular, banks are extremely 'flexible' in setting the fees for privatizations in the hopes that leading high-profile transactions will give them an entrée to the corporate market in that country.

During the early part of the 1990s, fees dropped significantly, particularly for large emerging markets privatizations. In 1993, Credit Suisse First Boston accepted 4 per cent on the global offering of the Argentine oil company YPF. This was deemed (at least by bankers) to be fair compensation for the effort involved in bringing a developing market oil company to market. By 1996, the rate bid to win the mandate to privatize a Brazilian mining conglomerate, an equally complex task, had dropped to 1.91 per cent.

European privatization IPOs typically were set at around 3 per cent during the 1980s and 1990s. Secondary offerings for privatized companies carried commissions between 50 basis points and 100 basis points less. Corporate transactions in most European markets are slightly more lucrative to the arranging banks. Fees range from a low of 2 per cent in traditional-style UK offers to 5, and occasionally 6, per cent for bookbuilt offers.

### *Traditional UK fee structure*

Historically, the fee for underwriting equity new issues in the UK was 2 per cent, divided into three parts:

| | |
|---|---|
| Underwriting | 0.25% |
| Broking | 0.50% |
| Sub-underwriting | 1.25% |
| Total | 2.00% |

Prior to 'Big Bang' in the UK in 1986, traditional merchant banks and stockbrokers were largely employee owned and had relatively small capital bases. Combined with a 'hard underwriting' period of 5 to 15 days for public offerings, the merchant banks that were the primary underwriters for nearly all offerings had to find a method to minimize their balance sheet risk. This they did through the mechanism of sub-underwriting.

In sub-underwriting, City institutions agreed to purchase any shares that were not purchased in the offering. For this, they were paid a standard fee of 1.25 per cent of the amount that they sub-underwrote. As these City institutions were largely the purchasers of flotations, they found that the sub-underwriting arrangements were an attractive way of reducing the cost of the shares they acquired in the offering.

The standard 2 per cent commission continues to be used in the UK for traditional underwritten offerings, but many British IPOs have adopted bookbuilding and international-style syndicates with higher fees.

## *Components of the syndicate's commission*

> 'For every minute we spend negotiating the gross spread with the client, we probably spend well over 20 times negotiating the split of the gross spread among the various underwriters and co-managers.'
>
> Timothy Main, Equity Syndicate at JP Morgan (quoted in I. Picker, No more sticky fees, *Institutional Investor*, September 1998, p. 30)

Fees for US and international equity offerings typically have three components:

- Management fee
- Underwriting fee or commission
- Selling commission or selling concession.

The most common split among the three components is management (20 per cent), underwriting (20 per cent) and selling (60 per cent). Occasionally, an offering will split the commissions as management (20 per cent), underwriting (30 per cent) and selling (50 per cent).

During the 1990s, the average fee split for US IPOs was management (20.82 per cent), underwriting (21.79 per cent) and selling (57.39 per cent). As the size of an offering increased, so did the tendency towards the 20/20/60 fee split (i.e. larger offerings tended to have a higher proportion allocated to the selling concession) (Torstila, 2001).

The underwriting and management fees are paid based on the notional amount of stock that the syndicate member agrees to underwrite, while the selling fee relates to the amount of stock the syndicate member actually places.

The selling concession is paid out on closing of the offering, while the management and underwriting fees are paid in the months following the offering (usually within 90 days), after all the expenses of the issue have been tabulated.

### The management fee

The management fee is meant to compensate the bookrunner and other lead managers for the work they put into organizing the IPO, including structuring the offering, conducting due diligence, drafting the prospectus, dealing with regulators, organizing the syndicate, managing the roadshows, etc. The allocation of the management fee can be done in one of two ways:

- As a proportion of the underwriting commitment (most common in international offerings)
- Divided among the lead managers (co-managers in the USA) as determined by negotiation amongst the lead managers and possibly the issuer.

Occasionally, a *praecipium*, or 'step-up', is paid to the bookrunner to compensate it for the extra effort expended in managing the offering. Traditionally, the *praecipium* ranged from 20 per cent to 50 per cent of the total management fee. Although not common, I have included a *praecipium* in the examples to illustrate how it affects the distribution of fees to other syndicate members.

If, for example, the total commission was 5 per cent, the portion allocated to the management fee would be 1 per cent of the value of the deal. Assuming a $100 million deal, the total management fee would be $1.0 million. If a 20 per cent *praecipium* was in place, the bookrunner(s) would receive $200 000. The remaining $800 000 would be divided among all the managers (including the bookrunner) according to their proportionate underwriting commitment. So, if the bookrunner underwrote 50 per cent of the offering, it would receive 50 per cent of the $800 000 plus the $200 000 *praecipium*, for a total management fee of $600 000.

### The underwriting fee

The underwriting fee is paid to compensate managers for the underwriting risk. In bookbuilding offerings, as we have seen, this risk is minimal. All expenses, including those related to stabilization (see Chapter 11), incurred by the managers in the completion of the offering are deducted from the underwriting fee before it is paid.

Usually, less than one-quarter of the underwriting fee remains to be distributed to the managers in small to medium-sized offerings. In jumbo offerings, a greater proportion of the underwriting fee will remain after the managers' expenses have been paid.

### Selling concession

Finally, the remainder of the commission is allocated to the selling concession. Almost all IPOs have selling concessions between 50 per cent and 60 per cent of the total commission.

If the syndicate includes a selling group, members of the selling group are eligible only for the selling concession relating to the shares that they have sold, but not any management or underwriting fees. Selling groups are an occasional feature of US offerings, but rare in international offerings.

In its purest form, the selling concession is paid to the bank that brings in an investor's order. The bookrunner has significant discretion on the allocation of shares and hence the selling concession among syndicate members. Over time, refinements to the allocation of the selling concession have been made. We will discuss these after looking at a basic example of a fee calculation.

## *Distribution of fees within syndicates*

That the lead manager/bookrunner should receive the highest fee from an IPO or secondary offering is not disputed. After all, it does the most work on the deal, both from an investment banking (documentation) perspective and in terms of sales and research (marketing). Torstila (2001) surveyed a small number of American syndicate professionals regarding the typical apportionment of fees to the lead manager/ bookrunner within an offering syndicate. On average, the lead manager received 61 per cent of the management fee (range: 50 per cent to 70 per cent); 52 per cent of the underwriting fee (range: 35 per cent to 60 per cent); and 72 per cent of the selling concession (range: 60 per cent to 90 per cent). We believe that the allocation of equity offering commissions to lead managers of international offerings is similar.

The remainder of this section works through a couple of examples as to how the fee apportionment calculation works under different systems.

### Illustration of distribution of fees

The following example looks at a possible fee distribution for a medium-sized corporate offering. It assumes the following:

| | |
|---|---|
| Issue price | €15.00 |
| Number of shares | 10 000 000 |
| Value of issue | €150 million |
| Commission per share: (gross spread) | 5.00% (€0.75 per share) |
| Total commission: | €7 500 000 |

The management, underwriting and selling fees are split in the most common manner:

| | | | |
|---|---|---|---|
| Management fee: (prior to *praecipium*) | 20% | €1.5 million | (€0.15 per share) |
| Underwriting fee: (prior to expenses) | 20% | €1.5 million | (€0.15 per share) |
| Selling concession: | 60% | €4.5 million | (€0.45 per share) |
| | 100% | €7.5 million | €0.75 per share |

Total fees available for distribution to the syndicate members are illustrated in Table 10.5. For completeness, it assumes that there is a 20 per cent *praecipium* to the lead manager and syndicate expenses are $1.0 million.

As Table 10.5 illustrates, after adjustments for the bookrunner's *praecipium* and expenses of the offering, the selling concession forms, by far, the largest component of the fees available to syndicate members.

#### *Example*

To keep things simple, we will look at only two members of the syndicate, the bookrunner and a co-manager. In this example, the bookrunner has an underwriting commitment of three million shares (30 per cent of the offering) and a co-manager has an underwriting commitment of 500 000 shares (5 per cent). Let's say that the

| | Gross fee (€) | Per share |
|---|---|---|
| Management fee | 1 500 000 | |
| *Praecipium* (to bookrunner) | (300 000) | |
| Management fee available to syndicate | 1 200 000 | €0.12 |
| Underwriting fee | 1 500 000 | |
| Syndicate expenses | (1 000 000) | |
| Underwriting fee available to syndicate | 500 000 | €0.05 |
| Selling concession | 4 500 000 | €0.45 |
| Total fees to the syndicate (excluding bookrunner's *praecipium*) | €6 200 000 | €0.62 |

**Table 10.5** Total fees available to the syndicate

bookrunner placed five million shares with investors, while the investors to whom the co-manager sold shares received an aggregate of 75 000 shares. See Table 10.6.

The largest component of the bookrunner's compensation (73.5 per cent) comes from the selling concession. In almost all offerings, the distribution of the selling concession among managers is the most important aspect of a firm's total compensation.

| Fee | Amount per share (€) | Bookrunner | | Co-manager | |
|---|---|---|---|---|---|
| | | Share basis | Total (€) | Share basis | Total (€) |
| Management | 0.12 | 3 000 000 | 360 000 | 500 000 | 60 000 |
| *Praecipium* | – | – | 300 000 | – | – |
| Underwriting | 0.05 | 3 000 000 | 150 000 | 500 000 | 25 000 |
| Selling | 0.45 | 5 000 000 | 2 250 000 | 75 000 | 33 750 |
| Total | | | 3 060 000 | | 118 750 |

**Table 10.6** Example 1: Fee distribution

## *Allocation of the selling concession*

Given the importance of the selling concession to a bank's remuneration from a deal, it is not surprising that there is considerable debate and negotiation over its allocation. The approach to the allocation of the selling concession has changed over time, with new methods designed to overcome the shortcomings of their predecessors. The remainder of the chapter examines different approaches to the allocation of the selling concession in international and American offerings.

The early days of international bookbuilding (1983–1995) experienced selling frenzies as 20 salesmen from 20 banks contacted every investor they knew to solicit orders. This meant that the largest institutions would receive 5, 10, or even 20 calls about the same deal. While frustrating for investors, the process could wreak havoc with the bookrunner's attempts to understand how the deal was proceeding.

Institutions had a choice to place their order with one bank or split their order among some or all of the syndicate members. Some institutions were scrupulous about distributing 'split orders'. CDC, a major French investor, would often split its order so that every syndicate member received at least a small order from CDC.

In order to secure a decent allocation in popular deals, institutions would regularly place orders with several different syndicate members. So if Capital Research believed that a deal was going to be four times subscribed, it might place an order for 100 000 shares with four different syndicate members in the hopes of ending up with a total allocation of 100 000 shares.

Prior to the early 1990s, syndicate members would submit orders to the bookrunner in bulk form – they did not disclose from whom they had received orders. In syndicate jargon, there was no 'visibility': the bookrunner would be unaware of the investor behind the order. This made the bookrunner's job extremely difficult in determining actual demand. Occasionally offerings that appeared to be several times oversubscribed would plummet in the aftermarket, because the oversubscription double, triple and quadruple counted orders from the same institution.

To resolve this problem, bookrunners began to demand 'visibility' of all orders over a certain value (around $250 000). Later in the decade, many offerings required the investor's name on all orders, even from retail investors. While the visibility of orders helped, it did not fully resolve the problem.

The system of split orders works as long as the syndicate is not too large and the deal size is manageable. As European deals got larger – remember the largest IPO was ENEL's €18 billion blockbuster – syndicates got larger and it became difficult to keep track of the underlying orders.

## Designations

In an effort to simplify the process, Euro offerings adopted a US practice known as 'designation'. Under the designation system, the investor places one order – usually, but not necessarily, with the bookrunner – and tells the bookrunner that it wants to split the commission on its order amongst several banks in the syndicate. Figure 10.2 is a sample designation form as used in a multi-tranche IPO.

Institutions will make designations between or among different syndicate members to reward the banks for ongoing research coverage of the secondary market or to help to ensure favourable allocations of shares in future offerings where the syndicate member is bookrunner.

**XYZ Co. Global Offering**

Confirmation of Selling Concession Designation

To: <Investor contact>
<Investing institution>
<Fax>

From: <Syndicate Member/Contact>
<Fax/telephone/email>
<Date>

Thank you for the order received for shares in the XYZ Co. global offering of shares. Please confirm that you wish the selling concession to be designated as set out below and advised to us by these managers.

This form will be confidential to the Regional Bookrunner for your tranche and the Global Co-ordinators of the global offering. Syndicate members will only see their own share of the designation.

| Manager | Share of Selling Concession |
|---|---|
| ______________________ | ________% |
| ______________________ | ________% |
| ______________________ | ________% |
| ______________________ | ________% |
| ______________________ | ________% |

Signed: ____________ Name: ____________ Date: ____________

Please return to: <Regional Bookrunner>
<Fax/email>

**Return at the latest of the closing of books**[1]

[1] Some issues require the designations to be made prior to allocations (as this form), others require investors to make designations after allocations (given 24 to 48 hours to complete the form).

**Figure 10.2** Sample designation form

For example, an institution places an order for 1 000 000 shares and designates as follows:

| | |
|---|---|
| Bookrunner | 50% |
| Bank A | 30% |
| Bank B | 10% |
| Bank C | 10% |

If the selling concession amounted to €0.45, and the institution received an allocation of 300 000 shares, the commissions that each bank would receive are illustrated in

Table 10.7. If designations are made prior to the allocation of shares, the bookrunner may be tempted to give larger allocations of shares to investors who have designated the bookrunner rather than other syndicate members. It is not unknown for salesmen to call institutions and tell them that their allocation will be increased if the designation is changed to favour the bookrunner.

To address this situation, some offerings allocate the shares prior to asking institutions for designations. In such instances, the 24 or 48 hours following allocations resemble the old-style sales frenzy with salesmen from all syndicate members begging, cajoling, threatening institutions for favourable designations. Thus the feeding frenzy described above is postponed to the days following pricing, rather than during the bookbuilding period.

| Bank | Allocation to investor | Proportion (%) | Notional shares sold | Commission/ share (€) | Total (€) |
|---|---|---|---|---|---|
| Bookrunner | 300 000 | 50 | 150 000 | 0.45 | 67 500 |
| Bank A | 300 000 | 30 | 90 000 | 0.45 | 40 500 |
| Bank B | 300 000 | 10 | 30 000 | 0.45 | 13 500 |
| Bank C | 300 000 | 10 | 30 000 | 0.45 | 13 500 |

**Table 10.7** Selling concession designation

The designation system did not solve all the problems. Refer again to Figure 10.2. Note that an institution's designation is disclosed only to the regional bookrunner and the global coordinator. Unless it checks directly with the institution, a junior syndicate member will be in the dark as to its designation.

Checking designations is vitally important: sometimes the bookrunner(s) will only pay out the selling concession on designations that the junior syndicate member has claimed. That is, a co-manager will be asked, 'What designations did you receive on this deal?' If the co-manager's response misses a designation that it was unaware of, an unscrupulous bookrunner (and there are some) will be tempted not to pay that commission.

An additional problem for co-lead and co-managers is knowing the monetary amount of the designated selling concession. A syndicate member may know that it has received a 30 per cent designation on an Institution A 500 000 share order and therefore be able to calculate its share of the selling concession. However, unless the syndicate member knows how many shares were actually allocated to Institution A, it is unable to calculate the amount of selling concession that it deserves.

## Pre-agreed economics

To address these shortcomings, the syndicates in some offerings agree on the allocation of the selling concession prior to sales commencing. This is another US practice, and is known by the inelegant phrase 'pre-agreed economics'.

One of the most common ways to share the selling concession is to divide it among each bank in proportion to its underwriting commitment. Other divisions can also be negotiated.

To return to the example, under the pre-agreed economics method fees would be distributed as illustrated in Table 10.8. In this example, assume that the shares are being offered exclusively to institutional investors and that the syndicate has agreed to share the selling concession according to the proportion of shares underwritten. The bookrunner's total earnings from the deal drop by nearly 30 per cent, while the co-manager's compensation increases by slightly more than 160 per cent.

| Fee | Amount per share (€) | Bookrunner | | Co-manager | |
|---|---|---|---|---|---|
| | | Share basis | Total (€) | Share basis | Total (€) |
| Management | 0.12 | 3 000 000 | 360 000 | 500 000 | 60 000 |
| *Praecipium* | – | – | 300 000 | – | – |
| Underwriting | 0.05 | 3 000 000 | 150 000 | 500 000 | 25 000 |
| *Selling* | *0.45* | *3 000 000* | *1 350 000* | *500 000* | *225 000* |
| Total | | | 2 160 000 | | 310 000 |

**Table 10.8** Distribution of fees under pre-agreed economics

Few international offerings operate on a full 'pre-agreed economics' basis. For example, an offering could allocate 50 per cent of the selling concession on a pre-agreed basis and 50 per cent on a 'jump ball' basis. Jump ball, a term highjacked from basketball, means that syndicate members compete for the designation of the selling concession. Every deal is different and there seems to be no standard split between pre-agreed economics and jump ball.

## Institutional pot

The pot system is a North American approach to selling new issues to institutional investors. The bookrunner is the only bank in the syndicate that solicits orders from the main institutional investors. In Canada, this group of institutional investors forms the 'Exempt List', which is included in all 'Agreements Among Managers'. The institutions will make designations among the managers and underwriters as described above.

The bookrunner(s) will decide the proportion of the offering to be allocated to institutions, usually around 65 per cent of the total (see the following chapter). Syndicate members compete for the retail orders that comprise the balance of the offering. In North America, syndicate members do not provide visibility for retail orders – they submit aggregate demand figures to the bookrunner. Similarly, on allocation, each syndicate receives shares for its retail order book with no direction from the bookrunner as to their distribution in most deals.

Under such a system, retail orders do not come entirely from individual investors. They include orders from smaller institutions and those large institutions seeking 'top-ups'. A 'top-up' order is an order placed with a syndicate member (not the bookrunner) in the retail portion of the offering by a major institution. The top-up order does not form part of its 'institutional pot' order and is only placed in hot deals as a way of increasing their total allocation.

Institutions that have placed top-up orders with a syndicate member may base the designations of their 'pot' orders on the number of shares that they receive as a top-up. For example, Institution M places a top-up order of 25 000 shares with each of Morgan Stanley and CSFB. On allocation it receives 6000 shares from Morgan Stanley and 2000 shares from CSFB in addition to its pot allocation. In designating the selling concession to be paid to Morgan Stanley and CSFB, Institution M may favour Morgan Stanley, because of the higher allocation of its top-up order.

When the prospectus is declared effective and allocations made by the bookrunner, the bookrunner should circulate to the rest of the syndicate the allocations made to investors in the pot. Many offerings allow institutions to make their designations for up to 48 hours after the allocations have been made. Thus there is a mad scramble by syndicate salesmen to contact the institutional investors to ensure a high designation on their order.

In reality, most bookrunners hold back the pot list for 24 to 48 hours. If the bookrunner holds back the pot allocation list it may lose fewer designations than if the syndicate knew the allocations right away. The pot system is not used in European offerings.

## Capped fees

In response to junior syndicate members' complaints about lead managers hogging the fees, since 1999 some offerings have imposed a cap on the proportion of total fees a lead manager can claim. The cap has usually been around 60 to 70 per cent. This helps to create an incentive for junior members of the syndicate to procure quality orders.

For example, a deal has one lead manager (bookrunner) and two co-lead managers. The lead manager has agreed to cap its fees at 70 per cent of the selling concession, no matter how many shares it actually places. Thus the two managers are competing for 30 per cent of the total selling concession.

To continue, let's say that the bookrunner allocates 97 per cent of the shares to orders it has brought in, 2 per cent of the shares to co-lead 1 and 1 per cent of the shares to co-lead 2. Without capping, the fees earned by the two co-leads would be minuscule. However, with capping, co-lead 1 receives 20 per cent of the selling concession and co-lead 2 receives 10 per cent of the selling concession. Knowing that there are meaningful fees up for grabs helps to provide an incentive to junior members of an IPO syndicate.

In the following chapter we will examine the decision criteria used in the allocation of shares in a new issue to investors.

# 11 Allocation, stabilization and lockups

The final aspects of an IPO are some of the most important in ensuring that a company's launch as a listed company is successful. Allocation ensures that shares are placed in the hands of long-term investors. Stabilization, when used, can mitigate price volatility in the opening days of trading. Imposing restrictions on the sale of shares by existing holders reduces the risk of overhang that might hold back the shares' performance in the secondary market.

## Allocation

Once the securities regulators give the nod, the issuer and bankers set the offering price. In a bookbuilding offer, the lead bank (bookrunner) immediately commences with the allocation of shares amongst the investors who have placed orders. Remember that until the price is set, orders are indicative, not firm. In a fixed price offer, the banks open the subscription period to investors for two days to three weeks, depending on the jurisdiction.

In fixed price offers, there is a risk that insufficient orders for the number of shares on offer will have been placed by the close of the offer. In the UK, this is the point at which the sub-underwriters step in. The sub-underwriters purchase any unsold shares, in addition to any shares that they might have ordered during the offering. This is a relatively infrequent occurrence and most offers are oversubscribed.

In bookbuilding offers, the managers adjust the offering price and number of shares on offer to ensure that there is oversubscription at the time of offering. The advantage of bookbuilding is that the books won't close if the offer is not oversubscribed. The disadvantage, of course, is that the deal might have to be pulled, while an underwritten fixed price offering would not.

Bookbuilding allows the lead manager to maintain a continuous dialogue with the issuer regarding the status of the offering. If the deal is in trouble (i.e. the book is not developing as expected), the price range or number of shares can be reduced. Similarly, if the deal is particularly hot, the price range and number of shares can be increased in most jurisdictions.

So, in the vast majority of new issues, there are orders for more shares than are on offer. The apportionment or allocation of shares among investors who have placed orders is a key element in ensuring the success of an offer. During the allocation process, the syndicate team at the lead manager will work with the issuer and selling shareholders to meet their objectives for the deal.

Common objectives of the allocation process include:

- Maximizing proceeds to the issuer.
- Favouring investors who will become long-term supportive shareholders of the company, known as 'core shareholders'.
- Encouraging a successful aftermarket:
  - Demand from the highest quality accounts will be scaled back as little as possible
  - Aftermarket prices are boosted by core accounts filling their unsatisfied demand
  - Small allocations to short-term investors.

We will discuss two types of allocation. The first is the allocation of shares among tranches: domestic retail, domestic institutional and international tranche(s). Once those decisions have been made, the allocations to the specific investors who have placed orders for shares must be determined. These allocations can be made either on a non-discretionary basis or on a discretionary basis.

### *Allocation among tranches*

At the beginning of the marketing for an offering, investment bankers set notional tranche sizes. They have to decide how many shares are going to be sold in the domestic market and in each foreign market where shares are to be marketed. Many US offerings set aside a uniform 15 to 20 per cent of the deal for international investors without further specifying the allocation. Theoretically, all shares could be allocated to investors in Switzerland, ignoring demand from elsewhere.

Other offerings, particularly privatizations and very large offerings, work out potential demand in each market before deciding on the tranche size. The global coordinator/bookrunner will retain flexibility to resize tranches based on realized demand during the bookbuilding period.

The other decision is to determine how much of the offering will be allocated to retail investors. The percentage will vary with perceived retail demand, institutional demand and international demand for the shares.

#### Retail vs. institutional

In many privatizations, retail investors are 'protected' and the retail tranche is separated from the tranche of shares available for domestic institutional investors. Often a 'clawback' mechanism is used if substantial retail demand is generated. In these cases, the lead manager has the ability to reduce the institutional offering in favour of the retail offering. The bookrunner may increase the retail portion even if there is greater proportionate demand for the institutional offering. In privatizations, retail clawback is seen as a political mechanism, not a syndicate mechanism.

Governments in many European countries were keen on building a 'share owner democracy' during the 1990s and regularly included the clawback mechanism. In fact, institutional investors look to the exercise of retail clawback as a factor in the likely success of the offering.

During the privatization of Spanish airline Iberia, the Government increased the retail tranche from 49.4 per cent to 59.4 per cent of the offering. Therefore, the institutional tranche (both domestic and international) was reduced from 45 per cent of the offering to 35 per cent of the offering. The remainder of the shares were allocated for the airline's employees.

Retail clawback is not universal in privatizations. The second privatization offering of Japan Tobacco in June 1996 featured a ring-fenced international tranche of 30 000 shares (11 per cent of the total). By ring-fencing a tranche, the global coordinator guarantees the number of shares to be offered. This can encourage bankers in the tranche to aggressively court investors, secure in the knowledge that they won't have to disappoint the investors if clawback is imposed.

Retail clawback does not occur in most corporate offerings. The retail allocation is set at the beginning and would only be increased if there was insufficient demand in the institutional or international offering. One exception was the June 1996 IPO from Asia Satellite Telecommunications in Hong Kong. The initial distribution of shares among tranches was: 50 per cent to the USA; 40 per cent internationally; and 10 per cent to Hong Kong retail investors. In structuring the offering, global coordinator Goldman Sachs added a retail clawback of 5 per cent in the event that the retail offering was oversubscribed by more than three times.

Ljungqvist and Wilhelm (2001) examined the allocation patterns between institutional and retail investors across 35 countries and 1015 IPOs between 1990 and 2000. On average, institutions received two-thirds of the shares available, although they found that the level of institutional allocation ranged from zero to 100 per cent. Table 11.1 features information from that study.

They were able to get information about the allocations from the local stock exchanges and securities commissions. However, no similar data is filed in the USA, so the researchers looked at 37 Goldman Sachs offerings for comparative purposes, identified by (L&W) in the table. An earlier study of the US market looked at 38 IPOs launched by an anonymous investment bank (Hanley and Wilhelm, 1995). These are identified as (H&W) in the table. The results are similar. The unweighted average allocation to institutional investors is 66.9 per cent, with the remaining 33.1 per cent going to retail investors.

## Retail investors

Although the vast majority of 'retail investors' are indeed individuals, in many markets, the category includes smaller (generally lower grade) institutions. As noted in Chapter 10, it is not uncommon for large institutions to submit orders to the retail book of many syndicate members. This is in the hope of topping up the order they receive from the institutional offer, as allocated by the bookrunner. The amount of top-up an institution receives from a manager can influence the level of selling concession designation.

The fact that syndicate members don't provide 'transparency' on retail orders (tell the bookrunner the identity of each order) makes this possible. Retail orders are submitted in aggregate by each syndicate member.

During bull markets, retail investors often feel hard done by. They believe that they are excluded from all the hot deals, and left with the dogs while the investment banks

| Country | Number of IPOs | Mean institutional allocations (%) | Mean retail allocations (%) |
|---|---|---|---|
| France | 261 | 68.4 | 31.6 |
| UK | 194 | 74.4 | 25.6 |
| Germany | 109 | 56.4 | 43.6 |
| Italy | 56 | 65.7 | 34.3 |
| Finland | 40 | 76.4 | 23.6 |
| Sweden | 39 | 68.1 | 31.9 |
| Belgium | 35 | 54.0 | 46.0 |
| Netherlands | 32 | 69.6 | 30.4 |
| Spain | 25 | 71.6 | 28.4 |
| Singapore | 56 | 57.5 | 42.5 |
| China | 12 | 69.5 | 30.5 |
| Hong Kong | 11 | 64.8 | 35.2 |
| South Africa | 8 | 37.9 | 62.1 |
| USA (L&W) | 37 | 64.4 | 35.6 |
| USA (H&W) | 38 | 66.8 | 33.2 |
| *Whole sample* | | *66.9* | *33.1* |

*Sources:* Hanley and Wilhelm (1995); Ljungqvist and Wilhelm (2001).

**Table 11.1** Institutional/retail allocations in selected countries

favour the large institutions. Although the perceived favouritism of institutional investors was particularly acute during the late 1990s, it was not a new issue. As long ago as 1992, commentators were likening the status of retail investors as being reduced to that of 'peasant(s) among a cartel of aristocrats' (*Forbes*, 25 May 1992). Two years later, *Business Week* (4 April 1994) estimated that institutional investors purchased 80 per cent of the shares in hot deals, but only 60 per cent of the shares in 'normal' deals.

In a study of retail/institutional allocations, Hanley and Wilhelm (1995) found that allocations are roughly stable at two-thirds of the offer, hot deal or not. They looked at 38 IPOs brought to market by a single (anonymous) American investment bank. Table 11.2 summarizes their findings.

As noted earlier, hot deals that price above the initial range tend to have better short-term performance than issues priced below or within the price range. When looking at the allocations of 'hot' vs. 'cold' deals, Table 11.3 indicates that from a *statistical perspective*, there is no favouritism of institutional investors.

Although the difference between 64.8 per cent and 70.4 per cent may seem large to the reader, because of the small sample size (38 deals), when the researchers applied statistical tests, 'institutional holdings appear to be largely independent of the degree to which an issue is underpriced'.

So, even if institutions are better at picking out deals that will be hot, it appears that they are unable to use this advantage to avoid investing in overpriced offerings.

| | Mean (%) | Median (%) | Standard deviation (%) | Maximum (%) | Minimum (%) |
|---|---|---|---|---|---|
| Institution (domestic) | 50.3 | 53.7 | 15.5 | 77.6 | 5.0 |
| Institution (international) | 16.6 | 14.3 | 9.8 | 40.4 | 0.0 |
| Total institutional | 66.8 | 71.7 | 15.8 | 88.6 | 6.6 |
| Retail | 28.0 | 24.3 | 15.3 | 93.4 | 11.4 |
| External retail | 5.1 | 3.0 | 5.7 | 22.3 | 0.0 |
| Total retail | 33.2 | 28.3 | 15.8 | 93.4 | 11.4 |

*Source:* Hanley and Wilhelm (1995: 242).

**Table 11.2** Distribution of allocation between institutional and retail investors

| | Initial return | | |
|---|---|---|---|
| | <0% | 0% | >0% |
| Number of issues | 9 | 5 | 24 |
| Initial return | | | |
| (average) | –1.7 | 0.0 | 14.7 |
| (median) | –1.4 | 0.0 | 12.7 |
| Percentage sold to institutions | | | |
| (average) | 64.8 | 53.4 | 70.4 |
| (median) | 71.6 | 63.4 | 73.3 |

*Source:* Hanley and Wilhelm (1995).

**Table 11.3** Allocation by initial return

Underwriters have the power to 'make' institutions support poorer offerings by threatening to exclude investors from the next hot deal. At the time of the lastminute.com new issue, a Morgan Stanley official was quoted as saying, 'We have a strong equities pipeline. If institutions misbehave on this deal, they will be punished in the next one.'[1]

One point is often ignored in the debate over institutional favouritism. Almost all large US investment banks and the majority of European and Asian banks have made considerable investment in their retail distribution capabilities. Although a single institution can pass millions in trading commissions to an investment bank, the collective volume of retail trades will be significant. Therefore, banks will always ensure that a proportion of all deals will go to retail investors. They would face a revolt from their stockbrokers otherwise.

[1] 'Last minute.com worth £732m on debut', *Financial Times*, 15 March 2000, p. 1.

### Friends and family

Most IPOs reserve a number of shares for friends and family members of the company's employees. Sometimes called the 'President's List', these people are given preferential allocations at the time of pricing. In deals that are perceived to be hot, there can be an undignified scramble to get on the list. People will call the lead manager, syndicate members, the company accountants – anyone connected with the issue – claiming to be old school friends, long-lost relatives or the CFO's auto mechanic, in the hopes of getting shares.

### Spinning

One of the many bull market excesses that has exercised the wrath of US regulators is that known as 'spinning'. Spinning can be regarded as the extension of preferential allocations as with 'friends and family' shares. The difference is that the lead manager allocates shares to corporate executives who are in a position to direct future lucrative corporate finance business to the lead manager of the IPO.

At the end of 2002, the FSA, the UK regulator was also looking into the practice of spinning and laddering (described above).

### Domestic vs. international

In privatization offerings, favouring domestic investors over foreign ones is accepted as the norm. Non-privatizations tend to be more hard-headed and allocate shares where there is the most demand at high prices. In countries with relatively small domestic equity markets, it would not be uncommon to find the international allocation to be greater than the domestic institutional allocation, or sometimes the entire domestic offering.

| | Allocated to public (retail) (%) | Allocated to Italian institutions (%) | Allocated to foreign institutions (%) | Demand to supply | |
|---|---|---|---|---|---|
| | | | | Public offer (times) | Institutional offer (times) |
| Main Market | | | | | |
| 1995 | 42.3 | 15.6 | 42.1 | 3.3 | 6.8 |
| 1996 | 40.5 | 24.3 | 35.2 | 4.0 | 5.9 |
| 1997 | 31.4 | 24.5 | 44.1 | 9.2 | 9.4 |
| 1998 | 44.4 | 27.2 | 28.4 | 4.5 | 18.0 |
| 1999 | 44.6 | 23.6 | 31.8 | 13.4 | 6.7 |
| 2000 | 48.7 | 26.4 | 24.8 | 2.9 | 4.5 |
| Neuvo Mercato | | | | | |
| 1999 | 27.3 | 32.6 | 40.2 | 28.0 | 9.5 |
| 2000 | 27.2 | 25.8 | 45.0 | 16.6 | 7.5 |

*Source:* CONSOB Annual Report, 2000.

**Table 11.4** Italian offerings summary

Table 11.4 (see page 196) indicates the allocation of shares in Italian IPOs during the period 1995–2000. This indicates the importance of international investors to the success of Italian offerings, largely because of the relatively small size of the Italian market.

The 'Demand to supply' column indicates an average oversubscription of 27 times retail offerings in 1999 – the peak of the high tech IPO boom. (*Note:* The ratio of orders to shares was 28:1, while the level of *over*subscription was 27:1, after the allocations have been made.) Institutions were somewhat more restrained, but the oversubscription of the institutional allocations was 8.5 times.

## *Allocating to investors*

When it comes to using discretionary or non-discretionary means for determining allocations, different markets follow different practices. In Australia, the fixed price offering system with pro rata allocations is the norm. In the UK market, both bookbuilding and fixed price offers are used and both discretionary and non-discretionary methods employed. In German offerings, the bookbuilding process is generally used, but the German Government has said that 'objective criteria' must be used in determining retail allocations. Finally, in the USA and Canada, the bookbuilding approach is coupled with universal discretionary allocation.

### Non-discretionary allocations

Non-discretionary allocations are used mostly in auctions and fixed price offers. In cases of oversubscription, the managers have two options: to scale down allocations on a pro rata basis or make random allotments using a ballot. In a ballot, some or all of the applications may be 'put into a hat' and applications drawn at random to be granted part or all of the shares applied for. Applications not selected are unsuccessful.

In March 2000, Infineon Technologies, the semiconductor business of Siemens in Germany, was brought to market in an equity carve-out. The offering, which was the largest non-privatization IPO in the country, attracted applications from 5.2 million retail investors. The retail demand of €35 billion exceeded total shares on offer by eight times (equivalent to €400 for every German citizen). Siemens, Infineon and their bankers, Goldman Sachs and Deutsche Bank, decided to allocate shares by a ballot, giving shares to one investor in six.

In pro rata allocations, the managers can either take a strict percentage and apply it across all investors or work with various allocation tiers. In the first instance, if orders for 6.7 million shares were collected for 1.5 million shares on offer, each order would receive 22.388 per cent of the shares requested. An individual who placed an order for 500 shares would receive 111 shares ($500 \times 0.22388$) and an institutional order for 65 000 shares would receive 14 552 shares ($65\,000 \times 0.22388$). Very few offers are allocated on a strict pro rata basis.

The March 2000 flotation of Britain's lastminute.com attracted 189 000 retail applicants. The £113 million IPO was oversubscribed by 40 times. Morgan Stanley, the lead manager, decided to allocate 20 per cent of the offering to retail investors, leaving 189 000 investors chasing 6.6 million shares. The company and Morgan Stanley decided to allocate retail investors on a strict pro rata basis: each individual investor received 35 shares, angering most, if not all. Institutional allocations, on the other hand, were done on a discretionary basis.

| Order (shares) | Allocation |
|---|---|
| >100 | number of shares ordered |
| 101–500 | 100 shares |
| 501–1000 | 500 |
| 1001–10 000 | 1000 |
| 10 001–25 000 | 8% of order |
| 25 001+ | 5% of order |

**Table 11.5** Hypothetical allocations

The allocation process used for lastminute.com was somewhat unusual. It is more likely that the managers will work out various allocation tiers. Generally, these tiers provide smaller investors with a larger proportion of their order than larger institutional orders. Table 11.5 is a hypothetical allocation grid.

Bankers have to make hard decisions. Do you anger five of every six investors as in the Infineon IPO, or do you anger every applicant, as in lastminute.com?

In March 1999, EFG Eurobank in Greece found that on closing of subscriptions, orders exceeded shares on offer by 40 times. More than 500 000 domestic investors placed orders in the Dr100 billion ($340 million) offering. It was decided to allocate 30 per cent of the offer to retail investors. The allocation process combined a pro rata system with allotment by ballot. The bankers decided to allocate 10 shares to each retail investor, with the remaining 2.77 million shares allocated by lot.

### Auctions

In auctions, there is no problem regarding which approach to use. Investors who bid for shares at levels above the clearing price receive their full allocations. Investors

| Price ($) | No of shares | Allocation (%) |
|---|---|---|
| 14.25 | 50 000 | 100 |
| 14.00 | 75 000 | 100 |
| 13.75 | 40 000 | 100 |
| 13.50 | 250 000 | 100 |
| 13.25 | 300 000 | 100 |
| 13.00 | 500 000 | 100 |
| 12.75 | 1 000 000 | 100 |
| 12.50 | 1 250 000 | 62.8 |
| 12.25 | 2 000 000 | 0 |
| 12.00 | 1 750 000 | 0 |
| 11.75 | 3 000 000 | 0 |
| 11.50 | 3 750 000 | 0 |
| 11.25 | 1 000 000 | 0 |
| 11.00 | 1 500 000 | 0 |

**Table 11.6** Willy's Wertberters order book

whose bids are at the clearing price exactly receive a pro rata allocation based on the size of their order and the number of shares required to clear the auction. For example, returning to the Willy's Wertberters IPO auction (see Chapter 4), after the marketing period the order book looks as in Table 11.6.

As the table illustrates, bids for a total of 2 215 000 shares were received at prices from $12.75 to $14.25. Of the 1 250 000 bids at $12.50, the company needs only 785 000 to meet its goal of selling three million shares. When allocating shares, the bank would give each investor who bid above $12.50 all the shares they asked for, at the price of $12.50. Those who bid $12.50 per share would receive a pro rata allocation of 62.8 per cent of their order, again at $12.50 per share.

## *Discretionary allocations*

In bookbuilding offerings, discretionary allocations are the norm. While the decision on price is fundamental to the success of the issue, the allocation policy has an important role, not only in the aftermarket, but also in the maintenance of a strong and stable shareholder base. Allocations are generally spread among three or four classes of investor: one or two core investors, other long-term investors, private clients and finally, short-term traders. Short-term traders (or stags) purchase new issues in the hopes of selling the shares immediately for a small profit and provide immediate liquidity in the shares. It is important to control the allocation of shares to the 'flippers' so as to ensure orderly trading during the first few days after issue.

In larger offerings, the syndicate manager at the bookrunner will evaluate the order submission sheets from members of the syndicate (see Figure 9.4). In smaller offerings, syndicate members may simply phone through the orders that they have received, which are then entered into the deal's spreadsheet. In either case, the syndicate manager's first job is to assess the real demand from investors and determine the potential aftermarket interest.

The primary goal of the syndicate manager is to allocate shares to top quality accounts that will be long-term holders of the shares, and who are likely to buy shares in the immediate aftermarket. The allocation of shares in a bookbuilding offering is subject to a number of criteria, some subjective some objective. The basis for allocations will vary offer by offer, depending on the goals of the issuer and the source and type of orders in the book. In no particular order, the following is a list of the most common criteria used by syndicate managers to determine individual allocations:

- Manager's ranking of investor quality
- Price leadership and sensitivity
- Timeliness/order history/consistency with pre-marketing feedback
- Participation in the marketing programme
- Order size (particularly relative to the investor's holding in the sector)
- Aftermarket behaviour.

Investor quality is the most subjective of the subjective criteria. It encompasses many of the other criteria, and often comes down to how long the investor is likely to retain its shareholding. Typical ranking criteria run on a scale of 1 to 6, with 1 being the best:

1 Important long-term investor/opinion leader/strong aftermarket expectations.
2 Consistent long-term investor.
3 Medium-term investor/may have specialist fund.
4 Short to medium-term investor. Possibly no applicable specialist fund.
5 Unknown investment strategy. Aftermarket behaviour unknown.
6 Speculative (i.e. stag or flipper).

Although investment banks may universally rank certain institutions as a 1 or a 6, all the categories in between can be subject to debate. Certain institutions may rank as a 1 for some types of transactions, but 4 or 5 for others. For example, 'value' investors placing orders for 'growth' stocks are likely to be ranked lower than when they bid for shares in the IPO of a 'value' company.[2]

Price leadership and sensitivity refer to whether the investor has placed a limit or step order vs. a strike (or market) order. As noted in Chapter 4, limit and step orders are preferred because they provide the bookrunner with more information. The favourable allocation that follows may be explained as compensation for the information contained in their limit bids (Cornelli and Goldreich, 2001).

Early orders are also ranked more highly than late orders. The bookrunner can place more reliance on the real demand of an order that comes in at the beginning of bookbuilding. If the market believes the deal is going to be hot, investors will pile in with inflated orders – making the determination of true demand more difficult. Similarly, the bookrunner takes comfort if the level of interest is consistent from pre-marketing to the day before pricing.

Many order increases in hot deals are simply made in an attempt to ensure that the investors' allocation will be protected. The syndicate manager is able to place more reliance on the 'actual' demand, evidenced by large early orders, than if the investor turns from lukewarm to red hot during marketing.

Early orders from retail investors are also valued. In Swisscom's privatization IPO in 1998, individuals who registered their interest in buying shares during the pre-registration period were guaranteed an allocation. In order to attract early orders from individuals, Swisscom and many other new issues have offered early orders a discount to the price paid by institutions and individuals who do not pre-register (IFR 1247, 22 August 1998).

Bookrunners believe that investors who have taken the time to attend a presentation or one-on-one are more serious about their demand. If a potential investor asks good (meaning tough, but not difficult) questions and displays a knowledge of the industry and an understanding of the company, it is viewed as a more likely bet as a long-term investor. After all, why do the homework if you intend to ditch the shares on the first day of trading?

During the hot new issues market of 1998, Transtec, a German IT company, listed on the Neuer Markt. Its DM71 million IPO was over 100 times subscribed, leaving the company and its lead manager with a difficult allocation decision.[3] The managers selected only top-tier German and foreign institutional investors and then graded them on the following basis: whether they had met for one-on-ones, had attended

[2] A 'growth' stock is one expected to grow its earnings at a faster rate than the overall market. A 'value' stock is one with a low price/earnings ratio or high dividend ratio.

[3] 'Transtec basks in the demand', *Corporate Finance Capital Markets Quarterly*, Summer 1998, p. 8.

general presentations, or had simply put in an order. All allocations were less than 10 per cent of the shares asked for, but an investor received a higher allocation the more proactive it was. The shares were priced at DM71 and traded as high as DM195 on the first day of trading, before falling back to DM100.

In the lastminute.com IPO, institutional allocations were done on a discretionary basis – how far institutions had 'done their homework' on the company and showed a real understanding of the business model and how they had performed in past Morgan Stanley (the lead manager) deals.

Order size is also a factor in allocations. The bookrunner will look at an investor's order relative to the size of the fund and its exposure to the market sector or country. Outsized orders may be viewed as a signal that the investor is a likely candidate for flipping some or all of its position. On the other hand, large orders, but not 'outsized', can be a signal that the investor intends to make the share a core holding. The syndicate manager will depend on his salesmen to tell him which is the case, understanding that a salesman will be balancing his own self-interest (commission or bonus) with what is good for the deal.

Anticipated support in the aftermarket is an important input into the allocation decision. In order to achieve immediate liquidity and an opening premium, the bookrunner must allocate shares so that there is unsatisfied demand. As investors enter the market to top up their position in a stock, they help to support the share price during the first few days.

Finally, although many syndicate managers will deny it, an investor's history with the bookrunner can be a deciding factor in the size of allocation. Investors who generate significant commissions in secondary trading will usually fare better than those who do not. In addition, if sales designations have been collected prior to allocations, the bookrunner might be tempted to favour investors who have given the bookrunner high designations.

### Directed allocations

In European offerings, the bookrunner tends to control the allocations for the entire offering. If there is a multi-tranche offering, each regional bookrunner will work with the global coordinator to make allocations in their region. The global coordinator and issuer are the only two parties who know where all the shares have been distributed. The regional bookrunners will know the distribution of shares in their region, but in no other region. All other managers will know only where they have placed shares, but not other managers' placements.

In US offerings, the institutional portion is allocated on a line-by-line basis (as above), while the retail allocation is left to individual managers. If the bookrunner decides that institutions will receive 70 per cent of a $100 million deal, it then doles out the remaining $30 million of shares to the other managers, who then allocate the shares to investors who have placed orders with them. Retail allocations tend to favour active traders and participants in a broad range of IPOs, not just the hot deals.

Most US offerings include an international tranche of 10 to 20 per cent of the total offering. The allocation of shares in the international tranche may be done on a line-by-line basis or, more frequently, like the domestic retail tranche. Each co-lead and co-manager receives a number of shares and then distributes them among its investors as it sees fit, with no overall control by the bookrunner.

## Problems with discretionary allocations

During the IPO bubble of 1998–2000, investors became desperate to obtain shares in the hottest deals. As we discussed, IPOs are priced by bankers in order to produce an opening premium of between 10 and 15 per cent. During the bubble, a TMT deal that opened 10 per cent above its offer price was deemed a failure.

We noted that the average one-day premium in German IPOs in 1998 was 80 per cent, in the USA the average peaked at 70 per cent in 1999, while in the UK IPOs opened an average 60 per cent higher than their offer price in 2000. When one-day returns of such magnitude are available, money managers feel under enormous pressure to participate in the offerings and obtain as large an allocation as possible. Institutional investors, particularly in the USA, desperate to receive favourable allotments agreed to pay inflated commissions on other trades or promise to buy the issuer's shares in the market after the offering.

An institutional investor might agree to pay a commission two, three, or even 10 times higher than normal on secondary trades in unrelated securities in order to get a shot at a decent allocation. The typical commission on a secondary market trade in the US market is between three and five cents a share. It was reported that some money managers were offering to pay 50 cents a share on trades the day before particularly hot offerings were priced in order to attract the favourable attention of the syndicate manager.

Fund managers who admitted to the practice justified their actions because the magnitude of returns on the IPO dwarfed the cost of obtaining a favourable allocation. Alternatively, the syndicate boss would extract promises from eager investors to buy more shares in the aftermarket. In a typical arrangement, an investor would commit to buying up to one or two times his allotment up to a pre-agreed price. If the share price soared past the agreed limit (often twice the offering price), the investor would not have to buy any more shares.

Individual investors became particularly aggrieved at missing out on the great returns that the IPOs offered. They had little or no leverage over their brokers, so tended to vent their frustrations in Internet chat rooms, or in the great American tradition, sued their brokers.

During 2001, the SEC began investigating the share allocation practices of US investment banks, particularly at Credit Suisse First Boston's (CSFB's) San Francisco technology group. Ultimately, CSFB agreed to settle with the SEC by paying a $100 million fine, but without admitting liability for anything. At the time of writing, numerous investor lawsuits were pending.

The bull market in Germany, particularly on the Neuer Markt, led to similar protests and subsequent Government action. In June 2000, the Exchange Expert Commission at the Ministry of Finance introduced allocation guidelines for allocations to individual investors. The guidelines were introduced in an attempt to eliminate the use of subjective criteria in determining allocations. They are largely aimed at increasing the transparency of the allocation process. The guidelines recommend that issuers or lead managers draw lots, allocate pro rata (within certain order sizes or across the offer as a whole), allocate according to time priority, or some other 'objective' criteria.

The €1.54 billion IPO for AGFA-Gaevert NV comprised public offerings in Belgium and Germany and private placements in many other countries. The prospectus (page

22) contained information on the basis of allocations for retail investors: 'In the event that the number of Shares is not sufficient to cover all retail purchase orders in the Belgian and German public offerings, the Underwriters reserve the right to refuse orders or accept them only in part. In such case, early subscriptions [made during the first week of bookbuilding] will be given preferential treatment . . . Such partial acceptance shall be made on an objective pro rata basis in accordance with the relative demand among retail investors in Belgium and Germany.'

## Allocations and flipping

No matter how careful syndicate managers are in allocating shares to long-term investors, many of those who receive an allocation, sell (flip) their shares in the first days of trading. Flipping may be motivated by a number of factors:

- Insufficient allocation
- Share price hits target in aftermarket
- Disguised intentions.

In a highly oversubscribed offering, allocations, even to the best investors, may be severely scaled back. If an investment manager has to distribute its allocation across a number of funds that it runs, the amount going to each fund may be minuscule. In such cases, it is not unusual for the manager to sell its entire allocation rather than attempting to build a meaningful position in the stock in the aftermarket.

Other investors may set an anticipated 12-month target return of, say, 30 per cent for the shares. If the stock gains more than 30 per cent on the first day and continues to rise, it is difficult to argue with investors' desire to take profits. This may be exacerbated in heavy new issues markets when attractive deals are being priced on a daily basis. The fund manager may decide to take profits and reinvest in next week's hot deal.

Finally, investors are not always entirely truthful with salesmen, and may indicate a long-term intention while planning to sell in the short-term. Likewise, salesmen are not always truthful with their syndicate managers, suggesting the same thing, but knowing differently. The salesmen have a vested interest as their new issue commission is inflated and they get the trade when the investor decides to sell.

So, flipping exists. What are its implications?

In an article exploring the relationship between investor uncertainty, divergence of opinion and the performance of IPOs, Houge et al. (2001) calculated the 'flipping ratio' of 2025 US IPOs during the period 1993–1996, as summarized in Table 11.7. The flipping ratio measures the trading volume (large blocks of 10 000 shares or more) generated by large institutional investors dumping their share allocation on the opening day. The flipping ratio is measured by dividing the total sales block volume by total share volume from the first day of trading.

The flipping ratio was fairly constant at around 30 per cent over the four years of the study. The ratio was also fairly consistent when looking at the market value of the company's shares, offer price per share, whether the company had venture capital backing and the 'prestige' of the lead manager (we discussed 'prestigious' underwriters and how the classification works in Chapter 2). Unfortunately, the study was conducted before the hot new issues market at the end of the decade. Anecdotal

| Year | Flipping ratio (%) |
|---|---|
| 1993 | 29.3 |
| 1994 | 30.0 |
| 1995 | 28.9 |
| 1996 | 31.1 |

*Source:* Houge *et al.* (2001).

**Table 11.7** Flipping ratio of US IPOs (1993–1996)

evidence suggested that institutions were large-scale sellers in the weeks after IPOs with large price run-ups.

One of the most interesting parts of the study was its examination of the short-run share price performance of IPOs by degree of flipping. The authors divided the sample of 2025 issues into thirds: low flipping, medium flipping, and high flipping. Companies with a low flipping ratio (the bottom third) tended to have a higher first-day return (average 20.1 per cent) than those with a high flipping ratio (average return of 8.6 per cent).

## Preventing flipping

In an attempt to limit allocations of stock to flippers, some US offerings permit the bookrunner to impose a *penalty bid*. Penalty bid provisions are included in the 'Agreement Among Underwriters', also known as the 'Syndicate Agreement', which governs the behaviour of the syndicate members.

Penalty bids permit the bookrunner to reclaim the selling concession from a syndicate member when shares originally sold by the syndicate member are purchased by the bookrunner as part of the stabilization of the share price immediately following the offering.

To illustrate, say Alpha Bank received an order from Prime Investors and Prime was allocated 10 000 shares at the $15.00 offer price. Assuming the standard 7 per cent commission for mid-sized IPOs and a 60 per cent selling concession, Alpha will receive $6300 in sales commission. If Prime sold all its shares in the immediate aftermarket and the bookrunner bought the shares as part of the offering's stabilization, under the penalty bid, the bookrunner could claw back the $6300 selling concession from Alpha Bank.

While commonly found in syndicate agreements, penalty bids are not frequently enforced in deals where prices shoot up. Heavy trading of hot new issues results in increased trading commissions for the managers of the offering. The penalty bid is really designed to encourage long-term holding of poorly received new issues.

By making the penalty bid a feature of the offer, the US bookrunner is attempting to impose discipline on the other members of the syndicate. 'The success of the penalty bid provisions depends on the ability of syndicate members to discourage their investors from immediately reselling shares into the syndicate's stabilizing bid' (Benveniste et al., 1996: 224).

An unusual and extreme attempt to prevent flipping occurred in the UK market during the summer of 2000. Carphone Warehouse, a retailer of mobile telephones and accessories, made its IPO on the London Stock Exchange towards the end of the high tech new issues bubble. The company and its bankers (Credit Suisse First Boston) were concerned about the level of retail stagging (as flipping is called in the UK) in recent TMT offerings. They devised an unusual structure that gave preferential allocation to retail investors who agreed not to sell their shares for three months.

The structure had the result that approximately 11 000 retail applications were made for the company's shares in the £185 million offering, far lower than normal for issues of this size. Eighty per cent of retail investors agreed to the lockup and received 100 per cent of their orders, higher than normal for an offering that was eight times oversubscribed. Those retail investors who did not agree to the lockup received an allocation of 60 per cent of their order.[4] By the time the three-month lockup had expired, the shares had lost 25 per cent of their value, making it unlikely that investors will fall for this ruse again.

## Stabilization

Another feature of international offerings adopted from the USA is stabilization. In stabilization, the lead manager tries to maintain, or stabilize, the price of the shares during the first days of trading. Stabilization is undertaken to facilitate the distribution of shares during the offering period, and typically is allowed for up to 30 days following allocation of the shares.

Following an IPO or secondary offering, heavy trading often takes place in the shares of the issuer, in some cases leading to significant volatility. Stabilization is meant to try to prevent, slow or halt a decline in the price of newly offered shares. As defined by the SEC, stabilization is 'the buying of a security for the limited purpose of preventing or retarding a decline in its open market price in order to facilitate its distribution to the public' (Securities Exchange Act Release 2446, 1940).

Only one manager in the syndicate is permitted to conduct stabilization on behalf of all syndicate members. In almost all instances, this is the bookrunner. Any losses or gains as a result of stabilization are shared among the syndicate according to each manager's underwriting commitment.

When an IPO's shares start trading, the bookrunner will enter a 'syndicate bid' at the offer price. If selling pressure is large enough to preclude buying any shares at the offer price, the lead manager may either decrease its bid to successively lower levels, or cease its efforts at stabilization altogether (Weiss et al., 1993: 178).

To assist in the stabilization efforts, the lead manager may 'overallot' shares (i.e. sell more shares than are being offered) to investors, thereby creating a short position in the market. (That is the lead manager has sold shares that it doesn't own.) If there is weakness in the price of the shares during the offering period, the lead manager can purchase shares in the market to 'fill' its short position, thereby creating demand for the shares and providing support for the market price.

[4] 'Quiet start for Carphone Warehouse', *Financial Times*, 15 July 2000.

To provide the lead manager and the underwriting syndicate with the maximum flexibility to support the offering in the aftermarket, it is typical for the issuer to grant the syndicate an option to purchase shares (the 'overallotment option'). The overallotment option is commonly called the 'greenshoe', reputedly after The Green Shoe Manufacturing Company of Lexington, MA, whose offering in February 1963 pioneered the use of the overallotment option. For trivia buffs, The Green Shoe Manufacturing Company is now part of Stride Rite, a publicly listed company.

This option enables the underwriting syndicate to purchase additional shares (up to 15 per cent of the total offering) from the issuer or an existing shareholder at the same price and on the same terms as the other shares offered in the deal, for a period of 30 days. If the share price rises in the month following the new issue, the lead manager exercises the greenshoe, purchasing the shares and covering its short position. If the share price falls, the greenshoe option would not be exercised, and the lead buys shares in the market to cover its short position.

If the greenshoe is exercised, the number of shares issued or sold increases, as does the amount of money raised in the transaction. This will increase the free float of the company's shares and increase the commissions earned by the bankers. To illustrate, assume the following. A new issue of 3.5 million shares at €10 per share has an overallotment option of 500 000 shares (14.29 per cent). The syndicate underwrites the issue of 3.5 million shares. At the time of allocations, the lead manager allots 4.0 million shares to investors (i.e. sells 500 000 shares that it doesn't own).

### Scenario A

During the immediate aftermath of the offering, the share price drops. In order to stabilize the transaction, the bookrunner buys shares in the market on behalf of the syndicate, hoping to slow or reverse any fall. During the stabilization period, the bookrunner buys 500 000 shares at an average price of €9.50. When stabilization ends, the syndicate delivers shares to investors from whom it borrowed them (i.e. it covers its short). The syndicate earns €0.50 per share, or an aggregate of €250 000 less any expenses incurred during the stabilization exercise.

### Scenario B

In the second scenario, the shares rise above the issue price and stay above €10.00. The syndicate has sold shares that it doesn't own, and under normal market circumstances would have to cover its short position by buying shares in the market and taking a loss. However, the syndicate asks the company for shares in order to deliver them to the investors who have been allotted shares, thus covering the short position without cost to the syndicate. It earns its commission (say 4 per cent) on the extra shares issued – an extra €200 000.

### Covering the short position

The lead manager is faced with a timing problem when it overallots shares in an IPO. When the deal is priced and allocations made, the manager doesn't know whether it will close its short position by making purchases in the market or by exercising the greenshoe. However, it needs to deliver securities to investors on the closing date – usually three or four days after pricing and allocation. Given the standard 30-day period allowed for stabilization, there is a potential problem.

In order to deal with this, the lead manager typically borrows shares from an existing shareholder of the issuer, who is repaid, either with shares purchased in stabilization or shares acquired on exercise of the overallotment option.

### *'Naked shorts'*

Sometimes the syndicate will take a 'naked short' position on the stock, particularly in secondary offerings. A naked short involves selling more shares than the company is issuing, but without recourse to an overallotment option. When the market is volatile, it can be difficult to determine how large the short position should be, and most banks have got it wrong more than once.

In a high profile miscalculation, Goldman Sachs was forced to ask the 16 co-managers of its own $4 billion secondary offering to contribute to the $30 million in costs incurred in shorting its stock in August 2000. Goldman's had established a stabilization pool (short position) in the event of a declining share price. However, the deal was very successful. It was priced at $99.75 and the shares rose to $132 in the month that followed the offering. Because the price rose, Goldman's was forced to buy back the shares at a higher price than that at which they had been sold, causing the loss (Mullan, 2001).

### *Regulations regarding stabilization*

In the USA, stabilization activities are governed by Rule 10b-7 of the 1934 Act. The rule requires the syndicate to disclose in the prospectus that stabilization might occur. For IPOs, the initial stabilizing bid cannot exceed either the offering price or the bid of the highest independent dealer. There is no specific time limit on how long stabilization might last, but the SEC has ruled to 'relatively brief time limits'. Industry practice gives the lead manager up to 30 days to exercise the overallotment option – indicating a maximum period. In fact, most stabilization activities take place in the first few days of trading.

In December 2001, new rules regarding stabilization were introduced in the UK by the Financial Services and Markets Act 2000 (FMSA 2000). While the rules are many, some of the most important are:

- *Disclosure:* the terms of the proposed stabilization must be included in the prospectus.
- *Stabilization period:* begins on the date of the first public announcement of the offer, stating the share price. Ends on the earlier of the 30th day after closing or the 60th day after the date of allotment.
- *Record keeping:* the stabilizing manager must create a register recording each transaction in order to provide an 'audit trail'.
- *Price limits:* the initial stabilizing price (or bid) cannot be higher than the offer price. Subsequent stabilizing bids cannot exceed the initial stabilizing bid unless:

- An independent buyer and seller trade on the company's principal stock exchange at a price that is between the initial stabilizing bid and the offer price. If so, this becomes the new stabilizing price limit.

### *Does stabilization work?*

It is difficult to obtain information on how many offerings are stabilized without asking the managers of the offerings. However, estimates suggest that 10 to 20 per cent of IPOs and secondary offerings are stabilized (Ruud, 1993). This is supported by the observation that 16 per cent of US IPOs close the first day of trading at the offer price. The low figure is partially explained by the fact that most IPOs are priced below the anticipated opening price and that more IPOs and secondary offerings tend to take place in rising markets. Ritter (1998b) suggests that one-third of IPOs are stabilized.

Hanley et al. (1993) examined 1523 IPOs on Nasdaq from 1982 to 1987. In deals where stabilization is believed to have taken place, they found that bid–ask spreads were lower and stabilized offers decline in value after stabilization ends. Ritter (1998b) suggests that stabilized offerings drop by 4 per cent in the first month of trading.

### *Research support for new issues*

Other support comes in the form of research reports. In the USA, syndicate members are precluded from issuing research for 40 days following pricing of an IPO (10 days for a follow-on deal). In the absence of national regulations on research blackout periods in Europe, best practice is evolving that suggests syndicate members should not publish any research for 25 days following the offer.

## The lockup period

Most IPOs and subsequent equity issues feature a lockup agreement among insiders, selling shareholders and the company, on the one hand, and the lead manager, on the other, prohibiting the former from selling any of their shares for a specified period without the lead manager's permission. The terms of the lockup including its expiry date are included in the prospectus.

Lockups are included in order to support the price of the offering during the months immediately after closing. They are meant to:

1 Ensure that shareholders, such as venture capitalists, will not 'dump' shares on the market in the immediate aftermath of the IPO (or subsequent equity offering).
2 'Provide a credible signal that insiders are not attempting to cash out in advance of imminent bad news' (Field and Hanka, 2001).
3 Aid stabilization by temporarily constraining the supply of shares.

If there is a lockup, the disclosure language in the prospectus will normally be found in the 'Underwriting' or 'Plan of Distribution' section. Sample language can look as follows:

> 'We and our selling shareholders will agree as part of the underwriting agreement, subject to certain exceptions, not to transfer or dispose of, directly or indirectly, any shares or any securities convertible into or exercisable or exchangeable for shares, for a period of <180> days after the date of this prospectus without the prior written consent of <lead manager/bookrunner/global coordinator>.'

Most risk factor sections of prospectuses also contain a warning that 'Future sales of [common stock] may affect the market price of our common stock', or similar language.

After the lockup expires, insiders and existing shareholders are permitted to sell shares. In the USA, there are restrictions on the number of shares that an insider/existing shareholder may sell during any three-month period. Under the SEC's Rule 144 (not Rule 144a), as long as a shareholder has held the shares for at least one year, in any quarter an insider can sell no more than a maximum of 1 per cent of the total shares outstanding, or the average weekly trading volume. When sold, the shares are deemed registered (i.e. can be bought or sold by anyone). Sales of more than 500 shares, or $10 000, must be disclosed to the SEC on Form 144 no later than the date of the sale, but there are exceptions for private sales to qualified investors, sales of stock acquired in incentive plans, and sale of stock held by non-insiders for more than three years (Field and Hanka, 2001).

In a large-scale study of 1948 lockup agreements following US IPOs, Field and Hanka (2001) found that when lockups expire, there is a 40 per cent increase in trading volume and 'a statistically prominent three day abnormal return of minus 1.5 percent'. That is, the share price declines.

The impact can be much greater. When Fran Rooney, CEO of Baltimore Technologies, sold 13 per cent of his holding in the company for £5.8 million on termination of his lockup, the stock tumbled 40 per cent in one week.[5]

In general, the price reaction and volume increase are larger when the firm has been financed by venture capital. VCs are known by the investment communities to be sellers, holding shares in public companies is not their business.

Through the 1990s, the lockup period became concentrated on 180 days (six months), as illustrated in Table 11.8. If the lockup is not 180 days, the other common periods are 90, 270 and 365 days. See Table 11.8.

Investors can be released from the lockup on the say of the offering's lead manager(s). This occurs in less than one in 10 cases, but when it does, it usually involves sales by venture capitalists.

Those companies or shareholders that do negotiate an early lockup release, suffer an average 23 per cent drop in market capitalization (i.e. share price) in the 10 days following announcement (Keasler, 2001). Interestingly, those companies that announce an early release for some of their shareholders do not suffer the same stock price decline on the day the other shareholders' lockup expires.

In order to minimize the fall in price at the end of the lockup period, it is not uncommon for the manager of the offering to administer a 'booster shot' just prior to

[5] 'When lockups end, it can still be hard to cash in', *Financial Times*, 29 August 2000.

| Year | Mean lockup period (days) | <180 Days (%) | 180 Days (%) | >180 Days (%) |
|---|---|---|---|---|
| 1988 | 172 | 45 | 43 | 13 |
| 1989 | 168 | 39 | 54 | 7 |
| 1990 | 165 | 43 | 52 | 5 |
| 1991 | 183 | 22 | 68 | 10 |
| 1992 | 196 | 9 | 77 | 13 |
| 1993 | 188 | 8 | 84 | 9 |
| 1994 | 196 | 6 | 80 | 14 |
| 1995 | 191 | 4 | 88 | 9 |
| 1996 | 184 | 4 | 91 | 5 |

*Source:* Field and Hanka (2001).

**Table 11.8** Common lockup periods in the USA

the expiry. The booster shot is a positive research report intended to raise the value of the stock.

## *Evading lockups*

There are a number of methods available to insiders to raise capital without breaking the provisions of a lockup. They may use zero cost collars, use their shares as collateral for loans, or use a variable forward sale (a forward contract). For US companies, these derivative positions must be reported to the SEC, and hence the public. However, these transactions do not appear on insider sales databases. At the time of this writing, a good source of information on these hedging techniques can be found at www.RestrictedSecurities.com.

Websites such as www.IPOlockup.com, www.IPOHome.com and www.UnlockDates.com have been established to keep track of forthcoming expirations of stocks listed on US exchanges. The *Wall Street Journal* also prints a weekly table.

# 12 Secondary equity offerings

For some public companies, the initial public offering is the one and only time they approach the equity markets. But for many newly listed companies, the IPO is the first transaction in a developing relationship with investors. Growth requirements mean that firms return to the equity markets either sporadically or regularly in the years following their initial listing. Another common reason for a follow-on offering, as secondary offerings are sometimes called, is when an existing shareholder wishes to raise more cash from its investment.

Fresh equity capital can be raised through a:

1 Marketed secondary offering
2 Rights issue
3 'Bought deal'
4 Accelerated bookbuilding.

Existing shareholders can reduce their positions through a:

1 Marketed secondary offering
2 'Bought deal'
3 Accelerated bookbuilding.

The volume of secondary offerings kept pace with IPOs in the 1990s, as illustrated in Figure 12.1.

A company whose share price has appreciated since its IPO will have an easier job of raising capital than a company whose share price is below its IPO price. Obviously, investors who have made money off a stock are more likely to be interested in purchasing more shares. Investors who missed out on the IPO may be more inclined to take a second chance to build a meaningful stake in a company.

We looked at the experience of Fairchild Semiconductor in Chapter 1. To recap, Fairchild raised $425 million in an IPO to fund its operations and pay down debt. Five months later, Fairchild returned to the markets, this time raising $903 million. In the deal, the company raised a further $200 million. But its shareholders were the real beneficiaries, selling $700 million worth of shares at a price per share that was 81 per cent higher than the IPO price. The fact that the company's share price had increased made the secondary offering that much easier.

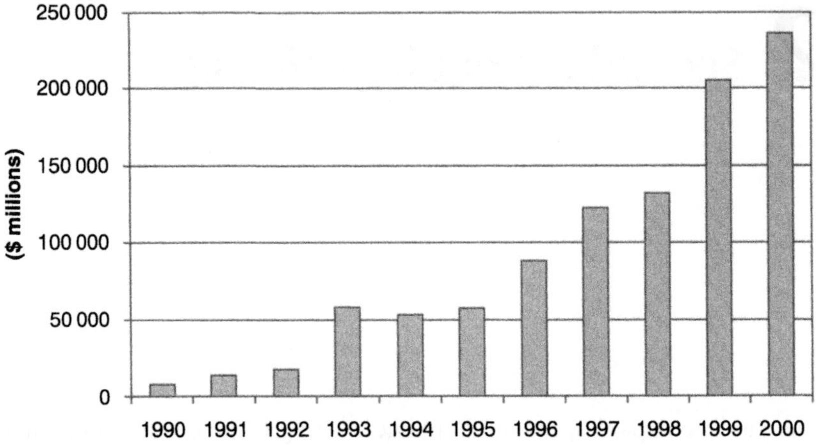


*Source*: Various.

**Figure 12.1** Secondary offerings

An offering that combines primary and secondary shares is often called a 'piggyback offering'. It benefits selling shareholders primarily, allowing them to sell shares in a large block, rather than dribbling them out to the market. By organizing a secondary offering, management can increase liquidity in an orderly fashion and ensure placement with long-term investors.

Corporate financiers and their equity capital markets colleagues perform much the same role in rights issues and secondary offerings as they do in flotations. They coordinate the work of the other advisors, lead the preparation of documentation, and advise the issuer or vendor on the pricing of shares. There is one complication, and it can be a large one. During this process, the company's shares are trading in the stock market every day and the fluctuations in price can be large. The biggest disaster in secondary offerings was the offer of BP shares just before the stock market crash of 1987. Prior to the announcement of a sale of shares at 330p, BP's shares had been trading in the 345–355p range. The stock market crash occurred after the offering was underwritten, but before it closed. Following the crash, BP shares traded well below 300p each, resulting in hundreds of millions of pounds of losses to the underwriters and sub-underwriters in the UK and internationally.

This chapter takes us through the four main methods of 'further issues'. For the most part, documentation and regulation are similar to those required for IPOs. Rights issues and marketed secondary offerings benefit from a shortened marketing programme (compared with the IPO), while accelerated bookbuildings have minimal marketing and bought deals, none.

## Reasons for secondary offerings

Companies raise money in order to invest in new capital expenditures or projects, to make acquisitions of other companies, to repay debt, or simply when the market is good and they can opportunistically raise funds. One study of US secondary offerings (Masulis and Korwar, 1986) suggested the following uses of proceeds:

| | |
|---|---|
| Debt reduction | 14% |
| Capital expenditure | 16% |
| Mixed use | 14% |
| Other/not disclosed | 56% |

All the same reasons that are applicable to shareholders/investors selling shares in an IPO continue to be relevant to secondary offerings. Existing shareholders may wish to raise cash, diversify holdings, VC exit, no longer have a strategic holding, or dispose of shares received in an M&A transaction.

## Rights offerings

In the UK and the rest of Europe, almost all subsequent equity offerings are done by way of a rights offering. On the other hand, rights issues are almost unknown in North America. In a rights offering (the term is used interchangeably with rights issue), all shareholders receive notification of the fundraising. They are entitled to purchase new shares in the company in the proportion that they hold at the time the offer is announced. So if Saturn Investment Management holds 1.75 per cent of the ordinary shares of Holmes Place, it will be entitled to purchase 1.75 per cent of the new shares on offer. If they wish to purchase the new shares, they do so (i.e. they exercise or take up their rights). If the shareholder does not wish to purchase the shares to which he is entitled, he can sell his rights on the stock exchange.

Rights issues can raise substantial capital for companies, as Table 12.1 illustrates.

### *Pre-emption rights*

Investors in UK stock exchange quoted companies are protected from the dilution of their ownership stake through pre-emption rights. This means that if a firm wishes to raise new equity capital, it must first offer the shares it is planning to sell to its existing shareholders. The protection from dilution is as a result of both law and strong tradition in the City. Assuming a shareholder 'takes up' his rights to subscribe to the new issue, he will maintain his proportionate share of the equity in the company. Such pre-emption rights are not part of the corporate finance landscape in Canada or the USA.

Limited exemptions to the pre-emption practices exists in the UK. Seventy-five per cent of shareholders must vote in favour of a resolution waiving their pre-emption rights (at a general meeting of shareholders) and the shares may not be sold at more than a 10 per cent discount to the prevailing market price. Companies infrequently seek this permission. More common is the '5 per cent exemption' in which companies are permitted to make an issue of up to 5 per cent of shareholders' capital without offering the new shares first to existing shareholders.

| Company | Year | Amount raised (£m) |
|---|---|---|
| British Telecommunications | 2001 | 5927 |
| Pearson | 2000 | 1705 |
| BP | 1987 | 1500 |
| Zeneca | 1993 | 1300 |
| Eurotunnel | 1994 | 858 |
| ICI | 2002 | 800 |
| Allied-Lyons | 1994 | 670 |
| RMC Group | 1995 | 493 |
| Spirent | 2000 | 528 |
| Logica | 2000 | 463 |
| EMAP | 1998 | 368 |
| Scottish & Newcastle | 1995 | 364 |
| Misys | 1997 | 334 |

**Table 12.1** Large UK rights issues

Continental European companies regularly seek, and receive, permission from their shareholders to waive pre-emption rights as a matter of course. For example, agenda item 5 at the 15 June 2001 Annual General Meeting of Shareholders of Telefónica, S.A., Spain's largest telephone company, asked shareholders for:

> 'Authorization of the Board of Directors to increase the share capital under the terms and conditions of Article 153.1(b) of the Corporation Law, for the maximum period of five years, *with or without preferred subscription rights*, in this latter case, the shares being issued at an issue price corresponding to the actual value resulting from the mandatory report of the Accounts Auditor of the Company and, in all cases, in accordance with the stipulations of Article 159 of the Corporation Law.' [italics added]

Similarly, Dutch companies TPG NV and KPN included the following agenda item in their 2002 Annual General Meetings:

> 'Extension of the authorisation of the Board of Management to:
>
> a) issue shares;
> b) restrict or exclude pre-emptive rights'

During the mid to late 1990s, corporate financiers were at the centre of a debate over whether UK companies should change their approach to fund raising. Many people believe that pre-emption rules prevent new investors from achieving meaningful stakes in companies, thus narrowing the shareholder base and increasing dependence on a few investors. Others argue that the status quo should be maintained because pre-emption rights protect existing shareholders from a potential transfer of value to new shareholders if new shares are sold at a large discount to the prevailing market price.

A survey of UK finance directors into the system of rights issues and raising equity capital was conducted by MORI in 1998. It reported that nearly 80 per cent of finance directors believed that they should have access to a greater variety of financing methods. When it came to the system of pre-emption rights, most supported the system, but thought that the 5 per cent exemption, as described above, was too low. One-third believed 10 per cent was more appropriate, while 23 per cent supported an exemption of up to 25 per cent (Martinson, 1998).

Large company finance directors generally found the current system most restrictive and half the FDs surveyed (61 per cent of FTSE 100 FDs) believed that companies in other countries had a competitive advantage because of the flexibility of their capital raising systems.

In response to the news report about this survey, the *Financial Times*' influential LEX column wrote on 20 October 1998, 'The idea [of increasing the exemption to 25 percent] has merit and could sometimes cut companies' cost of capital.' But the column suggested that if firms were to gain this freedom, prior to launching an issue, they should be required to 'explain why any non-pre-emptive issue is in existing shareholders' interest'.

On the other hand, one of Britain's highest profile fund managers, Carol Galley, co-head of Merrill Lynch Mercury Asset Management, wrote in the *Financial Times* on 22 July 1998:

> '. . . Pre-emptive rights are enshrined in law. They give existing shareholders first refusal on any new shares in a rights issue. Two things are central to this principal: transfer of value and transfer of control. If shares are issued to new rather than existing shareholders there may be a transfer of value to the new shareholders from the existing ones. Whether this has actually happened can only be known with hindsight. In a pre-emptive issue no such transfer of value can take place. We therefore believe that pre-emptive issues are the correct way for companies to raise new equity and that proposals to permit more non-pre-emptive issues are misplaced.'

At the time of writing, no changes to pre-emption rights have been made in the UK.

### *Setting the price*

One of the most important aspects of a rights offering is setting the terms and price of the new shares. Typically the new shares are offered at a discount to the prevailing trading price on the stock exchange. In most instances, the discount is set between 10 and 20 per cent. For assurance, the issuing company will have the offer 'underwritten' – as in a fixed price flotation. This means that if the share price falls below the purchase price and the shareholders do not subscribe to the issue, the company is guaranteed to receive the funds.

In the UK, underwritten rights offerings must remain open for 21 days. That is investors have 21 days in which to make up their minds about whether to exercise their rights or to sell them in the market. It is possible that the shares will fall below the issue price during this period. If so, no rational investor would purchase new shares when she could buy them in the market at a lower price.

## *Investors' options*

An investor has four options when a company in which he is a shareholder decides to launch a rights offer. He can either:

- Exercise the rights and purchase the new shares he is entitled to
- Sell the rights in the market
- Exercise a portion of his rights and sell the remainder in the market
- Do nothing.

### Exercising rights

When an investor exercises all his rights and purchases the shares he is entitled to, the investor maintains his proportionate interest in the company. While he will end up with more shares, if the investor held 0.34 per cent of the company before the rights issue, he will continue to hold 0.34 per cent of the company after the issue.

### Selling rights

Share purchase rights trade on the same stock exchange as the shares they entitle the holder to buy. During the period that the rights trade, investors may sell their rights, called 'nil paid rights' in the UK. Investors who sell their rights may do so because they have no confidence in the company, do not have sufficient cash on hand to increase their investment, or for another reason.

### Do nothing

If the investor chooses to do nothing, either through ignorance or deliberately, his rights will be sold on the last day of trading with all other unexercised rights. The company will then send the investor a cheque for the value of his rights that were sold. The purchasers of the rights will then exercise their entitlement to buy the new shares.

If there are no takers for the existing rights, the underwriter and sub-underwriters are required to purchase any shares that are not taken up (sometimes referred to as 'eating the tail').

## *Rights issue timetable*

Rights issues follow a fairly standard timetable in the UK, giving investors 21 days in order to decide to exercise their rights or to sell them in the stock market. (The rights become listed on the London Stock Exchange or AIM for their lifetime.)

### Timetable for typical rights issue

The following is the timetable of a rights issue undertaken by Monument Oil and Gas in April 1998. It starts with the announcement of the proposed issue and ignores the weeks or months of work by corporate financiers and brokers prior to announcement:

| | |
|---|---|
| Announcement of proposed issue | 2 April |
| Record dates for rights issue | Tuesday 14 April |
| Latest time and date for receipt of forms of proxy | 12 noon, Saturday 18 April |
| Extraordinary General Meeting | 12 noon, Monday 20 April |
| Provisional allotment letters despatched | Monday 20 April |
| Dealings expected to commence in new ordinary shares, nil paid | Tuesday 21 April |
| Latest time and date for splitting nil paid allotments | 3pm, Monday 11 May |
| Latest time and date for acceptance and payment in full and for registration of renunciation | 3pm, Wednesday 13 May |
| Definitive share certificates to be despatched and credits made to appropriate CREST stock accounts in respect of new ordinary shares | Thursday 21 May |

The following more detailed timetable is for the £5.9 billion rights offer launched by British Telecommunications plc in the spring of 2001:

| | |
|---|---|
| Record date for the rights issue | Close of business on 9 May |
| Nil paid rights and fully paid rights enabled in CREST | By 8am on 21 May |
| Dealings in new BT shares, nil paid, commence on the London Stock Exchange | 8am on 21 May |
| Recommended latest time for requesting withdrawal of nil paid rights from CREST | 4:30pm on 7 June |
| Latest time for depositing renounced provisional allotment letters, nil paid, into CREST or for dematerializing nil paid rights into a CREST stock account | 3pm on 11 June |
| Latest time and date for splitting provisional allotment letters | 3pm on 12 June |
| Dealings in new BT shares, fully paid, commence on the London Stock Exchange | 8am on 14 June |
| Latest time and date for acceptance | 9:30am on 15 June |

| | |
|---|---|
| Recommended latest time and date for requesting withdrawal of fully paid rights from CREST | 4:30pm on 22 June |
| Latest time and date for splitting provisional allotment letters, fully paid | 3pm on 27 June |
| Latest time for depositing renounced provisional allotment letters, fully paid into CREST or for dematerializing fully paid rights into a CREST stock account | 3pm on 27 June |
| Latest time and date for registration of renunciation of provisional allotment letters, fully paid | 3pm on 29 June |
| New BT shares credited to CREST stock accounts | 2 July |
| Despatch of definitive share certificates for new BT shares | By 16 July |

### *Restrictions on sale*

Difficulties can arise when a company that is undertaking a rights issue has shareholders in foreign countries. The difficulties are greatest when there are US resident shareholders. If the issuer decides not to register the offering for sale to the public, the issuer will have to exclude retail investors. In these cases, the international shareholders' rights are sold in the market on the last day of trading. The international shareholder then receives the proceeds of the sale of the rights.

The following is excerpted from Villiers Group's rights issue in 2000 which was not registered under the 1933 Act in the USA:

> 'Rights Shares which would have been provisionally allotted to North American persons will, if a net premium (after deduction of expenses of sale) can be obtained, be sold, nil paid and the net premium will be distributed *pro rata* by cheque, and at the risk of those shareholders to whom the Rights Shares would otherwise been provisionally allotted, subject to the retention by the Company of individual amounts of less than £3.00.'

### *Fees and commissions*

Traditionally, UK rights offerings carried a 2 per cent commission. The total commission paid by the company raising the funds is divided as follows:

| | |
|---|---|
| Primary underwriter | 0.50% |
| Broker to the issue | 0.25% |
| Sub-underwriters | 1.25% |

The traditional fee structure mirrors that of the fee structure for UK flotations. The primary underwriter is typically the investment bank sponsor of the offer. Other professional service firms can and do act as sponsors, but usually only for smaller offerings. Sub-underwriters are financial institutions that agree to underwrite a small proportion of the offering. If the underwriting period is to last longer than the standard period, a higher commission for the sub-underwriters is customary. An additional 0.25 per cent is added to the sub-underwriting commission rate for every additional seven days of underwriting.

In the mid-1990s, competitions authorities in the UK turned their eye to the rights issue. They were responding to a study conducted by academics at the London Business School, which found that sub-underwriters were 'overpaid' for the risks taken in underwriting during the period 1986–1994 (i.e. the standard underwriting commission provided higher compensation to the underwriters than the risk they were taking warranted).

Frightful of regulation, the industry responded with an innovation to setting the sub-underwriting fee. The fee, or a portion of it, was put out to tender. In this situation sub-underwriters are invited (by the primary underwriter or sponsor) to 'bid' for the fee they require to take up any shares that remain as a result of unexercised rights. Some sort of tendering occurs in approximately 50 per cent of rights issues, resulting in an overall decrease in the sub-underwriting portion of the total commission. Table 12.2 shows the money saved by companies in some of the early tenders in 1996 and 1997.

Another response was found in the increased number of deep discount rights offerings that do away with underwriting entirely. Deep discount rights issues are discussed in the next section.

The first issue which included a tender for sub-underwriting occurred in 1996 as part of a £222 million rights issue for Stakis, the hotels group. Corporate financiers at Schroders devised a method whereby institutions interested in sub-underwriting the issue tendered for the fee that they would receive for doing so. One-third of the sub-underwriting fee was put out to tender, which resulted in bids that saved the company approximately £400 000 in underwriting commissions.

The following year, in October 1997, Schroders put the sub-underwriting for all of a £125 million rights issue for Berkeley out to tender. In that offer, the shares were offered at a discount of 26 per cent to the previous market price in order to reduce the risk to the sub-underwriters. In most cases, the discount is set at 15 to 20 per cent. This resulted in the sub-underwriting commission being cut from the 'standard' 1.25 per cent to 0.3 per cent, saving Berkeley nearly £1.2 million.

In April 1998, Monument Oil and Gas did away with underwriters all together by getting its leading shareholders to underwrite the issue, rather than engaging an underwriter and sub-underwriters. In doing so, the company saved itself £1.3 million in commissions on its £96 million rights issue. Monument was able to do so because it had relatively few, large shareholders that were long-term supporters of the company and willing to increase their ownership if necessary. Institutional investors representing 54 per cent of share capital had taken up their rights, leaving only 46 per cent of the issue to be underwritten. The commission on the remainder of the issue was 0.625 per cent, less than half the 1.75 per cent combined underwriting and sub-underwriting fees. The one-for-four rights issue was priced at a 10 per cent discount to the pre-announcement share price.

| | Gross size (£m) | Discount | Proportion of sub-underwriting offered for tender (%) | Actual commission paid (£m) | Actual commission paid (%) | Reduction in commission (£m) | Reduction in commission (% of normal costs) | Normal commission payable (%) |
|---|---|---|---|---|---|---|---|---|
| Stakis | 222.0 | 10.6 | 33.3 | 4.20 | 1.89 | 0.40 | 8.4 | 2.00 |
| More Group | 49.6 | 11.1 | 33.0 | 0.89 | 1.72 | 0.11 | 10.9 | 2.00 |
| Bodycote | 115.5 | 12.2 | 53.0 | 1.69 | 1.41 | 0.70 | 29.3 | 2.00 |
| Biocompatibles | 45.5 | 12.1 | 33.3 | 0.94 | 1.95 | 0.08 | 8.2 | 2.12 |
| Finelist | 37.3 | 7.5 | 50.0 | 0.56 | 1.61 | 0.32 | 37.7 | 2.25 |
| Great Portland Estates | 98.8 | 1.6 | 50.0 | 1.70 | 1.72 | 0.28 | 14.2 | 2.00 |
| Grantchester | 67.1 | 6.2 | NA | 0.88 | 1.05 | 0.46 | 30.5 | 2.25 |

*Source: The Treasurer*, May 1997, p. 23. Original data from SBC Warburg.

**Table 12.2** Selected underwriting tenders

### Deep discount rights issues

One way to avoid paying underwriting commissions is the use of a deep discounted rights issue. This type of issue sets the price of the new shares at a much greater than standard discount to the prevailing share price. Companies have tended to shy away from deep discounted rights issues for several reasons. In particular, many believed they would be under pressure to maintain the level of dividends on the enlarged equity, thereby increasing their cost of capital.

Deep discounted issues are relatively uncommon in the UK, although some of the largest rights issues have used the deep discount structure during the years between 1999 and 2001.

On Monday, 31 July 2000, Pearson announced an offer of $2.5 billion (£1.66 billion) for a US company called National Computer Systems (NCS), which is involved in education services. To finance the acquisition, one of many made by Pearson in 2000, the company announced a £1.7 billion rights issue on the basis of three new shares for every 11 owned at a price of £10 per new share. The price of £10 was a discount of approximately 50 per cent to the prevailing share price of £20.10. Not only was the discount large, but the size of the issue made the Pearson offering the largest ever rights issue in the UK at the time. It held this crown for just 10 months. In May 2001, British Telecommunications raised £5.9 billion.

One of the reasons Pearson decided to offer a deep discounted rights issue was that it was able to minimize the commissions paid. In deep discounted issues, it is unusual for an investor not to participate, reducing the risk to the company that the new shares are not taken up. In fact, some dispense with underwriting completely.

In Pearson's case, it decided to underwrite £1.5 billion (organized by Goldman Sachs and Cazenove), which ensured that the bulk of the funds would be available on closing. The cost of the underwriting was 0.5 per cent of the funds raised, or £7.5 million in total. If the issue had been underwritten on standard terms (i.e. 2 per cent), Pearson would have paid £34 million in commissions. At the time, institutions backed the move, which they described as 'innovative' and 'cost-effective'.

British Telecommunications, perhaps encouraged by the success of Pearson's offering, also opted for a deep discount in its 2001 rights offering. BT priced its new shares at 300p each, a 47 per cent discount to the prevailing market price. The total expenses of the issue (including legal, accountancy fees and printing fees) represented 0.877 per cent of the record £5.9 billion raised, or £52 million. Because BT had a long established US shareholder base and a listing on the New York Stock Exchange, a prospectus was filed with the SEC, permitting US investors to participate in the offering.

During 2001–2002, numerous other UK companies including Kingfisher, Imperial Tobacco, ICI, easyJet and Enterprise Inns launched deep discount rights issues.

### At market rights issues

At the other end of the spectrum to the deep discount rights offering is the 'at market' issue, where the new shares are offered to existing shareholders at or very near to the prevailing market price. At market issues are even less common than deep discount rights issues, but can meet a company's specific needs, as the following example illustrates.

In July 1998, Adecco, the Swiss personnel services company, raised SFR310 million ($206 million) by issuing 500 000 shares through an at market rights issue. The rights issue was needed in order to refinance debt incurred in a recent acquisition. This was the first of its kind in Switzerland and caused a stir in the market on its successful completion.

Adecco decided against a traditional rights issue at a discount to the market price because it assumed that shareholders would have exercised their rights. This would have raised the funds that Adecco required, but would not have met the second objective of broadening the company's shareholder base. The company's bankers, Credit Suisse First Boston (CSFB), suggested a structure that allowed existing shareholders to subscribe for shares, while it engaged in an institutional bookbuilding to elicit demand for the shares that were not taken up by existing shareholders.

CSFB assessed the likely demand from existing shareholders and then tailored its marketing efforts accordingly. The bank knew that an at market pricing would mean fewer existing shareholders subscribing for new shares than if the offer had been priced at a 15 to 20 per cent discount to the prevailing share price. So it had to estimate the number of shares that would not be taken up by existing shareholders in order to determine the potential size of the offer for new investors and tailor its marketing approach accordingly.

The company made investor presentations over the course of a five-day roadshow stopping in Zurich, Geneva, Paris, Edinburgh and London. On completing the roadshow, the offering price was set at SFR620, a discount of 3 per cent to the day's closing price, but a 5 per cent premium to the share price (SFR590) when the subscription period began.

Allocations were made two-thirds to existing shareholders who had exercised their pre-emption rights and one-third to new investors. CSFB generated demand for over 400 000 shares with the approximately 165 000 shares that were available to new investors.

## Marketed offerings

Marketed secondary offerings are structured in a manner very similar to an IPO. The marketed offering is the most common method of raising funds in the USA. The company appoints an investment bank and assembles a team of lawyers, accountants and PR experts. Typically, but not always, the same team that took the company public is in place for the secondary offering. Corporate financiers coordinate the preparation of a prospectus and take soundings in the market regarding investor appetite for the new shares. Confidentiality is important in marketed offerings, as information regarding a firm's impending sale of shares would cause a fall in the company's share price as described in the following section (arbitrageurs would sell the shares, causing the price to fall and purchase shares in the new issue at a lower price to cover their short position).

Once the preliminary prospectus is prepared and filed with the regulator, a marketing campaign commences. Marketing for a secondary offering is less extensive than that for a company's IPO as investors are generally familiar with the firm's business. Where an IPO often has a four- to six-week marketing period, a secondary offering typically uses one to three weeks.

The marketing period will be extended if the issuer decides to target investors in new markets. This may add to the length of the roadshow and the number of calls the analysts and salesmen will make.

Once the regulator approves the offering documents, and the lead manager has sufficient orders, it closes the book and prices the new issue. The price of the new shares is usually set at the closing price on the pricing day, or at a very small discount to it. For example, the Norwegian Government reduced its stake in Christiania Bank from 51 per cent to 35 per cent in a NOK2.7 billion ($348.6 million) secondary offering in 1999.

When the offer closed on Friday March 19, the selling price was set at NOK30.60 – the closing price in the market. One analyst noted, 'the absence of a discount from the market is a sign of strong investor demand' (Lee and Revheim, 1999). The strong interest continued on the following Monday, when the 90 million shares were allocated to investors. Contrary to many secondary offerings, the share price closed up on the day at NOK31.10, a 1.6 per cent increase, indicating that there had been significant unsatisfied demand.

Commissions on secondary offerings are typically lower than on IPOs, reflecting the lower amount of marketing effort required. As with IPOs, larger deals will earn lower percentage commissions than small deals. The commissions charged will range from approximately 0.75 per cent for the underwriting of a deep discount rights offering to 4.00–4.25 per cent for a medium-sized marketed transaction in the USA.

Banks may stabilize the price of secondary offerings, as they do for IPOs. Therefore a greenshoe (overallotment option) is usually, but not always, included.

### *What happens when a marketed deal is announced?*

Secondary offerings logically follow a period of strong stock performance by the issuer as well as the market as a whole (Marsh, 1979). Asquith and Mullins (1986) document that industrial companies raising primary funds experience a 40.4 per cent cumulative excess return (i.e. market adjusted) during the two years prior to the offering. Companies that issue secondary shares experience a 21.4 per cent market adjusted return during the prior two years, while combined primary secondary offerings follow a 41.8 per cent cumulative excess return.

However, a 1983 study of secondary offerings found that companies' share prices dropped by approximately 2.5 per cent when they announced a further equity offering. Three years later, Asquith and Mullins looked at the price drop over a two-day period following the announcement of a new equity issue. Their research showed that industrial companies issuing shares experienced an average price decline of 2.7 per cent. For companies raising primary equity only, the decline was greater at 3.0 per cent, while secondary offers caused a drop of only 2.0 per cent. Combination offerings caused the most marked investor reaction, causing the share price to fall by 3.2 per cent, possibly because they were larger offers. All these studies examined US secondary offerings.

While the decline in share price doesn't sound like much, when looked at in the context of the amount of money raised, the story changes. On average, when a company announced a primary issue, the monetary value of the share price decline equated to an average of 31 per cent (median 28 per cent) of the funds that were subsequently raised. For example, imagine a company with a market capitalization of $2.0 billion announces a $200 million secondary offering of shares. Assume that its share price declines by the average rate of 2.7 per cent. This would cut $54 million from the company's market capitalization. Note that $54 million is 27 per cent of the new offering of $200 million. 'These results imply that a substantial portion of the proceeds of an equity issue comes out of the pockets of old shareholders' (Asquith and Mullins 1986: 72).

The experience of secondary–secondary offerings (where existing shareholders sell) is worse still. The average drop in market capitalization equalled 78 per cent of the proceeds of the offering (median 43.4 per cent). In fact, in almost 30 per cent of secondary–secondary offerings the firm's value fell by more than the proceeds of the offering.

Mikkelson and Partch (1985) also found that the price drop at the initial announcement of a secondary offering is greater for offerings in which managers are sellers. Their research showed that when managers sold, the share price fell by 2.87 per cent, while when other shareholders sold in a secondary offering, the share price fell by only 2.57 per cent.

Masulis and Korwar (1986) found that companies that had larger stock price run-ups in the period before the announcement of the new issue experienced larger share price drops on the offering announcement. They also found that the use of proceeds had no statistically significant impact on the degree of decline: companies that announced the proceeds would be used for debt reduction fell by 3.84 per cent; capital expenditures by 3.75 per cent; and 'mixed use' by 2.52 per cent.

Firms that conduct secondary offerings experience a short-term outperformance and then go on to underperform in the two years following the announcement of the offering. Companies that make primary offers underperform by 3.1 per cent; secondary offerings by 10.1 per cent; and combination offerings by 5.7 per cent. The short-term outperformance may be a result of the marketing efforts involved in selling the new issue.

Loughran and Ritter (1995) attempt to explain the underperformance. They argue that secondary offerings occur when companies' shares are overvalued. Even after the post-announcement decline of 2 or 3 per cent, the shares remain overvalued. This contributes to long-term underperformance as investors discover the overvaluation and sell the shares, depressing the price. Spiess and Affleck-Graves (1995) suggest that underperformance is a result of managers' ability to time new issues when the firm's stock is overvalued. This benefits the firm through reduced dilution in primary offerings and the managers if they are selling shareholders.

Finally, Loughran and Ritter (1997) and McLaughlin et al. (1998) have also documented poor post-issue *operating performance* by firms that have raised equity in secondary offerings.

## Bought deals

A bought deal, sometimes referred to as a 'block trade', involves a bank buying shares in a company, then selling the shares as quickly as possible to institutional investors.

The difference between the buying and selling price is the investment bank's profit. The company does not pay a commission as it does in a marketed offer or rights issue. Bought deals have increased in volume dramatically since the early 1990s, as Figure 12.2 illustrates.

A bought deal entails greater risk for an investment bank (compared with a bookbuilding offering) because it can suffer losses if it is unable to sell the shares. Vendors like bought deals, because they are faster than formal offerings (rarely taking more than 24 hours for successful transactions). On the other hand, the vendor must accept that it will likely have to sell its shares at a discount to the prevailing market price. The discount is required because of the need for speed and secrecy as well as the fact that the investment bank is risking its own capital. In general, the all-in cost of a bought deal will be lower than that of a marketed secondary offering. However, not all companies are suitable candidates for bought deals.

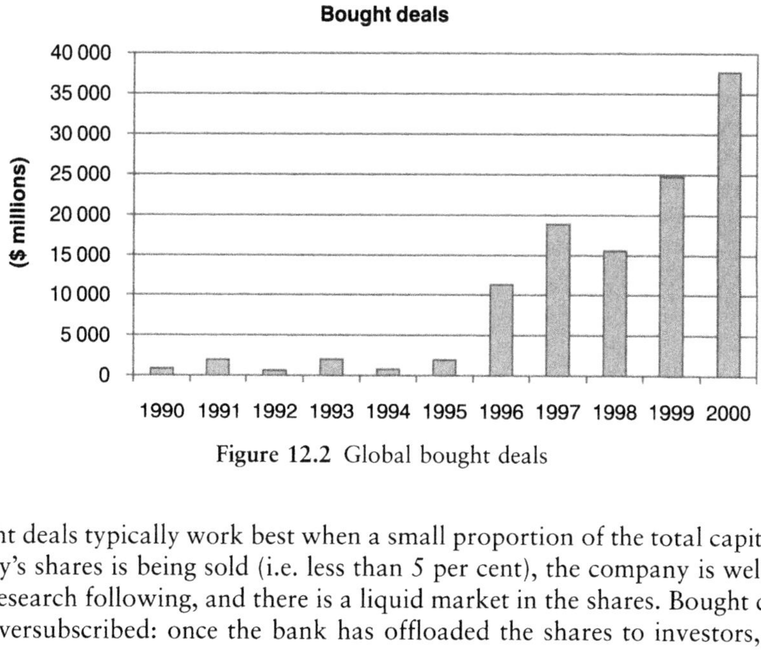


**Figure 12.2** Global bought deals

Bought deals typically work best when a small proportion of the total capital of the company's shares is being sold (i.e. less than 5 per cent), the company is well known with a research following, and there is a liquid market in the shares. Bought deals are rarely oversubscribed: once the bank has offloaded the shares to investors, it stops selling.

## *Examples of bought deals*

In 1995, the UK Government hired NM Rothschild, the merchant bank, to advise it on the sale of the state's remaining holdings in a number of privatized companies. These were worth approximately £1.2 billion. The largest holding was a 1.8 per cent stake in British Petroleum (BP), valued at over £500 million in December 1995.

By late in the year, Rothschild was ready to move. On Friday afternoon, December 1st, the firm received approval for its plan from the Treasury. Following a weekend of fine tuning their strategy, corporate finance and equity capital markets professionals were sure of its success.

On Monday, a number of leading investment banks in London were invited to Rothschild's offices at 8pm after markets in London and New York had closed. The firms were not told which of the stocks they were bidding for until after they had arrived. The only indication they had been given in advance was that they would be called upon to commit a large amount of capital.

Rothschild kept the bidders apart all evening. After being told that they were bidding for the Government's entire stake in BP, each investment bank was given two hours to respond. The winner was SBC Warburg (now UBS Warburg), which bid 508p per share for 101 million shares – just over £513 million. This compared with the closing price of 531p, a 4.15 per cent discount. Other bidders were said to be BZW, Merrill Lynch and at least one other American house, each of whom had offered less than 508p per share.

When trading opened on Tuesday 5th December, Warburg's salesmen called institutions throughout the UK and Europe and at lunchtime began to offer shares to US investors, as they arrived in their offices. The holding was placed with approximately 100 institutions, split evenly between the UK and Europe and the USA, at a price of 513p. BP shares closed at 517p, down 14p on the day, but still above the re-offer price.

For the day's work and the use of the firm's capital, Warburg earned approximately £5 million.

In November 2001, Sophus Berendsen, a Danish company with a large stake in Britain's Rentokil, disposed of 52 million shares by way of a bought deal. Sophus Berendsen sold the shares to Goldman Sachs' equity desk for 236p each, a 3.7 per cent discount to the previous day's closing price of 245p. Goldman Sachs then resold the shares to investors at a price of 238p. At the end of the day, after all the shares had been placed, Rentokil's share price closed at 244p. Goldman's earnings for distributing £123 million of shares was just over £1.0 million, or 0.81 per cent.

### *Bought deals in the USA: Rule 415*

Although most of the bought deals as described above have taken place in the European market, a form of bought deal exists in the USA and Canada. In 1983, the SEC adopted Rule 415, commonly referred to as the 'Shelf Rule'. The rule allows large firms to register all securities (both debt and equity) that they expect to issue over the next two years by preparing and filing a registration statement on either Form S-3 (domestic issuers) or Form F-3 (non-US issuers). These forms incorporate by reference the issuer's 10-K or 20-F, respectively, annual filing. The firm can then issue any portion of the securities included in the registration at any time during the two-year period.

> 'The procedure is called "shelf registration" because companies may put securities on the "shelf" (register) and pull securities off the "shelf" (issue) whenever the companies so choose.'
>
> (Kidwell et al., 1984: 183)

Under the traditional marketed offering, there is at least a 48-hour delay between the filing and pricing of an issue. In reality, an IPO takes from four to six weeks in registration, while a secondary offering from an established issuer will take from two to four weeks. The review process is shorter for secondary offerings because the company is already known to the SEC through its IPO registration statement and its annual 10-K's or 20-F's.

The shelf registration eliminates the 48-hour delay (except at the time the shelf itself is filed). An issuer can price and sell shares to a single bank, a syndicate of banks, or directly to investors. This improves the issuer's flexibility to opportunistically tap the equity markets. However, it reduces the bankers' ability to conduct due diligence.

The other benefit of Rule 415 is that it should reduce issuers' costs. At the time of introduction of the rule, SEC Chairman, John Shad, estimated the savings in paperwork to be $300 million per year, or about $50 000 per issue (Kidwell et al., 1984). Bhagat et al. (1985) found that an issuer could save 0.63 per cent in direct costs (i.e. out of pocket) for syndicated offers and 1.36 per cent for non-syndicated offers by using the shelf process. However, later research (Denis, 1993) suggests that issuers do not obtain lower costs by using shelf registration for equity offerings.

Research indicates that under Rule 415, share prices get knocked twice: first when the registration is announced (–0.98 per cent) and again at the time of the fund raising (–0.24 per cent) (Moore et al., 1986). In later research, Denis (1991) reports that the announcement of a shelf registered industrial company equity offering results in a share price decline that is 0.7 to 0.8 per cent greater than that of a similar non-shelf offer.

Although it continues to be available for equity offerings, fewer than 2 per cent of all deals since 1986 have been registered under Rule 415 (Denis, 1993). The primary use of Rule 415 is for debt issues by investment grade issuers.

In the Canadian market, almost all secondary offerings since 1983 have been completed as a form of bought deal. For mature issuers that are eligible to use a 'short-form' prospectus, a deal can be approved by the Ontario Securities Commission and completed within five days. A group of Canadian investment banks will bid for the shares at a slight discount to the prevailing market price. At this time, the issuer is guaranteed the proceeds of the issue. It is then the job of the banks to distribute the shares to investors and for the lead manager and issuer to get the prospectus approved. The issuer pays a standard commission of 4 per cent.

## Accelerated bookbuilding

Accelerated bookbuilding is a variant on the bought deal. A company that is reasonably well known, with good liquidity in its shares, may opt for a shortened marketing period, rather than the typical two to three weeks as in a traditional marketed offering. Accelerated bookbuilds may be done for either primary or secondary shares.

In the UK, an accelerated bookbuilding that raises funds for the issuer is often called a placing. The maximum size of a placing is 5 per cent of the company's pre-issue share capital. Placings are often conducted in conjunction with a corporate announcement, such as annual results or acquisitions. This gives the company's broker an opportunity to talk to investors and determine whether the market would support an offering.

Accelerated bookbuilds have been on the increase, in part because of the development of in-house research departments at the major investing institutions. Institutions are well informed about the attributes of the major stocks and don't require the information that is imparted by a full roadshow.

From the issuer/selling shareholder perspective, the ability to complete a deal in just a few days means that it can take advantage of short-term positive swings in market sentiment towards the stock or the sector. The short marketing period gives the issuer greater confidence in the price that it will receive compared with a two to three week period in which market conditions may materially change for the worse.

The key success factors for an accelerated bookbuild are similar to those of a bought deal: the ability to identify key institutions that are willing to take the stock; liquidity of the underlying stock; recent earnings performance and visibility; and stock and sector outlook. A key disadvantage is the bank's inability to access retail demand. Because there is no prospectus, retail investors are excluded from bought deals and accelerated bookbuildings.

Accelerated bookbuilds tend to have low levels of oversubscription relative to IPOs. Investors place orders for the number of shares they actually want – not an inflated figure designed to get a certain, lower number of shares. The number of investors who participate in accelerated bookbuilds is lower than in an IPO or marketed secondary offering, as only larger institutions, that can make immediate decisions on large purchases, are approached.

Typically any marketing takes place before the bookbuilding commences. So, a company can use its results presentation to analysts and investors as its 'roadshow'.

Investors are called and asked for a quick decision – 'how many shares do you want and do you have any limits on price?' The bookbuilding often takes place after the market closes; this gives investors a stable price to focus on. In a successful deal the book is closed, the offer priced and allocations made before the market opens the following morning.

When bookbuilding takes place with the market open and the stock trading, the banks have to be more careful in managing the process. Sometimes bookbuildings will continue for as long as three days if the issuer's investment case is less well known.

### *Examples of accelerated bookbuildings and placings*

In February 2000, National Grid reduced its holding in the telecommunications and Internet company, Energis, from 46 per cent to 36 per cent via an offer using accelerated bookbuilding. The sale of 30 million shares raised £1014 million (before costs, commissions and taxes) for the parent company.

During January and February, shares in all European telecommunications companies had been rising. The week before the sale of Energis shares was announced, its share price had increased by an extraordinary 30 per cent to £37.97 each. At the opening of the UK market on Wednesday 9th February, National Grid announced that it had hired ABN Amro Rothschild, leading a small syndicate of banks which included Cazenove, Dresdner Kleinwort Benson and HSBC, to sell up to 30 million shares.

On announcement of the accelerated bookbuilding, the shares dropped to £33.63, below the price at which the banks were offering them (£33.80). However, by the end of the day all 30 million shares had been placed at the offer price.

In November 2000, a simultaneous accelerated dual bookbuild of Reed International (a UK company) and Elsevier (a Dutch company) (the parent companies of Reed Elsevier, the Anglo-Dutch publisher) was completed. To add to the difficulty of an accelerated bookbuild, the shares of Reed and Elsevier are separately listed on the London and Amsterdam stock exchanges, but not fungible. Both shares are also listed on the New York Stock Exchange.

The company built interest through a three-week roadshow to market the acquisition of publisher Harcourt General, growing interest from institutions providing sufficient confidence for the bookrunners to bring forward an equity raising originally planned for the first quarter of 2001, and conduct a £1.3 billion ($1.8 billion) accelerated bookbuild.

The companies' financial advisors launched the deal days after the roadshow's end, and were able to raise a total of £1.3 billion, in just 14 hours, at a 0.7 per cent discount to each firm's share price. Sales were made to British, Dutch, American and other European investors.

On 21 February 2002, Centrica raised £426 million to finance acquisitions, mainly in the USA. The deal was handled by Hoare Govett (part of ABN Amro) and Cazenove, who placed 200 million new shares at a price of 215p per share. The shares, which represented 5 per cent of Centrica's capital, were placed at a 4p discount (1.83 per cent) to the previous day's close. The placing was done at the time of the company's annual results announcement and presentations.

## Other forms of offering in the UK

Two other forms of secondary offering are available to British companies in certain circumstances.

In an *open offer*, a firm sells new shares to a wide range of investors, but gives existing shareholders preference in allocations. An open offer is an infrequently used cross between a rights offer and a marketed offer and is generally used by smaller companies or in conjunction with a placing.

*Vendor placings* (not to be confused with plain old placings) arise in the context of acquisitions. In situations where the purchaser wants to pay for the acquisition with

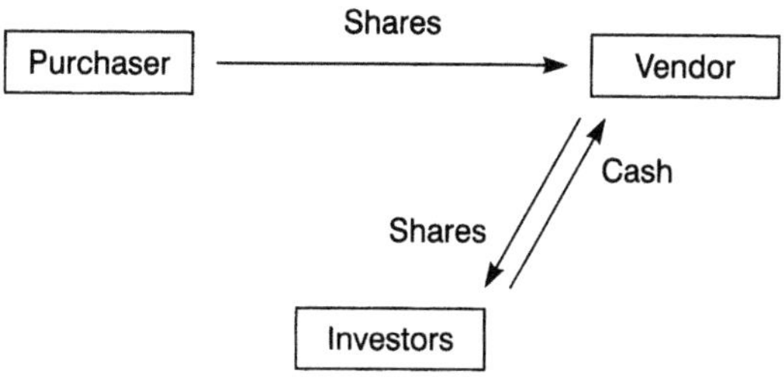


**Figure 12.3** Vendor placings

its own shares, but the vendor wants cash, the purchaser can organize a vendor placing. At the time of the acquisition, the purchaser issues shares, institutions buy the shares for cash and the vendor (or its shareholders) receive the cash as illustrated in Figure 12.3. Vendor placings only involve institutional investors because the deal must be completed quickly and a prospectus is not possible.

# Bibliography


(2001) *The Year 2000 in Review*, New York Stock Exchange.

Affleck-Graves J, SP Hegde, RE Miller and FK Reilly (1993) The effect of the trading system on the underpricing of initial public offerings *Financial Management* 22 (Spring): 99–108.

Aggarwal R and P Rivoli (1990) Fads in the initial public offering market? *Financial Management* 19 (4/Winter): 45–57.

Aggarwal R, R Leal and L Hernandez (1993) The aftermarket performance of initial public offerings in Latin America *Financial Management* 22 (Spring): 42–53.

Alcock A (2000) *The Financial Services and Markets Act 2000: A guide to the new law*. Bristol: Jordans.

Allen F and GR Faulhaber (1989) Signaling by underpricing in the IPO market *Journal of Financial Economics* 23: 303–323.

Arosio R, G Giudici and S Paleari (2000) What drives the initial market performance of Italian IPOs? An empirical investigation on underpricing and price support. Working paper, Politecnico di Milano.

Ashurst MC (2001) *The Financial Services and Markets Act: A practical legal guide* (ed. James Perry). London: Sweet & Maxwell.

Asquith P and DW Mullins (1986) Equity issues and offering dilution *Journal of Financial Economics* 15: 61–89.

Asquith D, JD Jones and R Kieschnick (1998) Evidence on price stabilization and underpricing in early IPO returns *Journal of Finance* 53 (5/October): 1759–1773.

Baker HK, JR Nofsinger and DG Weaver (1999) International cross selling and visibility. New York Stock Exchange Research Paper.

Bank of England (1990) New equity issues in the UK *Bank of England Quarterly Bulletin* May: 243–252.

Bank of New York (2002) *Depository Receipts: 2001 Year end market review*.

Barber BM and JD Lyon (1997) Detecting long-run abnormal stock returns: The empirical power and specification of test statistics *Journal of Financial Economics* 43: 341–371.

Barry CB (1989) Initial public offering underpricing: The issuer's view – A comment *Journal of Finance* XLIV (4): 1099–1103.

Barry CB and RH Jennings (1993) The opening price performance of initial public offerings of common stock *Financial Management* 22 (Spring): 54–63.

Barry CB, C Muscarella, J Peavy and M Vetsuypens (1990) The role of venture capital in the creation of public companies: Evidence from the going public process *Journal of Financial Economics* 27: 447–471.

Beatty RP and JR Ritter (1986) Investment banking, reputation, and the underpricing of initial public offerings *Journal of Financial Economics* 15 (1/2): 213–232.

Beatty R and M Vetsuypens (1995) Underpricing, overpricing and reputation: Are underwriters penalized for IPO mispricing? Working Paper, Southern Methodist University.

Beatty RP and I Welch (1996) Issuer expenses and legal liability in initial public offerings *Journal of Law and Economics* 39: 545–602.

Benveniste LM and WY Busaba (1997) Bookbuilding vs. fixed price: An analysis of competing strategies for marketing IPOs *Journal of Financial and Quantitative Analysis* 32 (4/December): 383–403.

Benveniste L and P Spindt (1989) How investment bankers determine the offer price and allocation of new issues *Journal of Financial Economics* 24: 343–361.

Benveniste L and W Wilhelm (1990) A comparative analysis of IPO proceeds under alternative regulatory regimes *Journal of Financial Economics* 28: 173–207.

Benveniste L and W Wilhelm (1997) Initial public offerings: Going by the book *Journal of Applied Corporate Finance* 10: 98–108.

Benveniste LM, WY Busaba and W Wilhelm (1996) Price stabilization as a bonding mechanism in new equity issues *Journal of Financial Economics* 42: 223–255.

Bhagat S, W Marr and GR Thompson (1985) The Rule 415 experiment: Equity markets *Journal of Finance* 40 (5/December): 1385–1401.

Billingsley RS and DM Smith (1996) Why do firms issue convertible debt? *Financial Management* 25 (2/Summer): 93–99.

Blackwell D, W Marr and M Spivey (1990) Shelf registration and the reduced due diligence argument: Implications of the underwriter certification and implicit insurance hypothesis *Journal of Financial and Quantitative Analysis* 25 (2/June): 245–259.

Booth JR and L Chua (1996) Ownership dispersion, costly information, and IPO underpricing *Journal of Financial Economics* 41: 291–310.

Booth JR and RL Smith (1986) Capital raising, underwriting and the certification hypothesis *Journal of Financial Economics* 15: 261–281.

Botosan C (1997) Disclosure level and the cost of equity capital *Accounting Review* 72 (3): 323–349.

Botosan C (2000) Evidence that greater disclosure lowers the cost of equity capital *Journal of Applied Corporate Finance* 12 (4): 60–68.

Boutchkova MK and WL Megginson (2000) Privatization and the rise of global capital markets *Financial Management* 29 (Issue 4/Winter): 31–76.

Bradley DJ, BD Jordan, H-C Yi and IC Roten (2001) Venture capital and IPO lockup expiration: An empirical analysis. *Journal of Financial Research* XXIV (4/Winter).

Brancato CK (1996) *Getting Listed on Wall Street: The Irwin Guide to financial reporting standards in the US*. New York: Irwin Professional Publishing.

Brav A and P Gompers (1997) Myth or Reality? The long-run underperformance of initial public offerings: Evidence from venture and non-venture capital backed companies *Journal of Finance* 52: 1791–1821.

Brealey RA and SC Myers (2000) *Principles of Corporate Finance*, 6th edn. London: Irwin McGraw-Hill.

Breedon F and I Twinn (1996) The valuation of sub-underwriting agreements for UK rights issues *Bank of England Quarterly Bulletin* May: 193–196.

Brennan M and J Franks (1995) Underpricing, ownership and control in initial public offerings of securities in the UK *Journal of Financial Economics* 45: 391–413.
Bruck C (1988) *The Predators' Ball: the inside story of Drexel Burnham and the rise of the junk bond raiders.* New York: Penguin Books. (Originally published New York: American Lawyer, Simon and Schuster, 1988.)
Bruner, RF, KM Eades, RS Harris and RC Higgins (1998) Best practices in estimating the cost of capital: survey and synthesis *Financial Practice and Education* (Spring/Summer): 13–28.
Caplen B, A Currie and P Lee (2000) Deals of the Year [1999] *Euromoney* February 2000.
Carrol GR (1983) A stochastic model of organizational mortality *Social Science Research* 12: 303–329.
Carter R and S Manaster (1990) Initial public offerings and underwriter reputation *Journal of Finance* 45: 1045–1068.
Carter RB, FH Dark and AK Singh (1998) Underwriter reputation, initial returns, and the long-run performance of IPO stocks *Journal of Finance* 53 (1/February): 285–311.
Chalk AJ and JW Peavy (1987) Initial public offerings: Daily returns, offering types, and the price effect *Financial Analysts Journal* 43: 65–69.
Chemmanur TJ and P Fulghieri (1994) Investment bank reputation, information production, and financial intermediation *Journal of Finance* 49 (1/March): 57–79.
Chen H-S and JR Ritter (2000) The seven percent solution *Journal of Finance* 55 (3/June): 1105–1131.
Chowdhry B and V Nanda (1996) Stabilization, syndication, and pricing of IPOs *Journal of Financial and Quantitative Analysis* 31: 25–42.
Chowdry B and A Sherman (1996a) International differences in oversubscription and underpricing of IPOs *Journal of Corporate Finance* 2: 231–250.
Chowdry B and A Sherman (1996b) The winner's curse and international methods of allocating initial public offerings *Pacific Basin Finance Journal* 4: 15–30.
Chung KH (2000) Marketing stocks by brokerage firms: The role of financial analysts *Financial Management* 29 (Issue 2/Summer): 35–54.
Clatworthy MA and MJ Peel (1998) The characteristics of new equity markets for SMEs *Journal of Small Business and Enterprise Development* 5 (1): 81–95.
Cornell B (1999) *The Equity Risk Premium.* New York: John Wiley.
Cornelli F and D Goldreich (1999) Bookbuilding and strategic allocation. Working Paper, London Business School.
Cornelli F and D Goldreich (2001) Bookbuilding: How informative is the order book? Working Paper, London Business School.
Cornett MM, H Mehran and H Tehranian (1998) Are financial markets overly optimistic about the prospects of firms that issue equity? Evidence from voluntary versus involuntary equity issuance by banks *Journal of Finance* 53 (6/December): 2139–2159.
Corwin SA and JH Harris (2001) The initial listing decisions of firms that go public *Financial Management* 30 (Issue 1/Spring): 35–55.
Cramer KD, SD Gunn, GT Johnson and DP Porter (2001) *Foreign Private Issuers of Equity Securities in the United States.* Chicago: RR Donnelley Financial.

D'Mello R and SP Ferris (2000) The information effects of analyst activity at the announcement of new equity issues *Financial Management* 29 (Issue 1/Spring): 78–95.

Dawson SM (1987) Secondary stock market performance of initial public offers, Hong Kong, Singapore, and Malaysia: 1978–1984 *Journal of Business Finance and Accounting* Spring: 65–76.

Dawson SM and T Hiraki (1985) Selling unseasoned new shares in Hong Kong and Japan: A test of primary market efficiency and underpricing *Hong Kong Journal of Business Management*: 125–134.

Dean C (1997) And then there were none *International Financing Review* Sept 6, 1997.

Denis D (1991) Shelf registration and the market for seasoned equity offerings *Journal of Business* 64 (2/April): 189–212.

Denis D (1993) The cost of equity issues since Rule 415: A closer look *Journal of Financial Research* XVI (1/Spring): 77–88.

Dhillon US, K Raman and GG Ramirez (1999) Does it matter who sells at the initial public offering: IPO pricing and secondary share sales. Conference paper, FMA International, Barcelona.

Dixon H (2002) Breaking views *London Evening Standard* 20 May 2002.

Dovkants A (1999) European firms find 'walk-ups' help boost share value in IPOs *Wall Street Journal Europe* 10 November 1999: 23.

Drake PD and MR Vetsuypens (1993) IPO underpricing and insurance against legal liability *Financial Management* 22 (Spring): 64–73.

Dunbar CG (1998) The choice between firm-commitment and best-efforts offering methods in IPOs: The effect of unsuccessful offers *Journal of Financial Intermediation* 6: 60–90.

Espenlaub S, I Tonks and A Gregory (1998) Testing the robustness of long-term under-performance of UK initial public offerings *LSE Financial Markets Group Discussion Paper 285.*

Fama E and KR French (1992) The cross section of expected stock returns *Journal of Finance* 47 (June): 427–465.

Fama E and KR French (1993) Common risk factors in the returns of stocks and bonds *Journal of Financial Economics* 33: 3–55.

Fama E and KR French (1997) Industry costs of equity *Journal of Financial Economics* 43: 153–193.

Field LC and G Hanka (2001) The expiration of IPO share lockups *Journal of Finance* 56 (2/April): 471–500.

Foerster SR and GA Karolyi (1999) The long-run performance of global equity offerings. Working Paper, Ivey School of Business.

Fox M (1984) Shelf registration, integrated disclosure, and underwriter due diligence: An economic analysis *Virginia Law Review* June: 1005–1034.

Galloway TM, CF Loderer and DP Sheehan (1998) What does the market learn from stock offering revisions? *Financial Management* 27 (1/Spring): 5–16.

Garfinkel JA (1993) IPO underpricing, insider selling and subsequent equity offerings: Is underpricing a signal of quality? *Financial Management* 22 (Spring): 74–83.

Garner DR, RR Owen, RP Conway (1994) *The Ernst & Young Guide to Financing Growth*. New York: John Wiley & Sons.

Geddes HR (1998) Corporate valuation methods used by UK corporate financiers. Unpublished working paper, University of Greenwich.

Gombola M, HW Lee and FY Liu (1997) Evidence of selling by managers after seasoned equity offering announcements *Financial Management* 26 (3/Autumn): 37–53.

Gompers PA (1996) Grandstanding in the venture capital industry *Journal of Financial Economics* 42: 133–156.

Greenstein IA, JN Korff, CV Reicin, PL Colbrand and JK Robinson (2000) *An Insider's Guide to Going Public.* Chicago: RR Donnelley Financial.

Habib MA and AP Ljungqvist (1998) Underpricing and IPO proceeds: A note *Economics Letters* 61 (December): 381–383.

Habib MA and AP Ljungqvist (2001) Underpricing and entrepreneurial wealth losses in IPOs: Theory and evidence *Review of Financial Studies* 14 (2): 433–458.

Hanley KW (1993) The underpricing of initial public offerings and the partial adjustment phenomenon *Journal of Financial Economics* 34: 231–250.

Hanley KW and JW Wilhelm (1995) Evidence on the strategic allocation of initial public offerings *Journal of Financial Economics* 37: 239–257.

Hanley KW, AA Kumar and PJ Seguin (1993) Price stabilization in the market for new issues *Journal of Financial Economics* 34: 177–197.

Hansen R, B Fuller and V Janjigian (1987) The over-allotment option and equity financing floatation costs: An empirical investigation *Financial Management* 16: 24–32.

Hassell D (2001) Danes cut their Rentokil link *The Times* 17 November 2001.

Hatchick K, K Smith and P Watts (2002) *The Alternative Investment Market Handbook*, 2nd edn. London: Jordans.

Hegde SP and RE Miller (1989) Market making in initial public offerings: An empirical analysis *Journal of Financial and Quantitative Analysis* 24 (1/March): 75–90.

Heinkel R and ES Schwartz (1986) Rights versus underwritten offerings: An asymmetric information approach *Journal of Finance* 41 (1/March): 1–18.

Hensler DA, RC Rutherford and TM Springer (1997) The survival of initial public offerings in the aftermarket *The Journal of Financial Research* XX (1/Spring): 93–110.

Hof RD (1999) Inside an Internet IPO *Business Week* 6 September 1999.

Houge T, T Loughran, G Suchanek and X Yan (2001) Divergence of opinion, uncertainty, and the quality of initial public offerings *Financial Management* 30 (4/Winter): 5–24.

How JCY and JG Low (1993) Fractional ownership and underpricing: Signals of IPO firm value? *Pacific Basin Finance Journal* 1: 47–65.

Hughes PJ and AV Thakor (1992) Litigation risk, intermediation, and the underpricing of initial public offerings *Review of Financial Studies* 5 (4/Winter): 709–742.

Hulbert HM, JA Miles and JR Woolridge (2002) Value creation from equity carve-outs *Financial Management* 31 (Spring): 83–100.

Ibbotson RG (1975) Price performance of common stock new issues *Journal of Financial Economics* 2: 235–272.

Ibbotson RG and JF Jaffe (1975) 'Hot isssue' markets *Journal of Finance* 30: 1027–1042.

Ibbotson RG, JL Sindelar and JR Ritter (1988) Initial public offerings *Journal of Applied Corporate Finance* 1 (2/Summer): 37–45.

Ibbotson RG, JL Sindelar and JR Ritter (1994) The market's problems with the pricing of initial public offerings *Journal of Applied Corporate Finance* 7 (1): 66–74.

Jain BA and O Kini (1994) The post-issue operating performance of IPO firms *Journal of Finance* 49: 1699–1726.

Jain BA and O Kini (1999) On investment banker monitoring in the new issues market *Journal of Banking and Finance* 23: 49–84.

Jain PC (1992) Equity issues and changes in expectations of earnings by financial analysts *The Review of Financial Studies* 5 (4): 669–683.

Jegadeesh N, M Weinstein and I Welch (1993) An empirical investigation of IPO returns and subsequent equity offerings *Journal of Financial Economics* 34: 153–175.

Jelic R, B Saadouni and R Briston (1998) The accuracy of earnings forecasts in IPO prospectuses on the Kuala Lumpur Stock Exchange *Accounting and Business Research* 29 (1/Winter): 57–72.

Jenkinson T and A Ljungqvist (1996) *Going Public: The Theory and Evidence on How Companies Raise Equity Finance*. Oxford: Clarendon Press.

Jenkinson T and C Mayer (1988) The privatisation process in France and the UK *European Economic Review* March: 482–490.

Jog VM and AL Riding (1987) Underpricing in Canadian IPOs *Financial Analysts Journal* 43 (6): 48–55.

Joyce T, M Gruson and PO Jungreis (1991) Offers and sales of securities by a non-US company in the United States. In P Farmery and K Walmsley (eds) *United States Securities and Investments Regulation Handbook*. London: Graham & Trotman.

Kandel S, O Sariq and A Wohl (1999) The demand for stocks: An analysis of IPO auctions *The Review of Financial Studies* 12 (2/Summer): 227–247.

Kaneko T and RH Pettway (2001) Auctions versus bookbuilding of Japanese IPOs. Working Paper, University of Missouri-Columbia.

Keasler TR (2001) The underwriter's early lock-up release: Empirical evidence *Journal of Economics and Finance* 25 (2): 214–228.

Keloharju M (1993) The winner's curse, legal liability, and the long-run performance of initial public offerings in Finland *Journal of Financial Economics* 34: 251–277.

Kelsall C (2001) Accelerated bookbuilds: The guide to European equities 2001 *Euromoney*: 8–9.

Kidwell DS, MW Marr and GR Thompson (1984) SEC Rule 415: The ultimate competitive bid *Journal of Financial and Quantitative Analysis* 19 (2/June): 183–195.

Kidwell DS, MW Marr and GR Thompson (1987) Shelf registration: Competition and market flexibility *Journal of Law and Economics* 30 (April): 181–206.

Kim J-B, I Krinsky and J Lee (1993) Motives for going public and underpricing: New findings from Korea *Journal of Business Finance and Accounting* 20 (2): 195–211.

Kim M and JR Ritter (1999) Valuing IPOs *Journal of Financial Economics* 53 (3/September): 409–437.

Klein A, J Rosenfeld and W Beranek (1991) The two stages of an equity carve-out and the price response of parent and subsidiary stock *Managerial and Decision Economics* 12: 449–460.

Koh F and T Walter (1989) A direct test of Rock's model of the pricing of unseasoned issues *Journal of Financial Economics* 23: 252–272.

Kothari SP and JB Warner (1997) Measuring long-horizon security price performance *Journal of Financial Economics* 43: 310–339.

Krigman L, WH Shaw and KL Womack (1999) The persistence of IPO mispricing and the predictive power of flipping *Journal of Finance* 54 (3/June): 1015–1044.

Lee C and A Revheim (1999) Christiania Bank's offering signals strong demand *Wall Street Journal Europe* 23 March 1999.

Lee I, S Lochhead and JR Ritter (1996) The costs of raising capital *Journal of Financial Research* XIX (1/Spring): 59–74.

Lerner J (1994) Venture capitalists and the decision to go public *Journal of Financial Economics* 35: 293–316.

Levis M (1989a) Stock market anomalies *Journal of Banking and Finance* September: 675–696.

Levis M (1989b) IPOs, subsequent rights issues and long-run performance. Working Paper, City University Business School.

Levis M (1990) The winner's curse problem, interest costs and the underpricing of initial public offerings *Economic Journal* March: 76–89.

Levis M (1993) The long-run performance of initial public offerings: The UK experience 1980–1988 *Financial Management* 22 (Spring): 28–41.

Ljungqvist AP and WJ Wilhelm (2001) IPO allocations: discriminatory or discretionary? *Journal of Financial Economics* 65 (2/August): 167–201.

Ljungqvist AP, T Jenkinson and WJ Wilhelm (2003) Global integration in primary equity markets: The role of US banks and US investors *Review of Financial Studies* 16: 63–99.

Ljungqvist AP, WJ Wilhelm and T Jenkinson (2002) Has the introduction of bookbuilding increased the efficiency of IPOs?

Logue DE, RJ Rogalski, JK Seward and L Foster-Johnson (1999) Underwriter bookbuilding methods, investment bank reputation and the return performance of firms conducting initial public offerings. FMA International, Barcelona.

London Stock Exchange (1999) *Listing Depository Receipts in London.*

Loughran T and JR Ritter (1995) The new issues puzzle *Journal of Finance* 50 (1): 23–51.

Loughran T and JR Ritter (1997) The operating performance of firms conducting seasoned equity offerings *Journal of Finance* 52 (5/December): 1823–1850.

Loughran T and JR Ritter (2002) Why don't issuers get upset about leaving money on the table in IPOs? *Review of Financial Studies* 15: 413–444.

Loughran T and JR Ritter (2001) Why has IPO underpricing increased over time? Working Paper, University of Notre Dame.

Loughran T, JR Ritter and K Rydqvist (1994) Initial public offerings: International insights *Pacific Basin Finance Journal* 2: 165–199 [updated April 2001].

Lucas DJ and RL Macdonald (1990) Equity issues and stock price dynamics *Journal of Finance* 45: 1019–1043.

Mann SV and NW Sicherman (1991) The agency costs of free cash flow: Acquisition activity and equity issues *Journal of Business* 64 (2): 213–227.

Marquardt CA and CI Wiedman (1998) Voluntary disclosure, information asymmetry, and insider selling through secondary equity offerings *Contemporary Accounting Research* 15 (4/Winter): 505–537.

Marsh P (1979) Equity rights issues and the efficiency of the UK stock market *Journal of Finance* 34 (4/September): 839–862.

Martinson J (1998) System for raising capital 'too restrictive' *Financial Times* 20 October 1998.

Masulis RW and AN Korwar (1986) Seasoned equity offerings: An empirical investigation *Journal of Financial Economics* 15: 91–118.

McGuinness P (1993) The post-listing return performance of unseasoned issues of common stock in Hong Kong *Journal of Business Finance and Accounting* 20 (2): 167–194.

McLaughlin R, A Safieddine and GK Vasudevan (1998) The information content of corporate offerings of seasoned securities: An empirical analysis *Financial Management* 27 (2/Summer): 31–45.

Megginson WL and KA Weiss (1991) Venture capitalist certification in initial public offerings *Journal of Finance* 46: 879–903.

Megginson WL, RC Nash, JM Netter and AL Schwartz (2000) The long-run return to investors in share issue privatisation *Financial Management* 29 (Issue 1/Spring): 67–77.

Mello AS and JE Parsons (1998) Going public and the ownership structure of the firm *Journal of Financial Economics* 49: 79–109.

Menyah K, K Paudyal and CG Inyangete (1990) The pricing of initial offerings of privatised companies on the London Stock Exchange *Accounting and Business Research* 21 (81): 51–56.

Michaely R and W Shaw (1994) The pricing of initial public offerings: Tests of adverse-selection and signaling theories *Review of Financial Studies* 7: 279–319.

Michaely R and WH Shaw (1995) Does the choice of auditor convey quality in an initial public offering? *Financial Management* 24: 15–30.

Mikkelson WH and MM Partch (1985) Stock price effects and costs of secondary distributions *Journal of Financial Economics* 14 (2): 165–194.

Mikkelson WH and MM Partch (1986) Valuation effects of security offerings and the issuance process *Journal of Financial Economics* 15: 31–60.

Miller EM (1977) Risk uncertainty and divergence of opinion *Journal of Finance* 32: 1151–1168.

Miller RE and FK Reilly (1987) An examination of mispricing, returns, and uncertainty for initial public offerings *Financial Management* 16: 33–38.

Moore NH, DR Peterson and PP Peterson (1986) Shelf registrations and shareholder wealth: A comparison of shelf and traditional equity offerings *Journal of Finance* 41 (2/June): 451–464.

Mulherin H and A Boone (2000) Comparing acquisitions and divestitures *Journal of Corporate Finance* 6: 117–139.

Mullan S (1999) ICICI bridges GAAP to NYSE *International Financing Review* 1302 (September 25): 81.

Mullan S (2001) Goldman shocks syndicate with fee demand *International Financing Review* 1366 (January 13).
Mullins K and N Toyama (1999) Toyota goes global with London New York listings *International Financing Review* 1303 (October 2): 74.
Munk N (2001) In the final analysis *Vanity Fair* August: 56–61.
Muscarella CJ and MR Vetsuypens (1989) A simple test of Baron's model of IPO underpricing *Journal of Financial Economics* 24: 125–135.
Nanda V and Y Yun (1997) Reputation and financial intermediation: An empirical investigation of the impact of IPO mispricing on underwriter market value *Journal of Financial Intermediation* 6: 39–63.
Nanda V, JH Yi and Y Yun (1995) IPO long-run performance and underwriter reputation. Working Paper, University of Michigan Business School.
OECD (2001) *Financial Market Trends* 79 (June): 43.
Pagano M, F Panetta and L Zingales (1998) Why do companies go public? An empirical analysis *Journal of Finance* 53 (1/February): 27–64.
Perotti EC and SE Guney (1993) The structure of privatization plans *Financial Management* 22 (Spring): 84–98.
Rajan R and H Servaes (1997) Analyst following of initial public offerings *Journal of Finance* 52 (2/June): 507–529.
Reese WA (1998) Capital gains taxation and stock market activity: Evidence from IPOs *Journal of Finance* 53 (5/October): 1799–1819.
Ritter JR (1984a) The 'hot issue' market of 1980 *The Journal of Business* 57 (2/April): 215–240.
Ritter JR (1984b) Signalling and the valuation of unseasoned new issues: A comment *Journal of Finance* 39 (4/September): 1231–1237.
Ritter JR (1987) The costs of going public *Journal of Financial Economics* 19: 269–281.
Ritter JR (1991) The long-run performance of initial public offerings *Journal of Finance* XLVI (1/March): 3–27.
Ritter JR (1998a) Initial public offerings. In D Logue and J Seward (eds) *Warren, Gorham and Lamont Handbook of Modern Finance.* New York: WGL/RIA [reprinted with modifications in *Contemporary Finance Digest* 2 (1/Spring): 5–30].
Ritter JR (1998b) Initial public offerings *Contemporary Finance Digest* 2 (1/Spring): 5–30.
Ritter JR (1999) Institutional affiliation and the role of venture capital: Evidence from initial public offerings in Japan. Working Paper, University of Florida.
Ritter JR (2001a) Big IPO runups of 1975–1999. Working Paper, University of Florida.
Ritter JR (2001b) Money left on the table in IPOs. Working Paper, University of Florida.
Ritter JR (2001c) Some factoids about the 2000 IPO market. Working Paper, University of Florida.
Ritter JR (2001d) Some factoids about the 2001 IPO market. Working Paper, University of Florida.
Ritter JR and T Loughran (2001) Why has IPO underpricing increased over time? Working Paper, University of Florida.

Rock K (1986) Why new issues are underpriced *Journal of Financial Economics* 15: 187–212.

Rogowski RJ and EH Sorenson (1985) Deregulation in investment banking: Shelf registrations, structure and performance *Financial Management* Spring: 5–15.

Roten IC and DJ Mullineaux (2001) Equity underwriting spreads at commercial bank holding companies and investment banks. Working Paper, University of Kentucky.

Ruud JF (1993) Underwriter price support and the IPO underpricing puzzle *Journal of Financial Economics* 34: 135–152.

Schipper K and A Smith (1986) A comparison of equity carve-outs and seasoned equity offerings *Journal of Financial Economics* 15: 153–186.

Schneider C, J Manko and R Kant (1996) Going public: practice, procedures and consequences. [This is an updated reprint of a 1981 *Villanova Law Review* article, available from Bowne.]

Schultz P (1993) Unit public offerings *Journal of Financial Economics* 34: 199–229.

Schultz P and M Zaman (1994) Aftermarket support and the underpricing of initial public offerings *Journal of Financial Economics* 35: 199–220.

Shaw DC (1971) The performance of primary common stock offerings: A Canadian comparison *Journal of Finance*: 1101–1110.

Sherman AE (1999) Underwriter certification and the effect of shelf registration on due diligence *Financial Management* 28 (1/Spring): 5–19.

Simon C (1989) The effect of the 1933 Securities Act on investor information and the performance of new issues *American Economic Review* 79: 295–318.

Smith CW (1977) Alternative methods for raising capital: Rights versus underwritten offerings *Journal of Financial Economics* 5: 273–307.

Smith C (1986) Investment banking and the capital acquisition process *Journal of Financial Economics* 15: 3–29.

Smith R, D Salomon and C Gasparion (2002) Swirl surrounds Salomon star *Wall Street Journal Europe* 1–3 March 2002: M1.

Spatt C and S Srivastava (1991) Preplay communication, participation restrictions, and efficiency in initial public offerings *Review of Financial Studies* 4 (4): 709–726.

Speiss DK and J Affleck-Graves (1995) Underperformance in long-run stock returns following seasoned equity offerings *Journal of Financial Economics* 38: 243–267.

Stoughton NM and J Zechner (1998) IPO-mechanisms, monitoring and ownership structure *Journal of Financial Economics* 49: 45–77.

Subrahmanyan A and S Titman (1999) The going public decision and the development of financial markets *Journal of Finance* 54 (3):1045–1082.

Teoh SH, I Welch, TJ Wong (1998) Earnings management and the long-run market performance of initial public offerings *Journal of Finance* LIII (6/December: 1935–1974.

Tinic SM (1988) Anatomy of initial public offerings of common stock *Journal of Finance* 43: 789–822.

Titman S and B Trueman (1986) Information quality and the valuation of new issues *Journal of Accounting and Economics* 8 (June): 159–172.

Torstila S (2001) The distribution of fees within the IPO syndicate *Financial Management* 30 (4/Winter): 25–44.

Vickers J and G Yarrow (1988) *Privatization: An Economic Analysis*. Harvard University Press.

Weiss K, A Kumar and PJ Seguin (1993) Price stabilization in the market for new issues *Journal of Financial Economics* 34: 177–197.

Welch I (1989) Seasoned offerings, imitation costs, and the underpricing of initial public offerings *Journal of Finance* 44 (2/June): 421–449.

Welch I (1991) An empirical examination of models and contract choice in initial public offerings *Journal of Financial and Quantitative Analysis* 26: 497–518.

Welch I (1992) Sequential sales, learning and cascades *Journal of Finance* 47: 695–732.

Welch I (1996) Equity offerings following the IPO: Theory and evidence *Journal of Corporate Finance* 2 (3/February).

# Useful websites

The following are some of the more interesting and/or useful websites that include information about IPOs and equity offerings. Readers should be aware that websites appear and disappear with regularity and some of the sites listed below may no longer be in operation. Nor is this list exhaustive. When one types 'IPO' into a search engine, one is faced with over three million references. *Note:* I have discarded the 'www.' in front of each web address.

## Academic information

One of the best sources for academic information regarding IPOs and secondary equity offerings is the home page of Jay Ritter, Professor at the University of Florida (www.bear.cba.ufl.edu/ritter). This is an up-to-date reference list of all academic papers published and being worked on.

Ivo Welch at Yale's School of Management also keeps a bibliography of IPO literature at www.iporesources.com. This site also contains links to various European researchers and articles.

## Stock exchanges

aex.nl (Amsterdam – Euronext)
asx.com.au (Australia)
bmv.com.mx (Mexico)
borsaitalia.it (Italy)
bourse.ch (Switzerland)
bourse-de-paris.fr (Paris – Euronext)
bovespa.com.br (Brazil)
exchange.de (Frankfurt)
klse.com.my (Kuala Lumpur)
kse.or.kr (Seoul)
nasdaq.com
nyse.com (New York)
sehk.com.hk (Hong Kong)
ses.com.sg (Singapore)
set.or.th (Bangkok)
stockex.co.uk (London)
stockexchange.be (Brussels – Euronext)
tse.com (Toronto)
tse.or.jp (Tokyo)

## Regulators

consob.it (Italy)
sec.gov (USA)
fsa.gov.uk (UK)
osc.gov.on.ca (Ontario, Canada)
fsa.go.jp (Japan)

For IPO and other regulatory documents, the following three sites are useful:

freeedgar.com (US prospectuses and regulatory filings)
sedar.com (Canadian prospectuses and regulatory filings)
europrospectus.com (a commercial site)

## General IPO websites (US oriented unless noted)

There are many, many more. These sites popped up near the top of a search of the term IPO on Google in July 2002.

Bloomberg.com (IPO Center)
direct-issue.com
edgar-online.com/ipoexpress
IPO.com
IPO.ft.com
IPO.onvista.de (German site)
ipofinancial.com
ipohome.com
ipomaven.com
ipomonitor.com
newissues-IPO.com (UK site)
thedeal.com (not just IPOs, information on investment banking activity)
UnlockDates.com

# Index

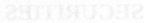

Printed and bound by CPI Group (UK) Ltd, Croydon, CR0 4YY
08/05/2025
01864776-0001